AF469915

WILFRED AVERY
AND THE UNPREDICTABLE IMAGE

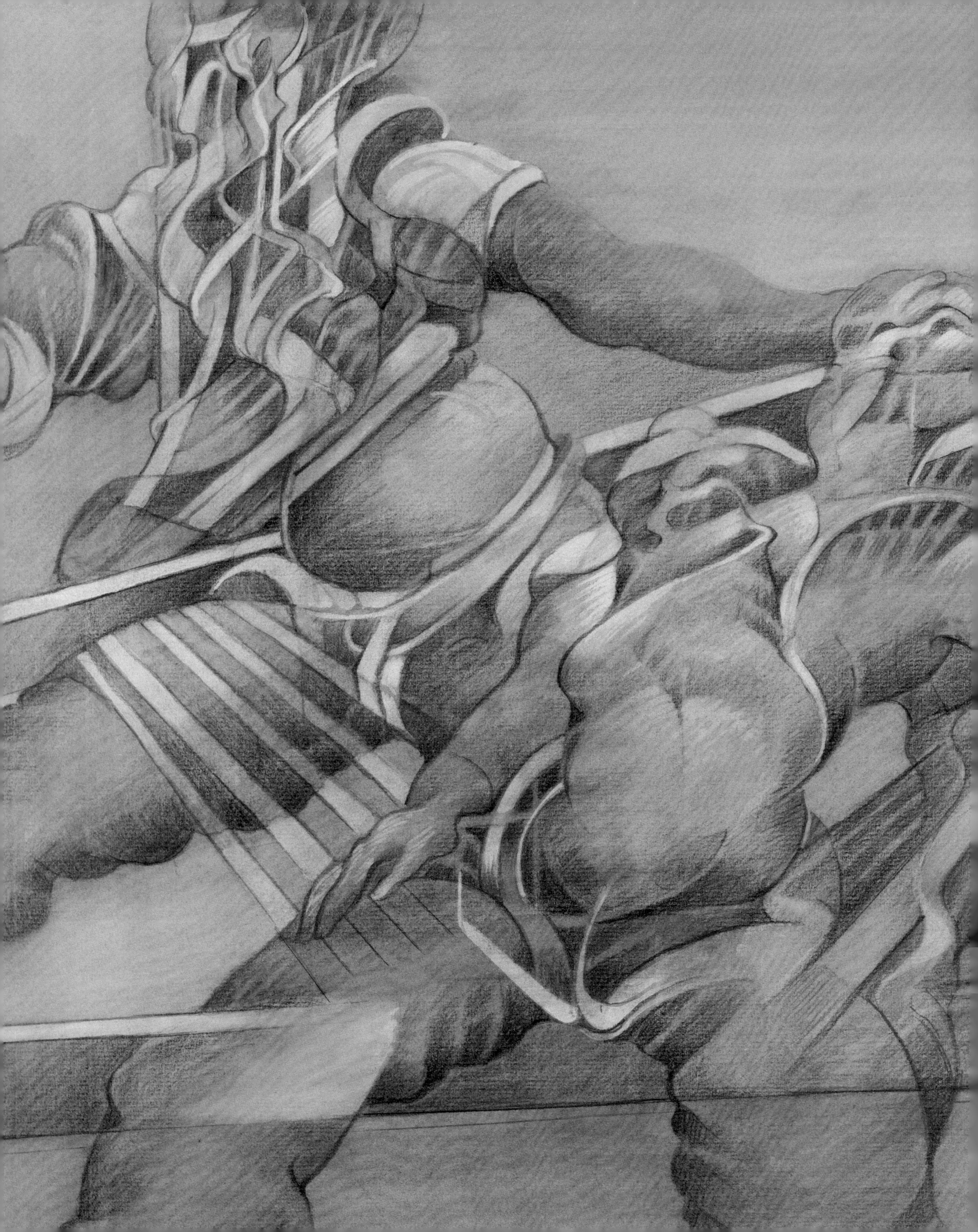

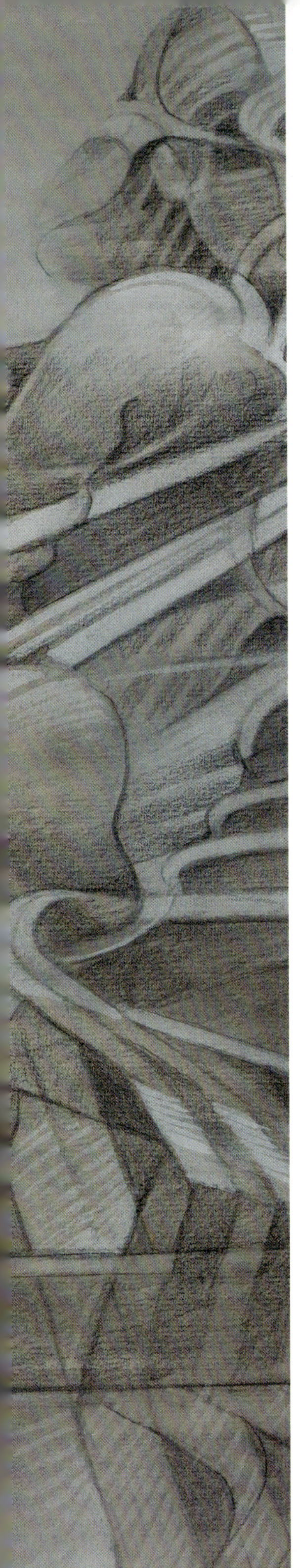

FRANCESCA RAMSAY

WILFRED AVERY

AND THE UNPREDICTABLE IMAGE

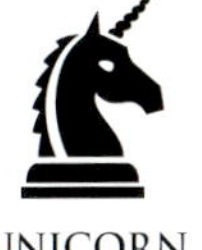

UNICORN

Published in 2023 by Unicorn
an imprint of Unicorn Publishing Group LLP
Charleston Studio
Meadow Business Centre
Lewes BN8 5RW
www.unicornpublishing.org

ISBN 978-1-911397-61-8

10 9 8 7 6 5 4 3 2 1

Designed by Guy Callaby
Printed by Fine Tone Ltd

CONTENTS

FOREWORD

I FIRST ENCOUNTERED Wilfred Avery when, with his brother Sam, he visited my parents at their bookshop in Eastbourne in the late 1950s. The young like to be noticed and engaged by adults, and Wilf, with his charming smile, kindness, sensitivity and engagement, did just that. Qualities that made him, by all accounts a brilliant teacher. They would assist his courageous battle with post-war prejudice and the British Establishment. Lacking contacts, finances, and an art school training, Avery encountered a Britain emerging from the war through the 1950s, changing slowly and retaining many of the pre-war Edwardian prejudices that Wilfred struggled with. His sexuality and lifestyle were isolating and made establishing himself as an artist with gallerists, public institutions and collectors difficult, and in his essay 'Paintings 1965–1969' he describes his despair at the fashion for American abstract art, but prophetically writes:

> *My work looks very unfashionable at the moment, but I must believe that the times will move towards me. I hope they will.*

George Melly and Brian Sewell were in the minority who believed in Avery's importance during his life, and now their good judgment is acknowledged by institutions and collectors who increasingly value the importance of Avery's paintings; a confection of technique, observation and narrative that although grounded in British post-war art has a freshness, relevance and significance today.

This fascinating book chronicles, in sometimes painful detail, the challenges that Wilfred Avery battled with. It gives belated acknowledgement to an important artist many have never heard of, living through a period considered to be liberating (the pill, the Beatles, Mary Quant) but which too often ignored the unfashionable.

I last saw Wilfred just before he died, again in Eastbourne. He was the same kind, serious and passionate artist that I had met so many years before. A man whose work deserves to be seen.

Gyr King 2023

For Wilfred Avery

INTRODUCTION

Images flow endlessly through one's mind. The complex web of thought that holds together the very essence of ourselves and of our ability to acknowledge our own existence, is the fabric of my work. In following and tracing their infinite pattern and variety, I touch continuously the rich heritage that is in us and stumble miraculously, it seems to me, on the images that may take us towards the future.[1]

DEVON-BORN WILFRED AVERY (1926–2016) was largely unrecognised in his lifetime. Untrained in any conventional sense, and working in self-imposed isolation from his creative contemporaries, his style evolved outside any popular movement.

In a career spanning over sixty years, only two subjects really interested him: landscape and the male body. An investigation into both developed from an increasing interest in the unconscious mind and an exploration (and acceptance) of his own sexuality. By the end of his long life – one led with a rare and intense creative focus – he had unified these two chosen subjects into one compelling whole.

Early work was painted in London in the 1950s. Although not outwardly sexual in tone, Wilfred's still lifes and quietly undressing male figures bear a queer intimacy that makes his practice just as radical as his contemporaries Francis Bacon and Keith Vaughan. Later work – paintings and collages made under the guidance of Jungian thought – are unsettled dreamscapes and semi-human configurations coloured foggy hues of blue and violet. These works teeter and tip between the figurative and the abstract, a position that made Wilfred difficult to place commercially, and exacerbated his sense of alienation from the art world. Mature work was made in Devon and later on the south coast. Here, landscape is fused with the male body; uncomfortably erotic configurations landlocked in passionate embraces. In his final years, suffering with ill health and unable to make new work, Wilfred set about destroying every piece that did not meet his full approval. In this sense, this monograph cannot be anything but written under his own hand.

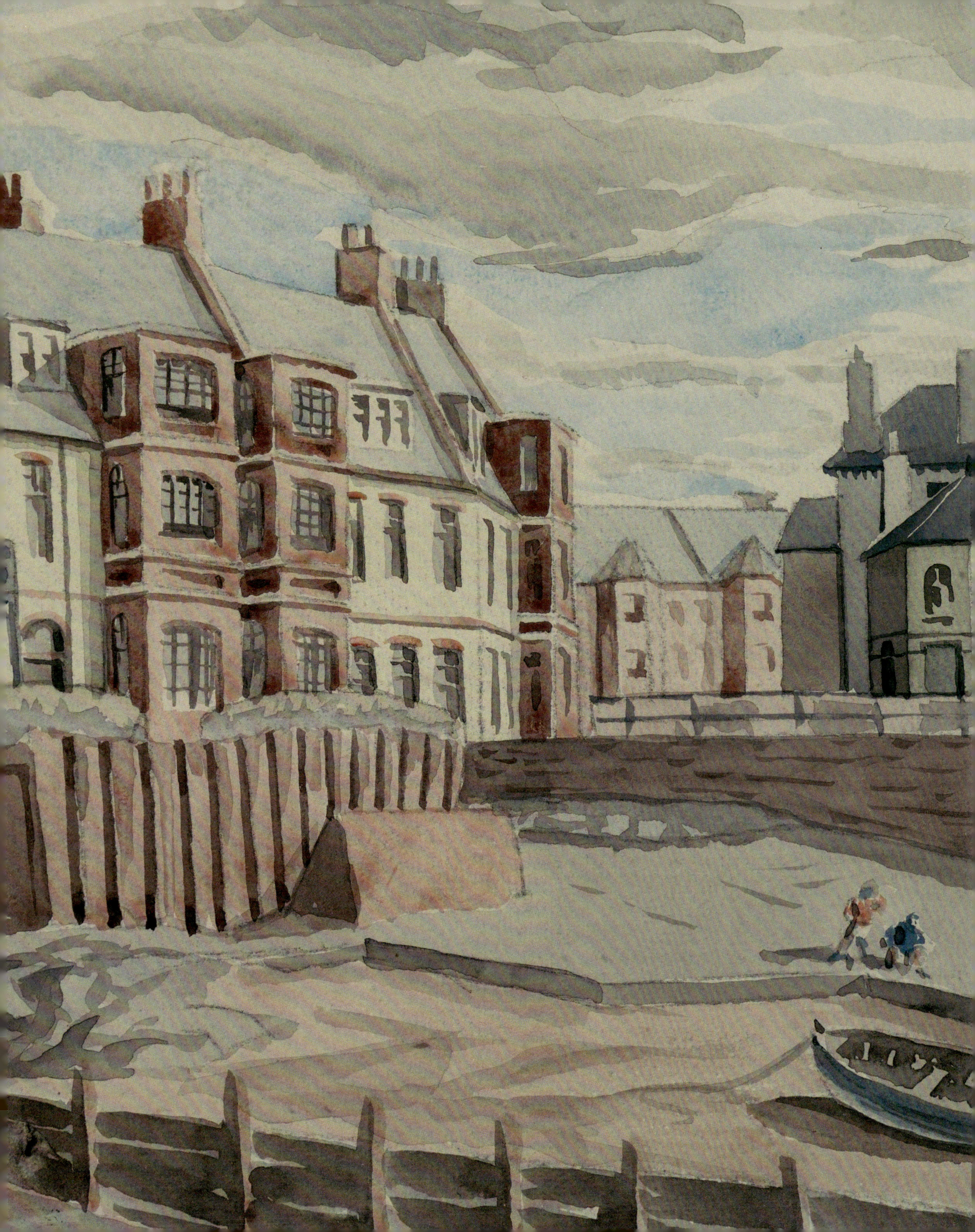

1 EARLY YEARS

'MY SENSE OF place does not lie here,'[2] Wilfred wrote while living in London in 1967. It remained instead, he would say, where it had always been, 'found long ago on the pink clifftops and green hillsides of my childhood'.[3] This salt-licked landscape got right under his skin and never really left; North Devon's snug hills and far distant coastal views continued to inspire the artist long after he had moved away. In essence, Wilfred never stopped painting home.

Wilfred was born on 24 April 1926 on the kitchen floor of the New Inn, the South Molton pub managed by his parents Sidney Avery and Edith Lock. The arrival of his identical twin brother, Sam, 20 minutes later was a surprise for all involved, and the first and middle names already chosen for the couple's one expected child were split between the pair. Often referred to only as 'the twins' by their parents and two siblings (Derrick at eighteen months older and Pat at four years younger), the boys were inseparable from birth. They lived together until the age of thirty-two, and remained a self-sufficient unit throughout their lives.

This bucolic rural upbringing of Wilfred's no doubt led to an early influence of Stanley Spencer. The pair shared the same infatuation with place – for Spencer, it was the Berkshire village of Cookham; for Wilfred, the landscape surrounding his home town of South Molton. This almost *religious* sense of landscape would go on to bring about further influence in Wilfred's early adulthood from visionaries such as William Blake and George Rouault. As a

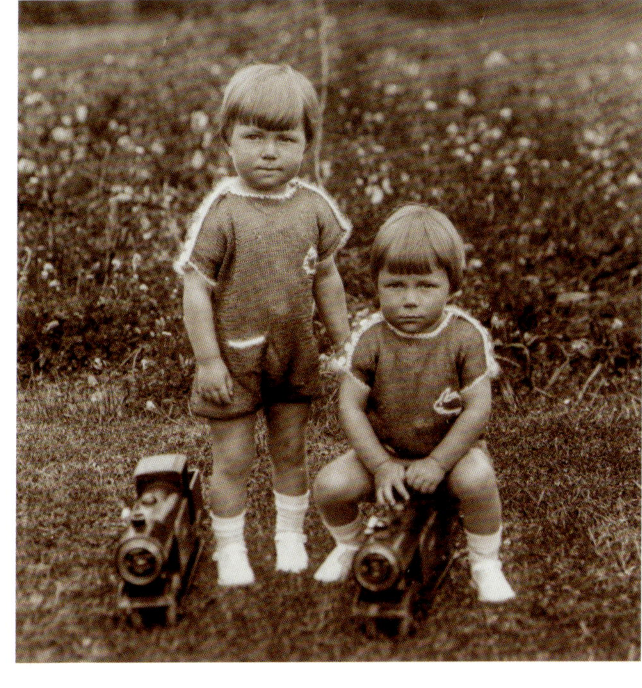

1:1 Sam and Wilfred as toddlers
1929
8.5 x 8.5 cm
Photograph
(Studio)

youth he was deeply involved with South Molton Church, at one point even considering entering the priesthood himself. He would later admit that he turned away from this idea after realising the church would not have allowed him to live, as he put it, 'truthfully'. His father also strongly advised him not to take this step, though his alternative suggestion of working in a bank would have been equally, if not more, unsuitable.

Wilfred's entire practice – really, his entire life – was imbued with a kind of spirituality; a sense, certainly, of an existence outside the empirical. This spiritual bent made him receptive to things unsaid, to certain feelings about people, both positive and negative. It was coupled with a propensity towards superstition and folklore. Wilfred remained insistent that he could cure warts, something he had learnt from his maternal grandfather Sam Lock (who was also a dowser). He claimed, in fact, to have healed the hands of actor Lee Montague, enabling him to get a TV role in which they were to feature prominently. In gratitude, Lee bought a small oil still life, *Plant and Lemons*, painted in the mid-1950s. For a time, Wilfred would also tell fortunes. However, he did later confess that this was more a way of getting across to people what he thought of them than a result of any psychic skill.

But Wilfred's childhood was not exclusively idyllic. He was susceptible to ill health, suffering both from chronic rheumatism and rheumatoid arthritis. Contracting diphtheria at the age of eight, he spent six months in an isolation hospital in Exeter. Wilfred was the sole child in the men's ward, and due to his contagion, his parents were only allowed to visit him from behind a glass window. Although always remembering the kindness with which he was treated by his fellow patients, this formative experience could not fail to have left him with a sense of abandonment, perhaps even of rejection, that would be hard to shake off.

•••

Aged seventeen in 1943, the twins moved to Cheltenham to embark on a two-year teacher training course at St Paul's College. This was Wilfred's idea, and with little discussion needed, Sam followed. As its name suggests, St Paul's College was a church foundation and Wilfred was thus able to nurture his interest in religion by studying Advanced Divinity as one of his chosen subjects. He had a natural gift for teaching; that rare ability in bringing out the best in people regardless of age, education or background. And although he moved away from it in a professional capacity in 1968, Wilfred did not stop acting teacher for a moment. In fact, the most unassuming dinner guest might as often find themself party to a well-considered lecture as to a well-cooked meal.

The boys had shown an interest and aptitude in painting from an early age. As there had never been any suggestion of going to art school when they were choosing a career, they both signed up to the Advanced Art module. The course was taught by James Salmon and, with the twins his only students that year, in effect, they received private tuition. It is hardly surprising that Wilfred would always refer to Salmon as such a significant influence – perhaps the earliest – in his development as an artist.

As students during the Second World War, the twins had little chance to encounter modern painting first-hand. Wilfred's developing interest in the art of his time was, however, reinforced by two pivotal experiences. In 1945, a touring exhibition of Parisian Cubism opened in the town. Reflecting on his visit over thirty years later in 1978, he wrote, '... I had little direct physical experience of modern painting. Galleries were closed and one learnt about art through books and reproductions. Then suddenly in 1945 the Arts Council sent an exhibition of Cubist paintings made in Paris during the War about the country. I saw it in Cheltenham and was immediately struck by the emotional power and presence that the plastic quality of those paintings held.'[4] In the same year, through his teacher James Salmon, Wilfred had the opportunity to meet the painter Paul Nash. Nash encouraged him to look to France rather than America for inspiration. Although brief, this conversation would come to shape Wilfred's entire career, instilling in him not only a deep appreciation for the work of Cézanne, Picasso and Braque, but a lifelong animosity towards American Abstract Expressionism.

The twins graduated at the age of nineteen, in the summer of 1945. Although the war was in its final stages, shortly after their graduation, both boys were called up. Wilfred failed his medical and after a short stint teaching back in South Molton, during which the weather worsened

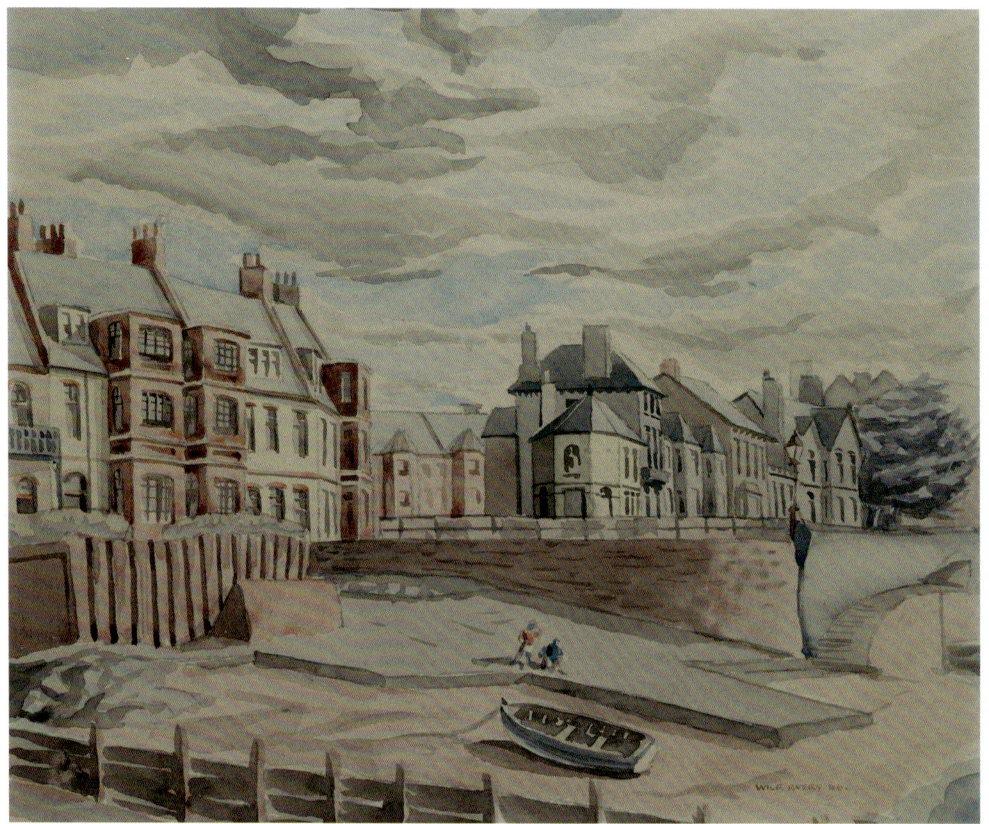

1:2 Exmouth Seafront
1946
24 x 29 cm
Watercolour
(Private collection)

his rheumatism, he moved alone to Exmouth in January 1946. This was the first time that the twins had been apart for an extended period. The two-year separation was not easy for Wilfred and as he would go on to do at so many points in his life, he turned to the land and sea to console and inspire him. Having secured a position at the County Primary School, he found lodgings with an elderly widow. Appalled at his slight form, she preoccupied herself with mothering him and feeding him up. The gratitude Wilfred felt towards his landlady is evident in his gift of a watercolour landscape, painted in the year he moved. The illustrative scene of an Exmouth street as seen from the beach has been painted in a subdued palette, and is one of the earliest works remaining in existence. It has been saved, one might assume, from destruction merely due to the fact that Wilfred gave it away almost as soon as he had finished it. In the same year he co-founded the Exmouth Art Club, still active today with over 200 members.

On Sam's return from National Service (much of it in India), the twins decided to remain in Exmouth, and moved to a flat on Morton Crescent. Sam found a teaching position in nearby Teignmouth, and in 1949 Wilfred joined the art department of the John Stocker Secondary Modern School in Exeter. In their free time, they volunteered with the theatre group, the Exmouth Players. Wilfred had first become involved with the theatre during his teacher training, and it would continue to occupy an important place in his life for many years to come. He took on myriad roles with the Players, painting scenery, producing and directing.

It was also around this time that he first began to seriously question his sexuality. This led in 1951 to a huge nervous breakdown, something undoubtedly compounded by working in a profession in which its discovery could lead to arrest. Wilfred's collapse can be interpreted as the first defining moment in his career, the point at which he discovered one of the themes that would come to characterise his practice, both an exploration of and a coming to terms with his own sexuality. He returned home to South Molton to recover, looked after by his supportive and unquestioning parents.

· · ·

Few works from this early period of Wilfred's career remain. The artist was intensely self-critical, destroying anything he did not feel matched his own high standards. This destruction could happen several years after completion or even after a work had already been exhibited. But what we are lacking in work is made up for with a whole trove of documentation written by the artist. It is through some of this writing that we know of the early religious quality of his work and his later interest 'in surrealism and tachisme via such "English" artists Nash, Sutherland and Frances Hodgkins'.[5] These many essays on art and art theory, as well as years of intimate diary entries, paint a portrait of someone who from the very beginning was thinking incredibly deeply about painting.

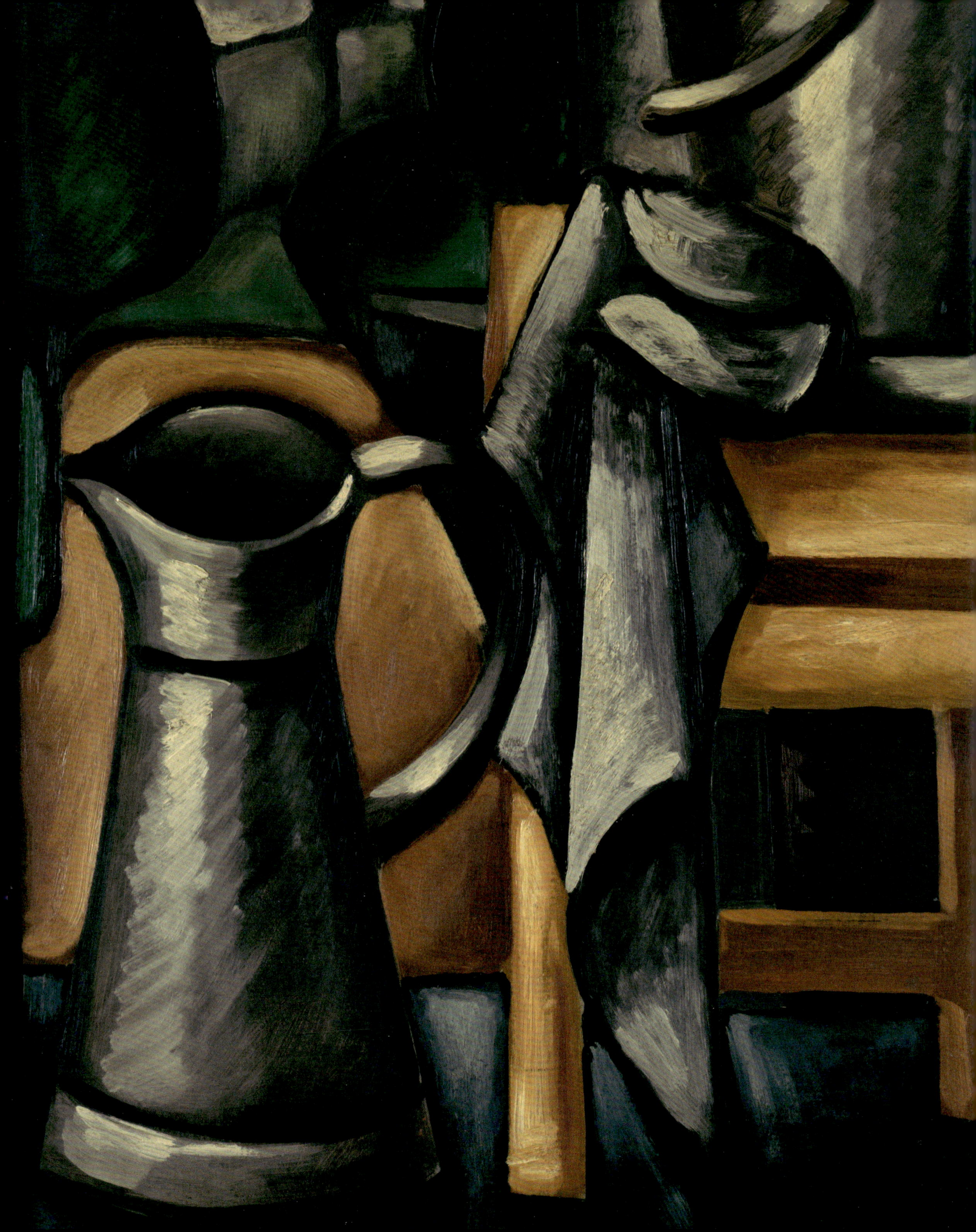

2 THE DOMESTIC INTERIOR

HAVING PAID OFF their student loans and completed the required period of teaching in Devon, Wilfred and Sam were keen to move to London, which they did at the beginning of 1952. At the cost of £7 per week, they rented a flat in Queen's Gate, South Kensington with their younger sister Pat. It was spacious enough for both of them to paint in, and all three siblings found work teaching with the London County Council. Although wanting with increasing compulsion to paint full-time, Wilfred took on a position at Campden Hill St George's School on Edge Street. It was out of continued financial necessity as much as his aptitude for teaching that he would remain here for the next eleven and a half years. Sam soon joined him and the pair were sometimes required to teach the same classes — much to the confusion of their pupils. In appearance, voice, even in the subject matter, style and success of their painting in this early period, the brothers were almost indistinguishable.

In London, and for the first time in his life, Wilfred had contact with the arts whenever he wanted it. Having recovered from his breakdown, he felt newly confident in his personal life and, moreover, in the direction he was taking his work. Instead of sitting back and waiting to be discovered, he approached the galleries he felt it would fit into, keen to find his place in the city's burgeoning avant-garde art scene. It was certainly the right time to move to the capital as an artist. Experimental commercial galleries had begun to crop up all over post-war London, and Wilfred showed some of his earliest work in two of its most important, Helen Lessore's Beaux Arts Gallery and Victor Musgrave's Gallery One. Both Lessore and Musgrave championed young and undiscovered artists, making their galleries two of the most influential nurseries of new talent in the post-war city.

The United Kingdom, however, was still deep in its post-war recovery, and 1950s London was a city of harsh contradiction, filled as much with vibrant creativity as it was with social and governmental intolerance. Reconstructive efforts placed equal importance in restoring cities as they did in rebuilding the nuclear family that years of conflict had broken apart. Rising divorce rates, coupled with a wartime slump in the British birth rate,[6] were considered a national threat, warranting restoration of the home — in its traditional format — as central in the drive towards reconstruction of the nation. 'The home,' as then Housing Minister Harold Macmillan declared in 1952, 'is the basis of the family, just as the family is the basis of the nation.' Macmillan's statement was demonstrated nowhere more obviously than in Clement Attlee's welfare state, the ideal citizen of which, as wittily hypothesised by broadcaster Kenneth Allsop, was the 'Sixteen pounds a week steady, pipe-smoking artisan with a safe job in the local works, a New Town house with a primrose front door, an attractive wife and two "kiddies" ...' Satirical, but with more than a grain of truth. By its very definition, the home was a heterosexual space, one that contained the traditional family unit and thus excluded queer men.[7] Those who did not fit the mould were characterised as threats to the very fabric of Britain, a danger not only to the structure of marriage and domesticity but at risk of leading astray the nation's youth.[8]

Despite the slow creep towards equality put into place by the 1957 Wolfenden Report, homophobia and sexual repression continued to loom large over Britain. Repercussions included social humiliation, loss of employment, arrest or institutionalisation.[9] Wilfred never defined himself as a gay artist, preferring instead to be known, as he put it, as 'an artist who happened to be gay'. But dismissing the suggestions of queer life in his 1950s works, made and exhibited within the context of such an inhospitable period in British history, would be a crucial error in interpretation.

• • •

It was into this bruised and conflicted city that Wilfred released the very earliest of his figure studies: three tender depictions of men undressing, painted between 1953 and 1956. Theirs are not erotic bodies — Wilfred's heavy and muddied impasto leaves it apparent that they were not

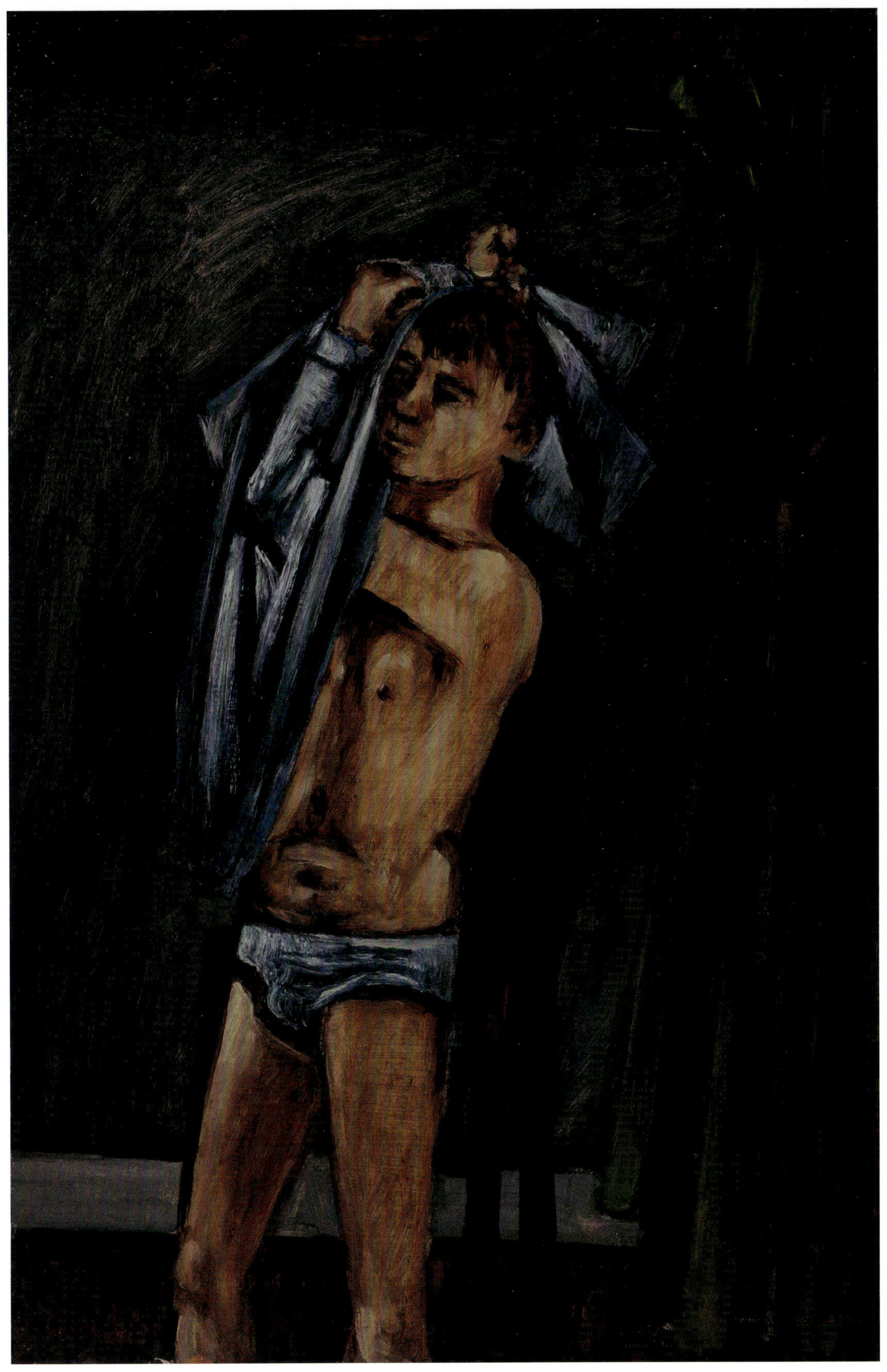

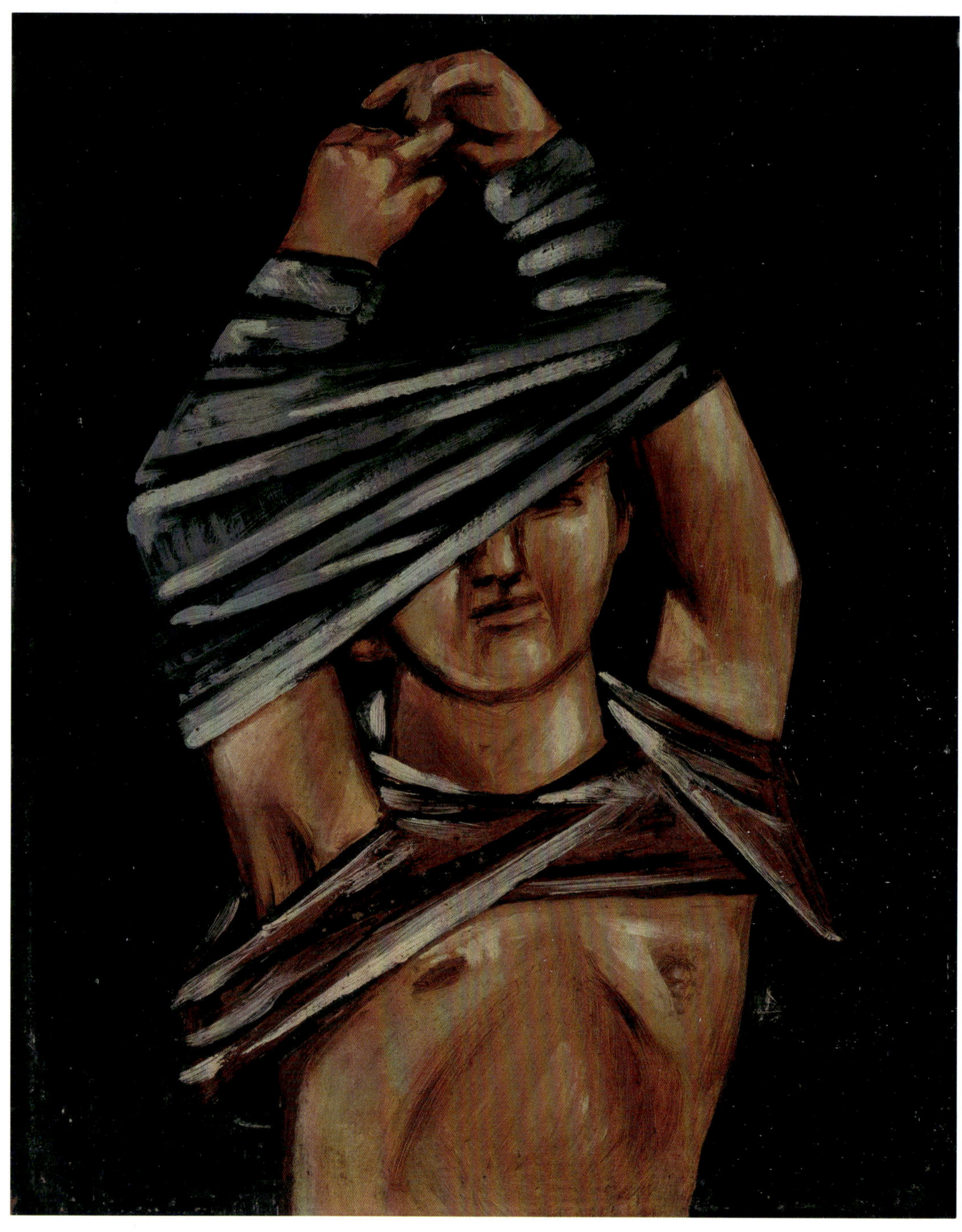

ABOVE
2:2 *Boy Undressing*
1955
51 x 46 cm
Oil on hardboard
(Private collection)

RIGHT
2:3 *Figure Undressing*
1956
112 x 81.5 cm
Oil on board
(Sheffield Museums Trust)

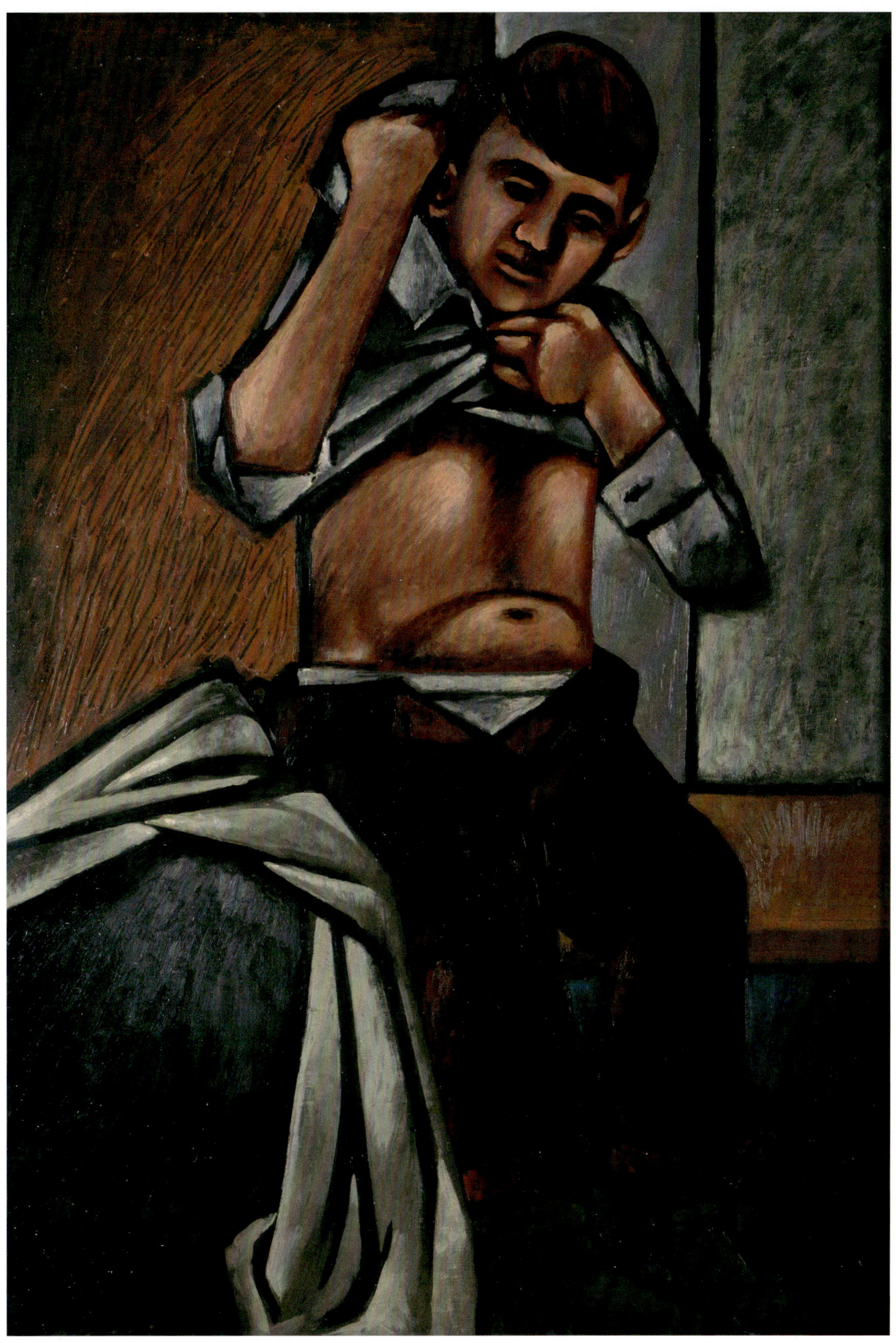

painted with sex on the mind. We are instead invited into the artist's domestic space, to experience the quietly intimate act of undressing. All three have been depicted lost in their own thoughts, each unaware of the presence of any viewer. Two further figures, drawn in 1959 in Wilfred's favoured Flomaster pen, share this avoidant pose. The same reserved facial expressions and closed-off body language continued to crop up throughout Wilfred's career (see *Figure* and *Male Portrait*, both made in 1959).

Work by the English artist Keith Vaughan bears a similar sense of melancholic intimacy. Vaughan's nudes lack a self-awareness in the same way as Wilfred's, a having to be 'on'. Both self-taught queer artists working in London in the same period, there are a number of interesting parallels between the pair. Vaughan was a conscientious objector, conscripted in 1941 into the Non-Combatant Corps. His record of life in the Wiltshire barracks makes repeated reference to the gratifying experience of living

BELOW LEFT
2:4 Figure
1959
33 x 20 cm
Flomaster pen on paper
(*Sheffield Museums Trust*)

BELOW RIGHT
2:5 Male Portrait
1959
38 x 28 cm
Flomaster pen on paper
(*Sheffield Museums Trust*)

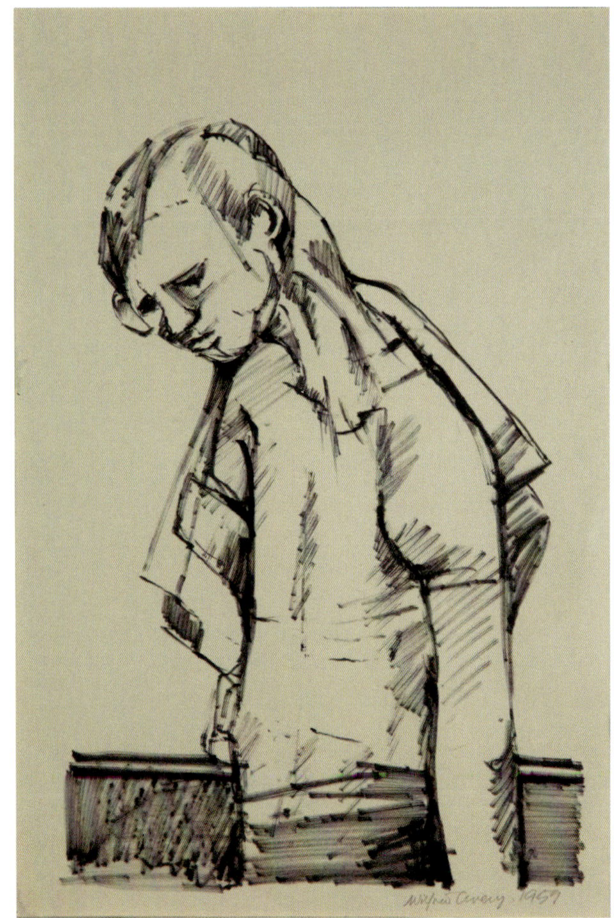

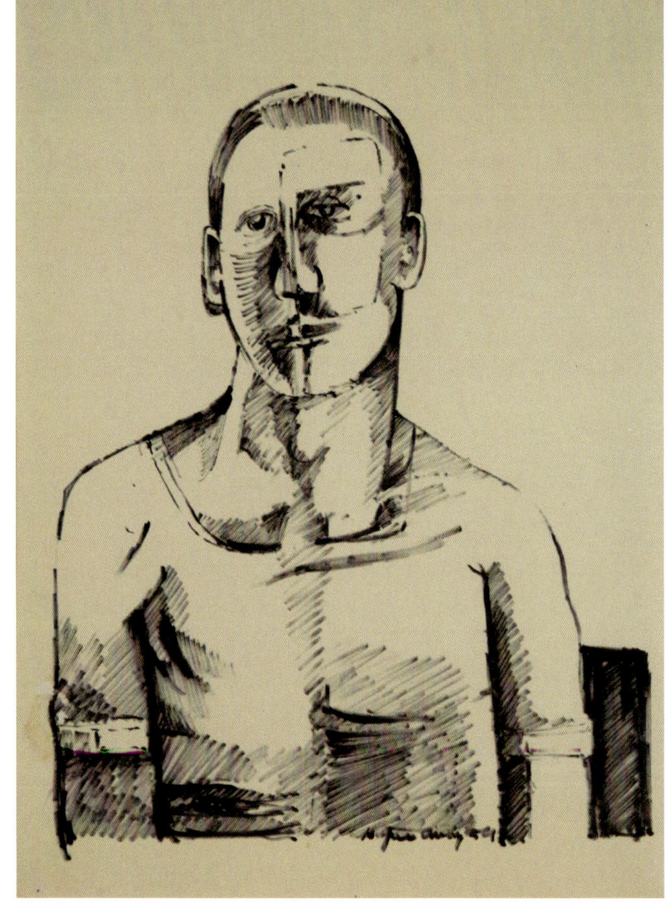

in close proximity with other men, an interpretation of domesticity unheard of in the outside world.[10] Sam had shared a similar experience during his own conscription, returning from India having not only lived with but also having had his first romantic relationship with a man. It seems likely that Sam's homecoming played into Wilfred's breakdown in 1951. Seeing his mirror image split for the first time and so drastically from his own trajectory must have caused him to seriously question his own sexuality and lack of sexual experience.

Wilfred's early figure studies are not erotic, but it is not much of a stretch to imagine the raised arms of the second of Wilfred's undressing boys to have taken some subtle influence from Michelangelo's *Dying Slave* (1513–16); the sculpture's lavish sensuality swapped for something more appropriate for 1950s London. Wilfred had not seen the original in Paris at this point, but would certainly have been familiar with its copy in the Cast Courts of the V&A.

The three studies are also indebted to Cézanne, each bearing a remarkable similarity both stylistically and in paint application to his *Man Standing Arms Extended* (c. 1878) and *The Bather* (c. 1885). In all three we see the same rubbery skin covering the same stocky form. The same hair colour and the same round face bearing the same melancholic expression. They are even all sharing the same pair of underpants.

In fact, those very same underclothes appear, too, in Piero della Francesca's *Baptism of Christ* (after 1437). Seemingly unaware of the sanctity of the occasion, a boy undresses just to the right of John the Baptist, revealing his white underwear as he pulls the tangled robes off over his head. Both Francesca's *Baptism* and *Crucifixion* of c. 1460 remained incredibly significant to Wilfred. He kept postcards of them in his studio, returning to the National Gallery for replacements when they got old and shabby. Just over a decade after completing his figure studies, Wilfred met his life partner John Raymond Crossley (known as Ray), and in their years together, made clear his preference for Ray to wear only white underwear. It was some years before Ray realised that this might be an attempt by Wilfred to recreate, morning and night, this background figure in Francesca's *Baptism*. There is no more visceral example, if so, of the sheer importance Wilfred took in the visual arts.

But who is the figure depicted in these three works? It might be easy to assume that Sam acted as some kind of model — his body as familiar to Wilfred as his own. However, Wilfred rarely, if ever, drew or painted the figure directly from life. And so although these figure studies are perhaps not directly inspired by lived experience, they *can* be interpreted as an expression of the domestic intimacy for which Wilfred was striving. Wilfred's long cohabitation with Sam is also evidence of this desire to live closer to their shared truths. Along with Vaughan and so many others in the queer community, he was negotiating his own version of heterosexual domesticity.[11] This domestic intent is mirrored, too, in the robust, flat-plane still lifes of the same period. Frying pans, glass bottles, a saucepan and spatula; domestic compositions set out on top of rumpled white tablecloths, some in Flomaster pen and others in the same thick and muted palette as Wilfred's undressing boys. Examples can be found in *Interior with Bucket and Jug* (1954) and *Room with a View 1* (1957).

Wilfred's depictions of the queer body within the domestic interior were made at a time it was rarely seen in the public sphere, let alone on the walls of a gallery. And even on gallery walls, the queer body was far from completely accepted. Francis Bacon's *Two Figures* (1953) — a homoerotic depiction of two nude men embracing in a dark room — was painted in the same year as Wilfred's *Figure Undressing*. It was exhibited in Erica Brausen's Hanover Gallery on completion. Fearing the provocation of a police raid should it be seen by the wrong eyes, Brausen hung it in the highest reaches of the space, half-hidden from any visitor who was not actively seeking it out.[12]

As previously discussed, Wilfred was not (as of yet) concerned with depictions of the *erotic* body. But what he did share with Bacon in this period was a preoccupation with the queer body depicted within an intimate domestic space. Viewed in this way, Wilfred's figure paintings become just as radical as this stalwart of the post-war London art scene. By painting the queer body within the domestic interior, Wilfred subverted the traditional concept of home, drawing attention to the fact that whatever one's sexual orientation, domestic life is inherently the same.

OPPOSITE

2:6 Interior with Bucket and Jug

1954

95 x 84.5 cm

Oil on board

(Sheffield Museums Trust)

• • •

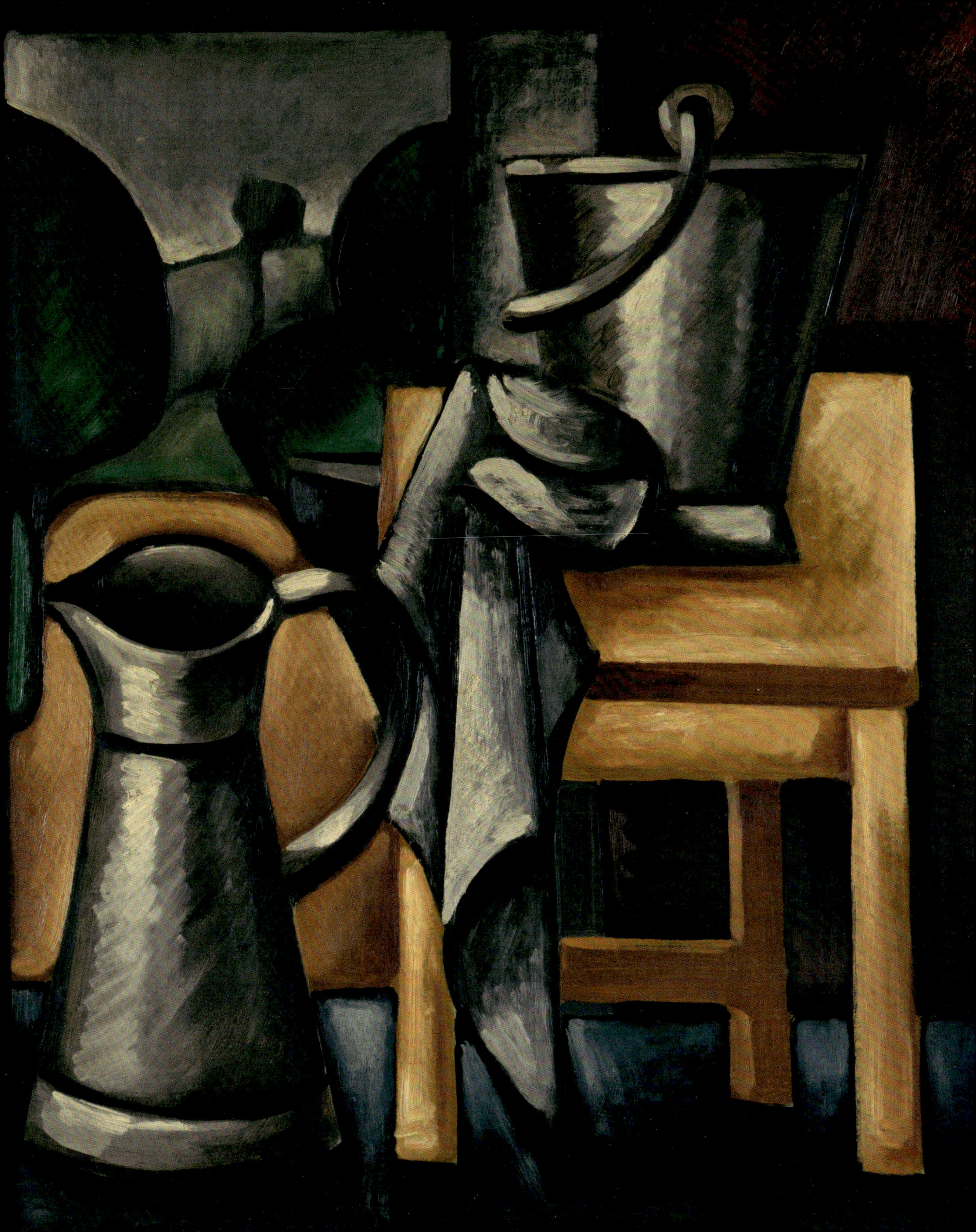

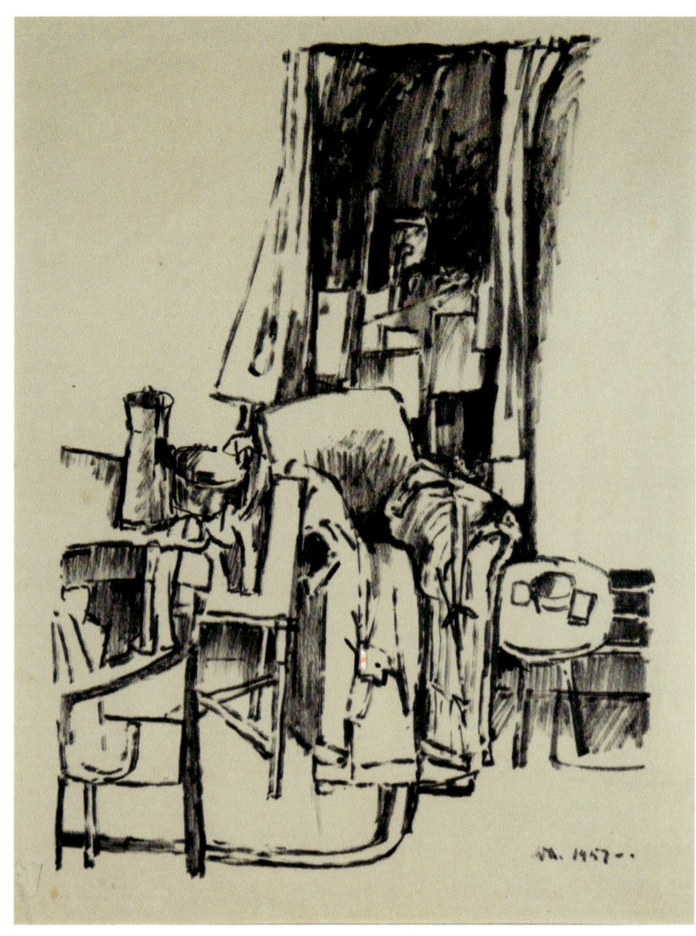

2:7 Room with a View 1
1957
40 x 32.5 cm
Flomaster pen on paper
(Sheffield Museums Trust)

Wilfred first exhibited in London in February 1953. *Family Group* (1953) was chosen for a group show at Helen Lessore's Beaux Arts Gallery on Bruton Street, Mayfair. Like much of Lessore's exhibition programme – due as much to financial pressures as her inclination to foster new talent, *Ten Young Artists* comprised only early career painters. Both Wilfred and Sam exhibited alongside Roderic Barrett, Diana Cumming, John Eyles, Donald Fraser, Peter Haigh, John Hart, George Manchester and Roy Pegram.

Although the only evidence we have of *Family Group* is its inclusion in the exhibition catalogue for Lessore's show, the work's name and date suggest it fits within Wilfred's early religious phase. Moreover, we know he destroyed it just two years later. Wilfred was considering – even at this very early stage – exactly how his work as a whole would be perceived in the long term. This makes his process of elimination just as fascinating – and telling – as the works that remain in existence.

It is interesting to note here that both *Family Group* and the first of his three male figures, *Figure Undressing*, were painted in the same year. The destruction of one but not the other is evidence enough of a decisive change in trajectory by 1955, and allows us to deduce that it was with his undressing boys that he wanted a future audience to see his career beginning. It also seems the most likely reason he exhibited with Lessore only once before moving to Victor Musgrave's Gallery One.

However fleetingly it may have been, Lessore's inclusion of Wilfred in her exhibition programme does pinpoint him right within the zeitgeist. Additionally, and for the first and only time in his career, his decision to approach Lessore's gallery marks a complete conviction of where his work sat in the art market. Wilfred's work into the late 1950s continued to fit well within Lessore's aesthetic, especially when viewed alongside her own group, the Kitchen Sink Painters. This commercially popular movement was active between 1952 and 1957 and comprised four male painters: John Bratby, Derrick Greaves, Edward Middleditch and Jack Smith. The group was originally named after Lessore's gallery and known as the Beaux Arts Quartet. They gained the name Kitchen Sink from critic David Sylvester, when in a 1954 review he queried their subject matter with the words, 'everything but the kitchen sink? The kitchen sink too.'[13] Their subject matter was described by critic John Berger at the time as everyday and banal. These were dingy interiors painted in heavy and muddy colours. Wilfred's own early London works are of a similar earthy robustness, still lifes and plain interiors occupied by simple figures.

Although in his turning away from Lessore's gallery, we can reasonably conclude a dramatic attitude shift in the direction Wilfred wanted his work to go in, association with the Kitchen Sink style lingered. He remained dismissive of this, insistent that his subject matter was a reflection of his rural origins rather than something honed through the mimicry of his contemporaries. This is the first example of a lifelong resistance to categorisation. And, anyhow, the casually misogynistic, heteronormative space of the Kitchen Sink was no home for him. It would be a detriment to Wilfred to uphold this 1950s critique. To reiterate, placing him instead within a queer context highlights a quietly radical practice and marks this as the crucial point from which his work would naturally progress into the confident and unabashed eroticism of his maturity.

● ● ●

Rent had begun to rise in London. The siblings' landlord, keen to increase the price of his property, accused Wilfred of breaching the terms of the lease by using it to paint in professionally; a particularly unfair claim, as Wilfred was holding down a full-time teaching job and earning barely anything from his practice. Still, his inclusion in this sole exhibition at the Beaux Arts Gallery was enough to be considered for one of Chelsea Council's artist studios, a block of flats on Hortensia Road with studio space on the top floor. The flats had just been built as part of the city's

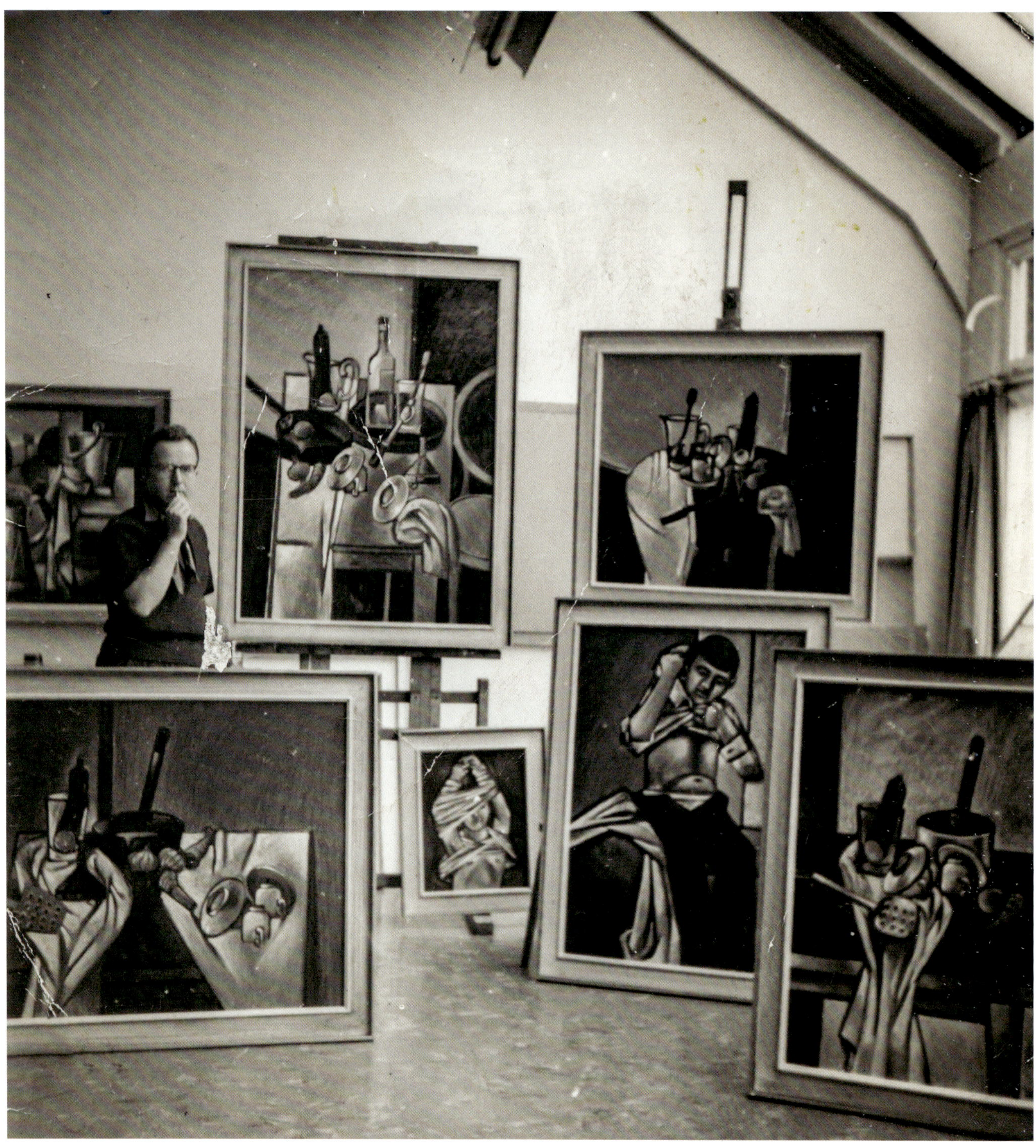

**2:8 Wilfred in his studio
at Knight's House**
1956
14 x 12 cm
Photograph
(*Studio*)

post-war reconstruction programme, attempting to encourage a revival of Chelsea's artistic links and let only to practising artists. The twins successfully applied for the largest of the three, and moved to Knight's House in 1955.

Just before this move, the twins found representation at Gallery One. The gallery's founder, Victor Musgrave, offered them two joint shows, one in 1954 (Litchfield Street) and then two years later in 1956 (D'Arblay Street). He also included them in a large 1954 summer group show of paintings and etchings. A black and white photograph shows Wilfred in his large, bright studio at Knight's House, surrounded by the work he exhibited in the 1956 exhibition. The selection includes two of his undressing boys, the only time either were exhibited.

The 1954 show was well reviewed by Stephen Bone in the *Guardian* and in *Art News* by the writer Oswell Blakeston. Blakeston's article mirrors Wilfred's own attitude to his work, taking note of the twins' rural upbringing: 'Their clearly designed work, has a simple, strong unity which is not the product of gallery conjurors with one-trick minds. It is a unity, a certain countryside philosophy, effectively communicated.'[14]

Musgrave's gallery was a place to socialise and network, a place where personal relationships were nourished as much as professional ones. Many of the gallery's roster of artists were captured on film by Musgrave's wife, the photographer Ida Kar. In 1956 she photographed Wilfred and Sam, posing in a casually theatrical manner behind a large painting of Wilfred's, *Table and Stool Against Landscape* (1954).

The social aspect of the gallery was a sticking point for Wilfred. Although he was not unsociable, the socialising he did was

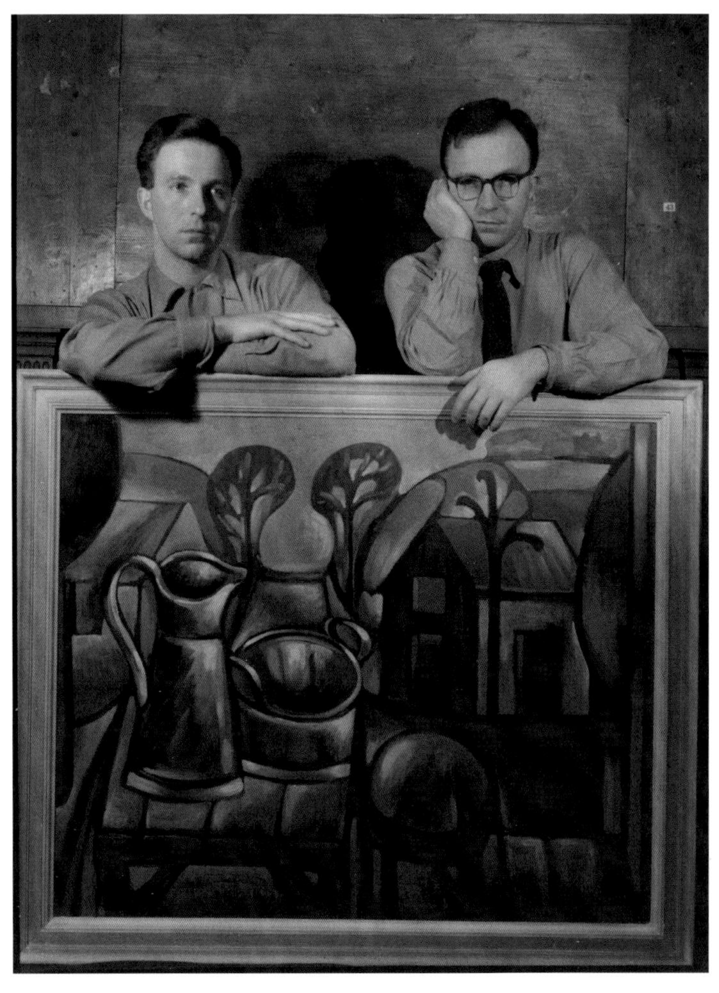

2:9 Ida Kar, *Samuel Lock (Samuel Avery); Wilfred Avery*
1956
Film negative
(*National Portrait Gallery, London*)

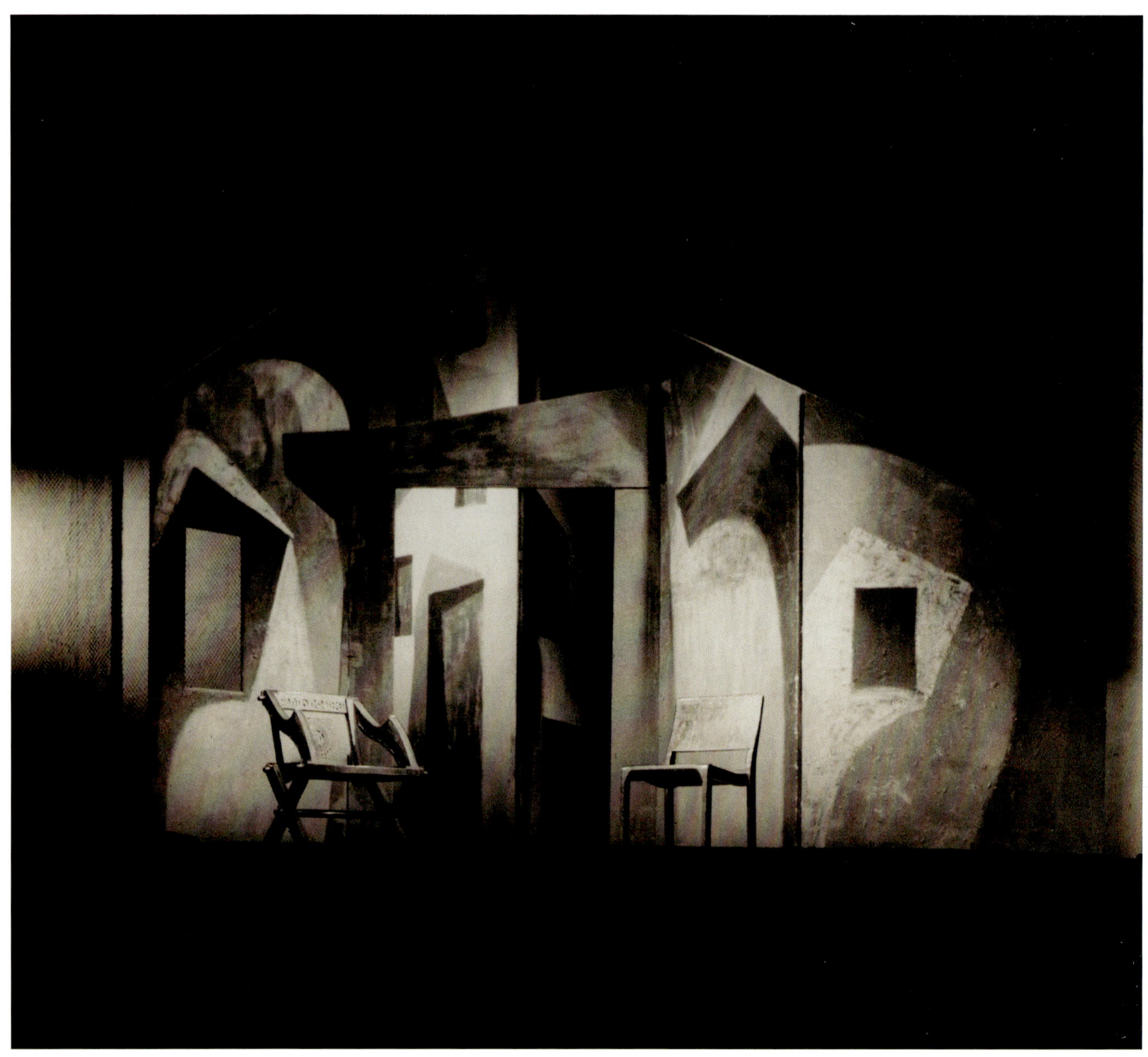

2:10 Stage set i for
The Numbered
1956
24 x 30 cm
Photograph
(Studio)

largely outside the art world and was instead far closer directed towards the theatre; something with which he continued to involve himself. In autumn 1956, Sam and he volunteered to design the stage sets for the reopening of the Oxford Playhouse. Set designs included Giraudoux's *Electra*, Cocteau's *Knights of the Round Table* (translated by W.H. Auden), and the premier of both *The Numbered* by Elias Canetti and Angus Wilson's *The Mulberry Bush*. (Interestingly, Wilfred's set designs were far more stylised and abstracted than his paintings of the same period, almost as if they were a premonition of what was to come in his work.) Although well-received,

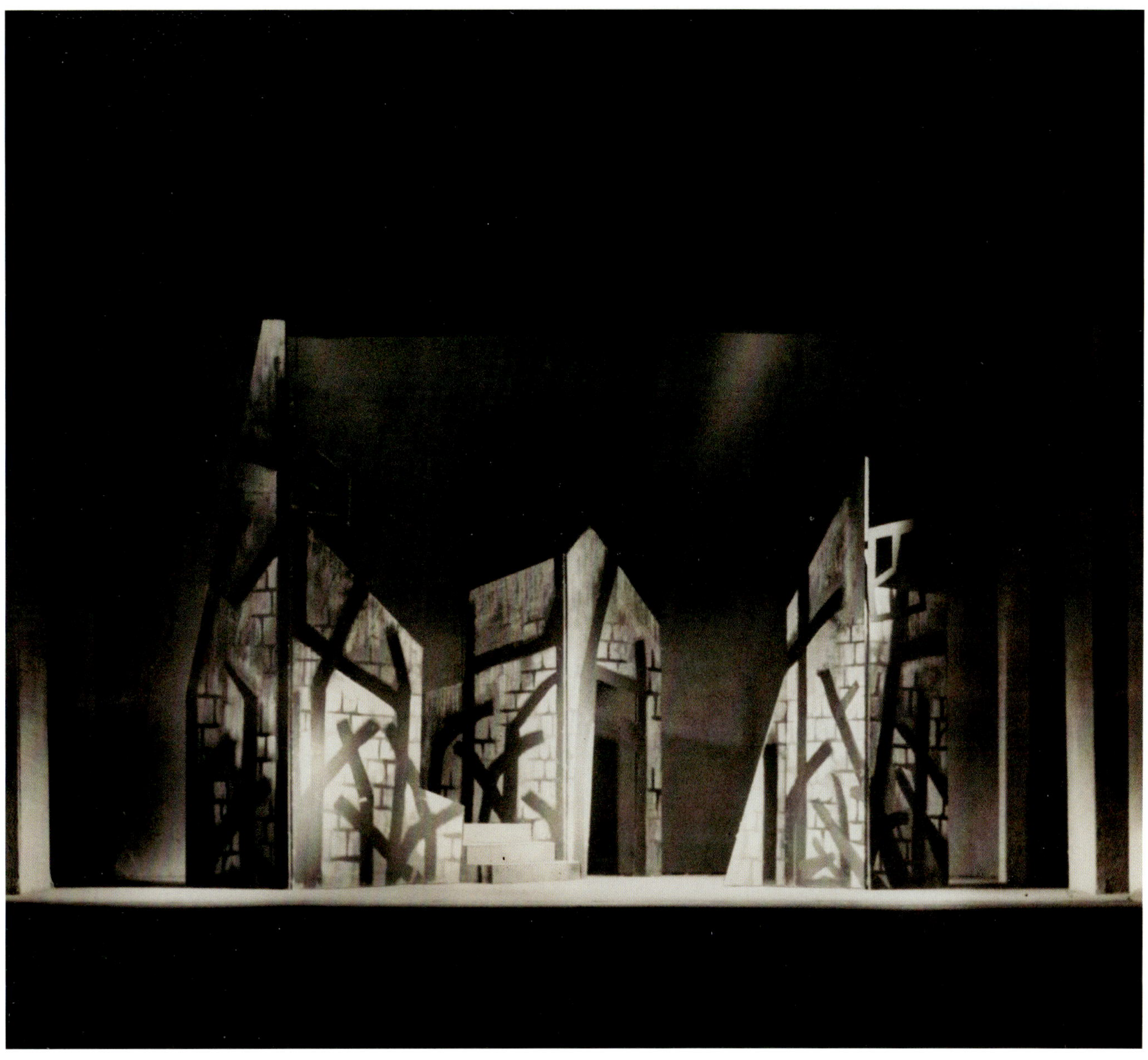

2:11 Stage set ii for
The Numbered
1956
25 x 29 cm
Photograph
(Studio)

Wilfred was reluctant to continue his work at the theatre at the expense of his painting, and so left after only one season. In strange synchronicity, Sam had at the same time decided to abandon painting to focus on writing, changing his surname from Avery to their mother's, Lock. The theatre, however, remained important to them both and their social circle would continue to centre around the stage.

After two years living together in Knight's House, the twins decided that if they were to have any personal life at all, they should split up. Wilfred moved out in 1957, leaving Sam to remain in the flat until his death in 2016. He found a derelict workshop in the back garden of the Down Under Club on Fulham Road, which the owner let for a tiny price on Wilfred's agreement that he refurbish it. Having an aesthetic eye, this Wilfred could do, but as he had never lived alone before, he did not know how to cook. He could not even make toast, and ate his meals in a local café every day. Unable to reciprocate the dinner parties to which he was often invited, and after realising that he only had to buy the very minimum of three bottles of wine in order to borrow 150 wine glasses from Barkers, a department store on Kensington High Street, Wilfred began holding a monthly open house. For one evening a month his home and studio became a mixing pot of young playwrights, novelists and actors who would often turn up to try out their acts for the first time. Guests included Kenneth Williams, Maggie Smith, J.B. Priestley, Peter Nichols and Sean Connery. Friends were allowed to bring friends, on the proviso that they *must* be someone interesting.

Wilfred lived at the workshop until its demolition in 1960. In any case, he had by that point decided it was too spartan for his living standards, and moved, after a temporary stay in the basement of a house in Brechin Place, with friends from his acting circle, to Swiss Cottage. Here he rented the top floor of 21 Fairfax Road from the actor Bernard Horsfall. A friend from the twin's Exmouth days, Jack Humphries, who was also an actor and had been the stage manager at the Oxford Playhouse, moved in at the same time and they shared a kitchen. This new accommodation must have been gratefully received by the artist — a basement flat can hardly have supplied him with the natural light that would become such a prominent feature of all his future studios.

• • •

Wilfred's social aversion already evident towards his own artistic circles undoubtedly had an adverse effect on his career. It was not that he did not want to be recognised; years' worth of rejection letters from museums and galleries makes this apparent. But of particular interest is the *sort* of recognition he wanted. Wilfred wanted his work to speak for itself. In essence, what he wanted to do was paint — in his own studio and alone.

At this point there was some momentum around his work, but by not taking networking seriously, he was left with far less opportunity to meet collectors and dealers. He found himself without an ongoing audience, and remained on the periphery of the London art scene. And the art world, of course, continued to mutate. Many of these changes can be seen in the later exhibition programming of Gallery One, which had moved away from painting and towards avant-garde sculpture and performance. Although his work continued to appear in various mixed shows in London, within just a decade it had become apparent to Wilfred that he no longer had a place in its creative heart.

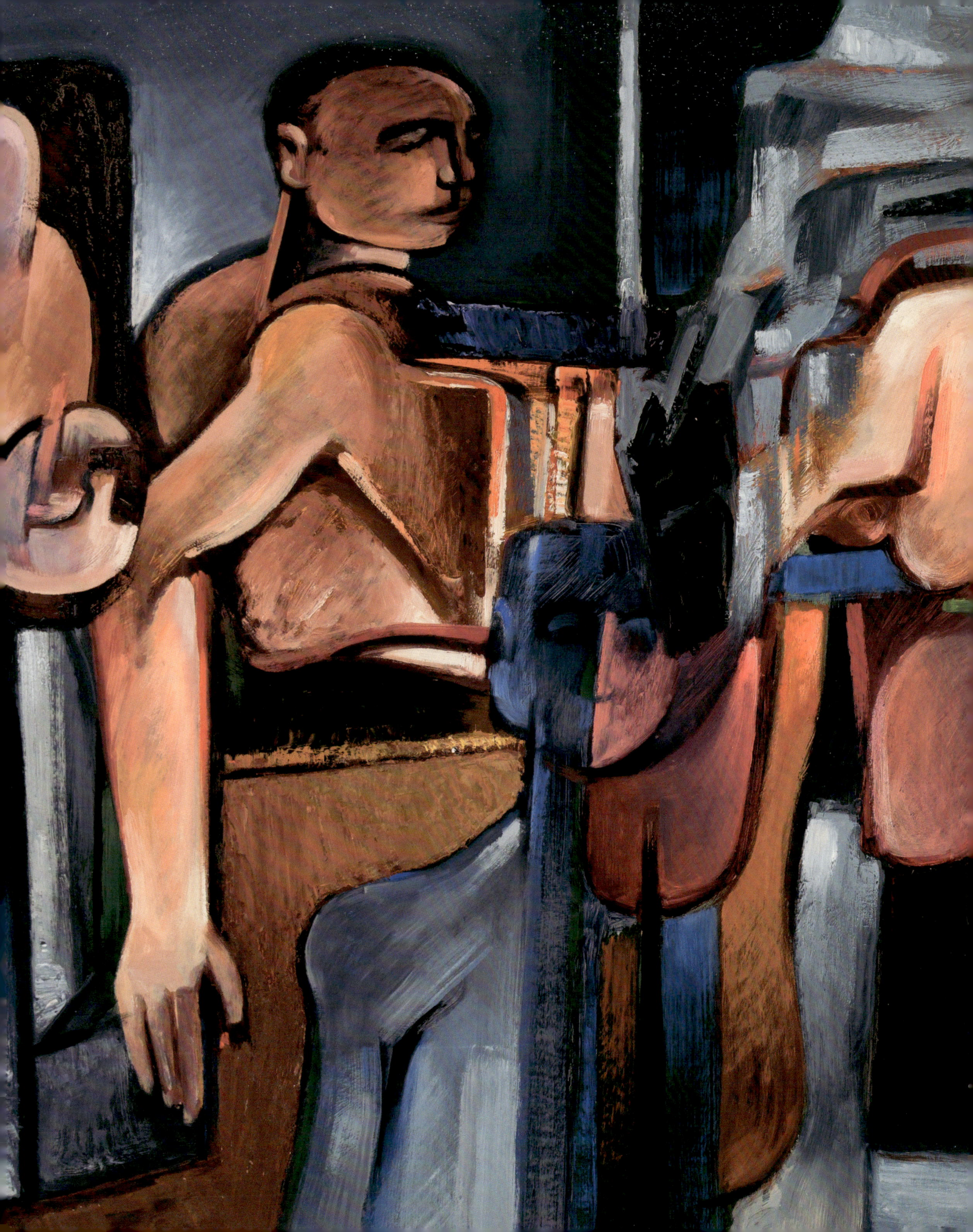

3 EXPERIMENTS IN FRAGMENTATION

THE LATE 1950S marked a second important shift in subject matter in which Wilfred turned away from the figure and surrounding domestic interior and looked instead to landscape. But these were no London scenes. They were landscapes sourced instead by turning inwards; views of Wilfred's Devon childhood and early adulthood in Exmouth. Having freed himself from the dreary colour constraints of the Kitchen Sink Painters, Wilfred's palette lightened and expanded into a vibrancy rare for the period; post-war art not being known for its colour schemes.

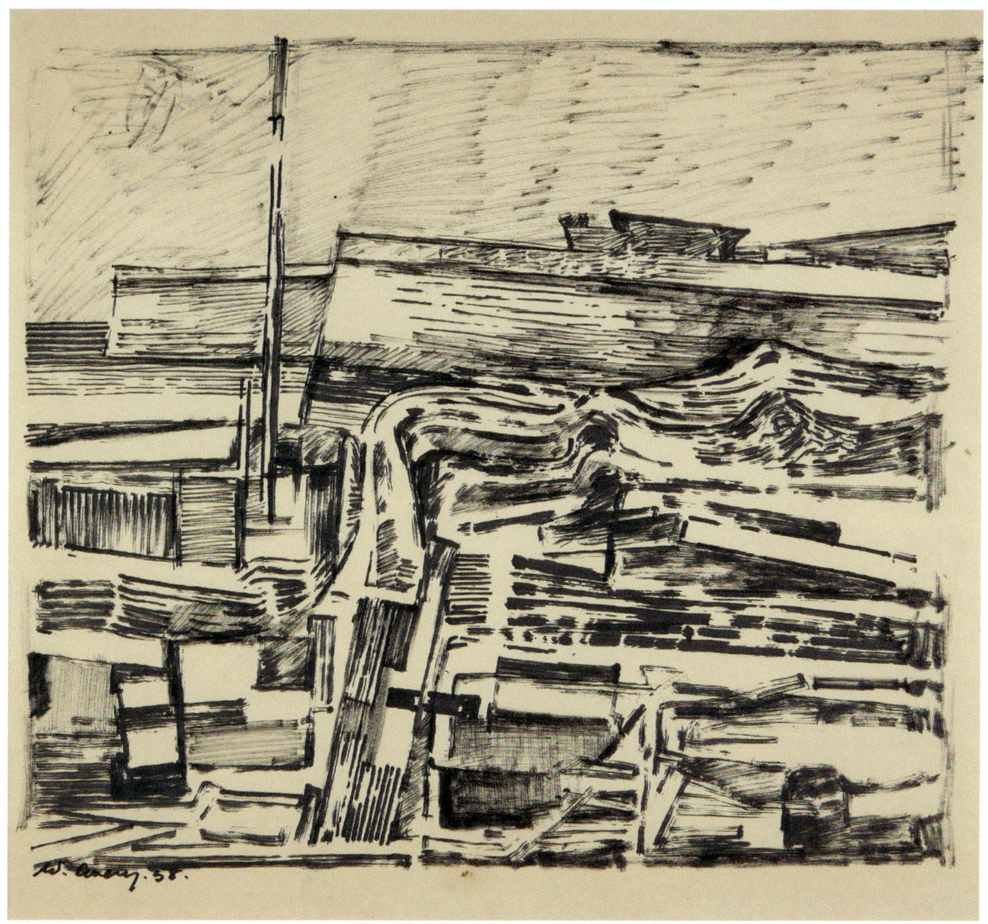

3:1 Coastscape 2
1958
33 x 40 cm
Flomaster pen on paper
(Towner Eastbourne)

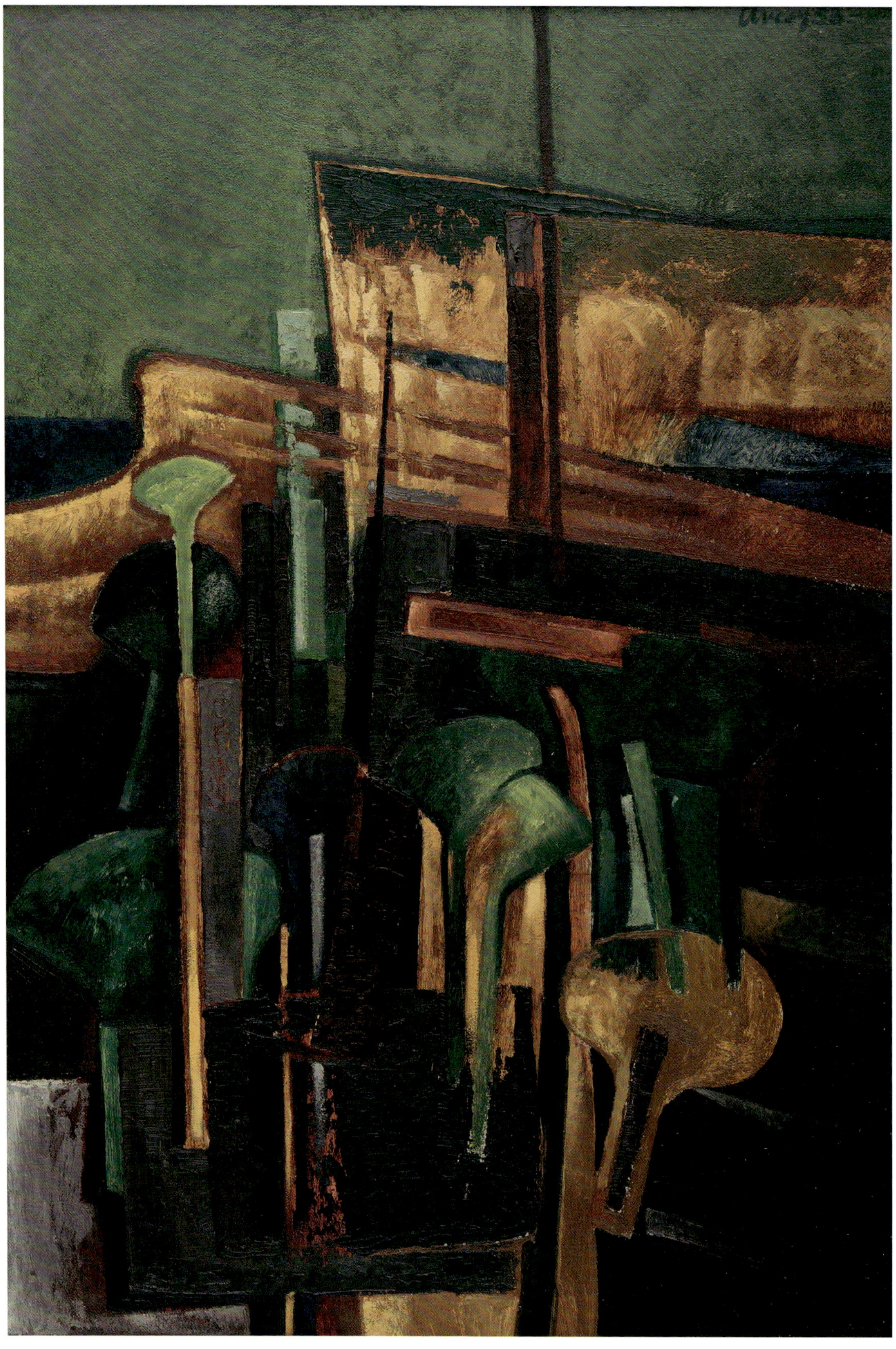

Landscapes painted between 1957 and 1960 are bright and claustrophobic. The latter, Wilfred claimed, was not artistic licence but reflected instead the tight-squeeze of the North Devon coastline. Stylistically, his work took on the central developments of early twentieth-century painting, favouring the formalised fragmentation of late Cubism. Still life was abandoned and did not reappear.

A large body of drawings in Flomaster pen precedes these paintings. Elements from many can be seen repeated in later oils. The stepped horizon line and patterned fields of *Coastscape 2* (1958), for example, are duplicated in *Landscape Near the Sea*, *Summer Landscape* and *Landscape with Cliffs* (all 1958). But it is clear on viewing these drawings in comparison to his oils that they are experimental work rather than

OPPOSITE

3:2 *Landscape Near the Sea*

1958

107 x 74.5 cm

Oil on board

(The Ingram Collection of Modern British and Contemporary Art © John-Paul Bland)

BELOW

3:3 *Summer Landscape*

1958

70 x 79 cm

Oil on board

(The Hepworth Wakefield)

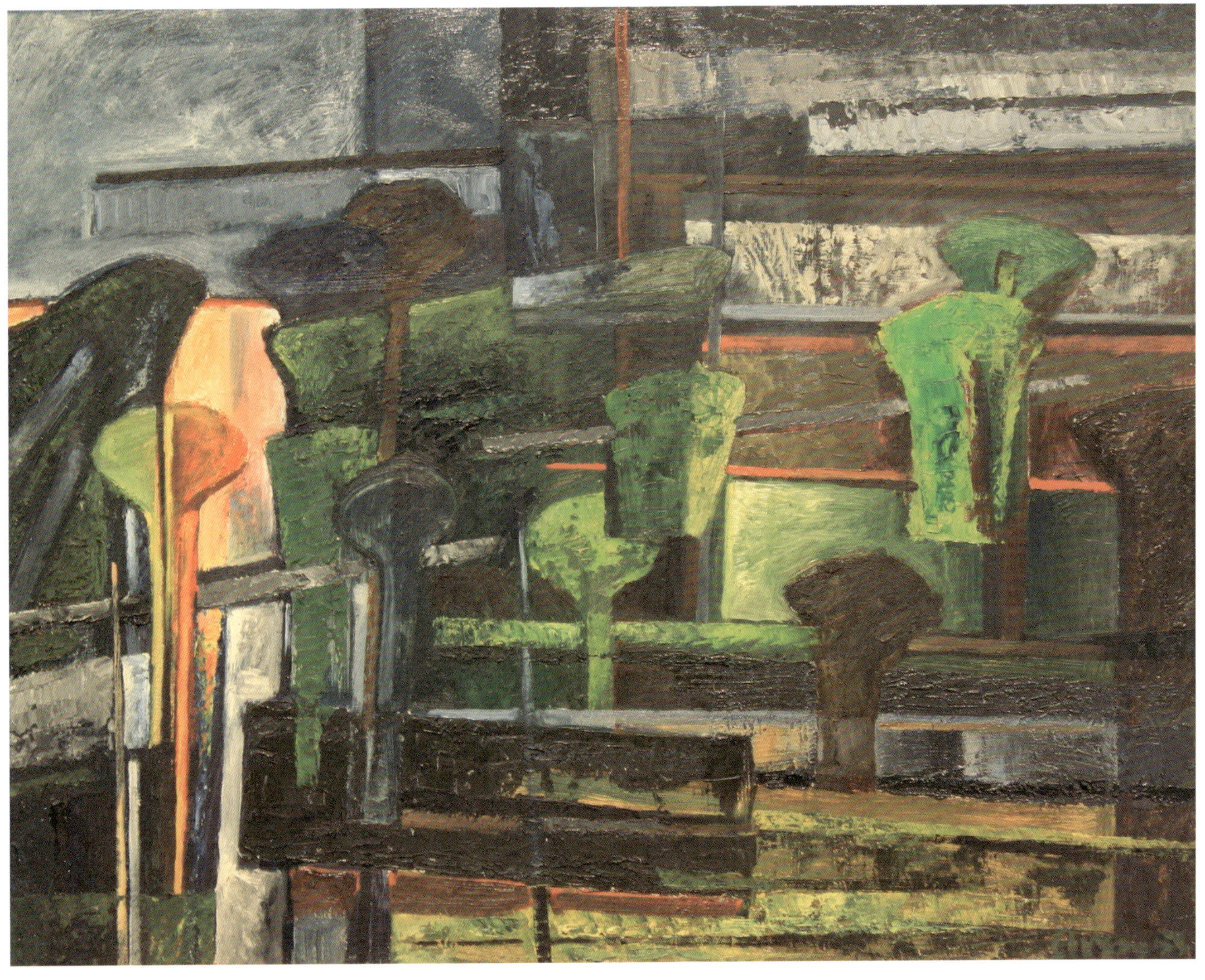

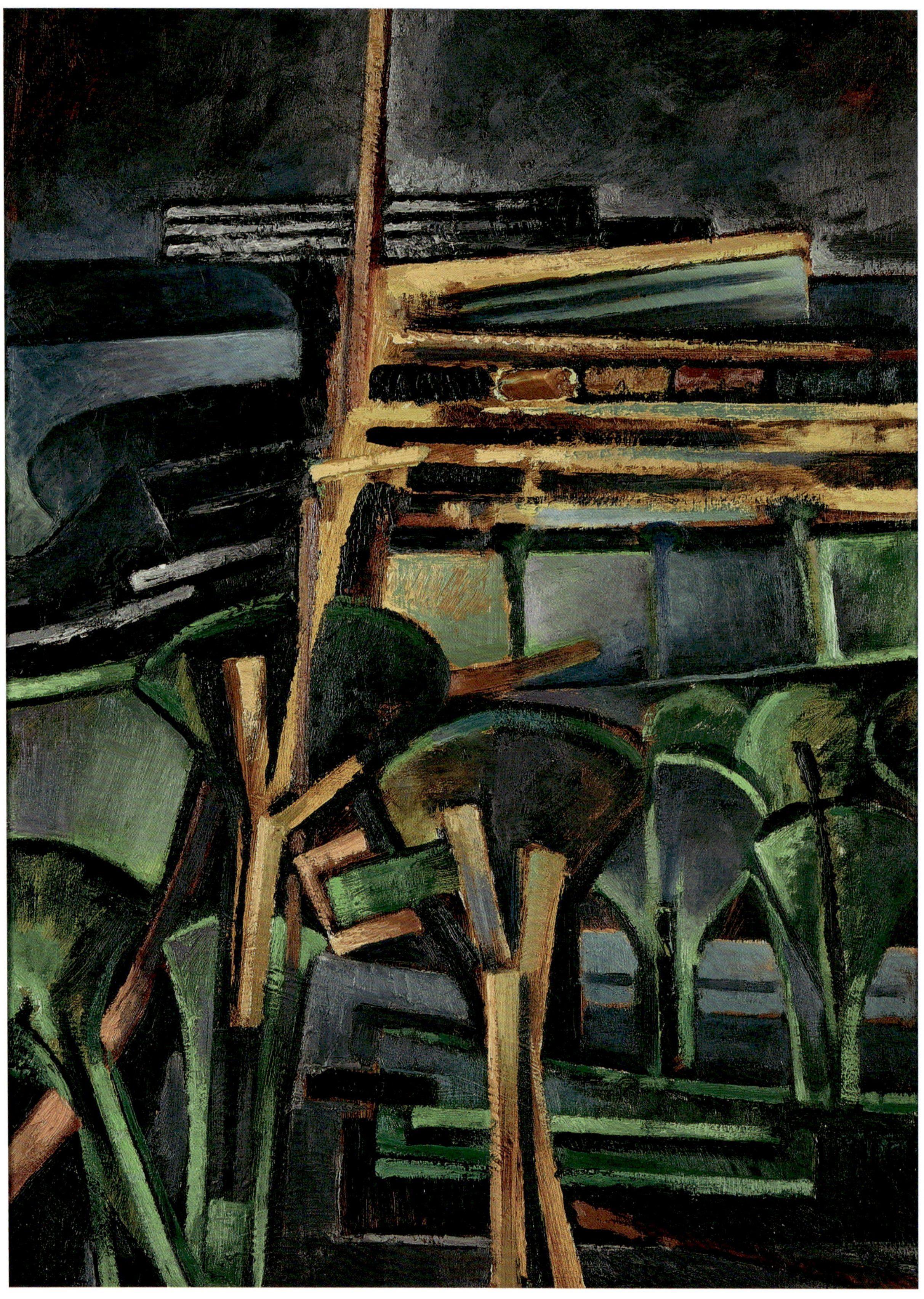

anything directly preparatory. Wilfred's paintings are conglomerations of his works on paper, assortments of memories overlaid to create semi-fictional landscapes.

This creative process is laid out more obviously in three sketches formally linked to *Summer Landscape* made in the preceding year (*Upright Landscape 1, 2* and *3*). The first is as true to life as we will ever see in Wilfred's landscape drawings — it is small but spacious, our eye drawn down what appears to be a tree-lined avenue. The latter pair are far more closely aligned to the painting. Trees have been simplified into lollipops and repeated. Open space gives way to intricate layering.

OPPOSITE
3:4 Landscape with Cliffs
1958
86 x 61 cm
Oil on hardboard
(*Towner Eastbourne*)

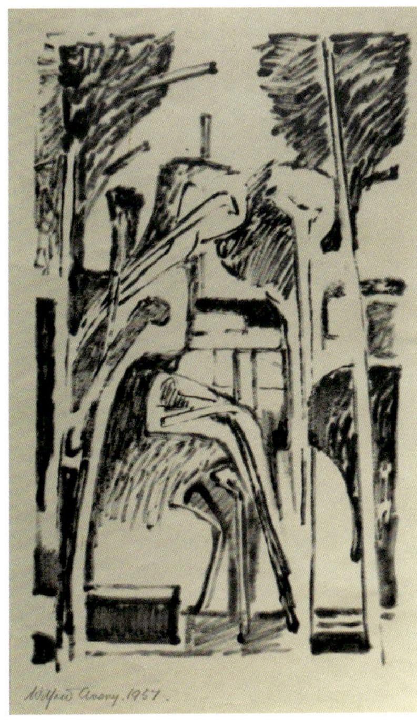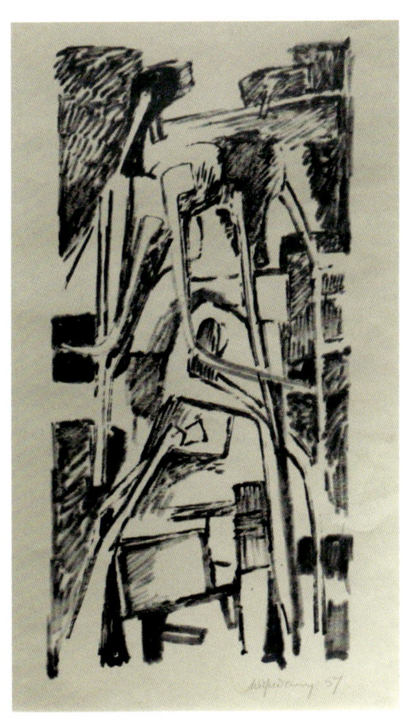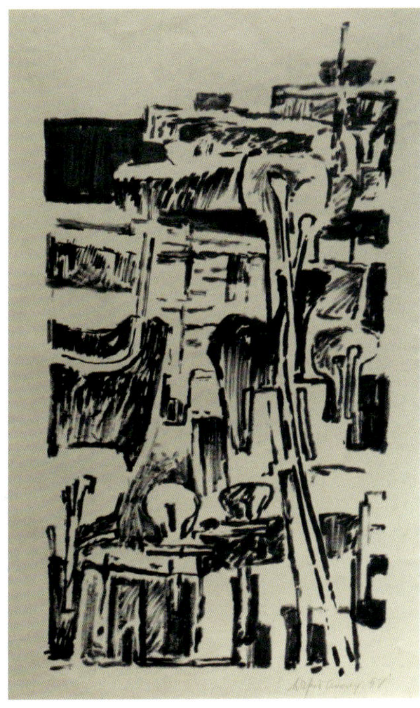

3:5 Upright Landscape 1
3:6 Upright Landscape 2
3:7 Upright Landscape 3
1957
33 x 18 cm
Flomaster pen on paper
(*The Hepworth Wakefield*)

The experimentation does not stop there, and even the painting that came after them shows signs of an ongoing thought process. All kinds of techniques are in evidence; paint applied with both brush and palette knife, and some partly rubbed off, allowing a luminous layer of underpaint to glow through. This same luminescence shines through in *Landscape Near the Sea*. In both, blocky trees layer up against a semi-geometric background. The ocean in the distance, a discoloured sky, but the whole vista radiant.

The lollipop shape appears again in *Fountains Abbey (Late Afternoon)* (1960). The Cistercian monastery was a source of great inspiration to Wilfred. After visiting for the first time in the winter of 1960, he painted two oils along with a series of studies in wax pastel — one of the only times he used this medium. One of this series was sold by Christie's a year later on behalf of the Aldeburgh Festival of Music and the Arts, amongst works by Stanley Spencer, Henry Moore, Barbara Hepworth and Duncan Grant. It was through the auction house that Wilfred met the outspoken art critic Brian Sewell, who bought one of the works from the series direct from his studio for £100.

Fountains Abbey (Late Afternoon) is an important example of an early foray into Cubist abstraction. The picture plane has been roughly quartered. This works to keep the eye in check and allows us to explore the scene without falling into discombobulation. A similar quartered composition can be found in *Coast Forms 2* (1957), drawn in Flomaster pen three years earlier. This makes evident the consistent trajectory of Wilfred's thought process, an ability to hold on to compositions and self-reference. Trees, in blue this time, stand close to what hints itself as an architectural structure (unusual to see a strong architectural influence in his work). Curved arches repeat and tumble over themselves. This is a deconstructed space, or even perhaps one seen from many angles, and in this sense it shares that particulate quality of Synthetic Cubism — how it is everything and all at once: an arm is as much part of a guitar as a human body, the placement of a nose on two (or even three) sides of one head all at the same time.

The Atelier paintings of late Braque were of particular importance in this period (see Wilfred's essay, *BRAQUE'S BIRD*, for detail of the broad and ongoing influence of the series, written in Brighton in 1999). A series of large interior still lifes painted over fifteen years from the later 1930s, Braque's flat-plane canvases are made up of fragmented and semi-recognisable shapes of sculpture and furniture. In some, a large white bird soars through, wings outstretched. Earthy tones have been mixed with fine sand and glow, as if sitting under a rich light source. Although he had by now moved away from the interior, Wilfred's use of Braque's technique of fragmenting and then layering, creates a dynamism, a

OPPOSITE
3:8 Fountains Abbey (Late Afternoon)
1960
59 x 49 cm
Oil on canvas
(Jerwood Collection)

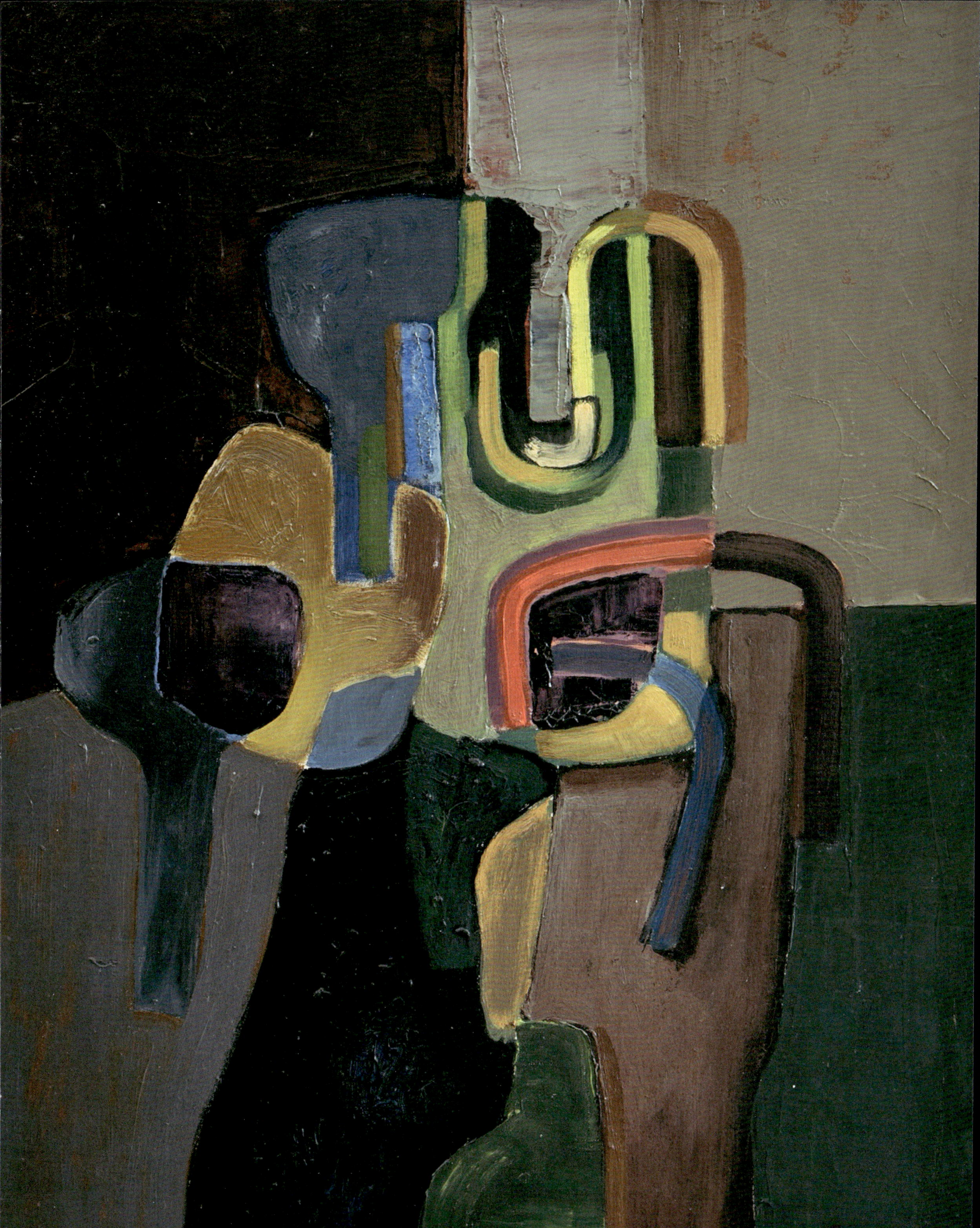

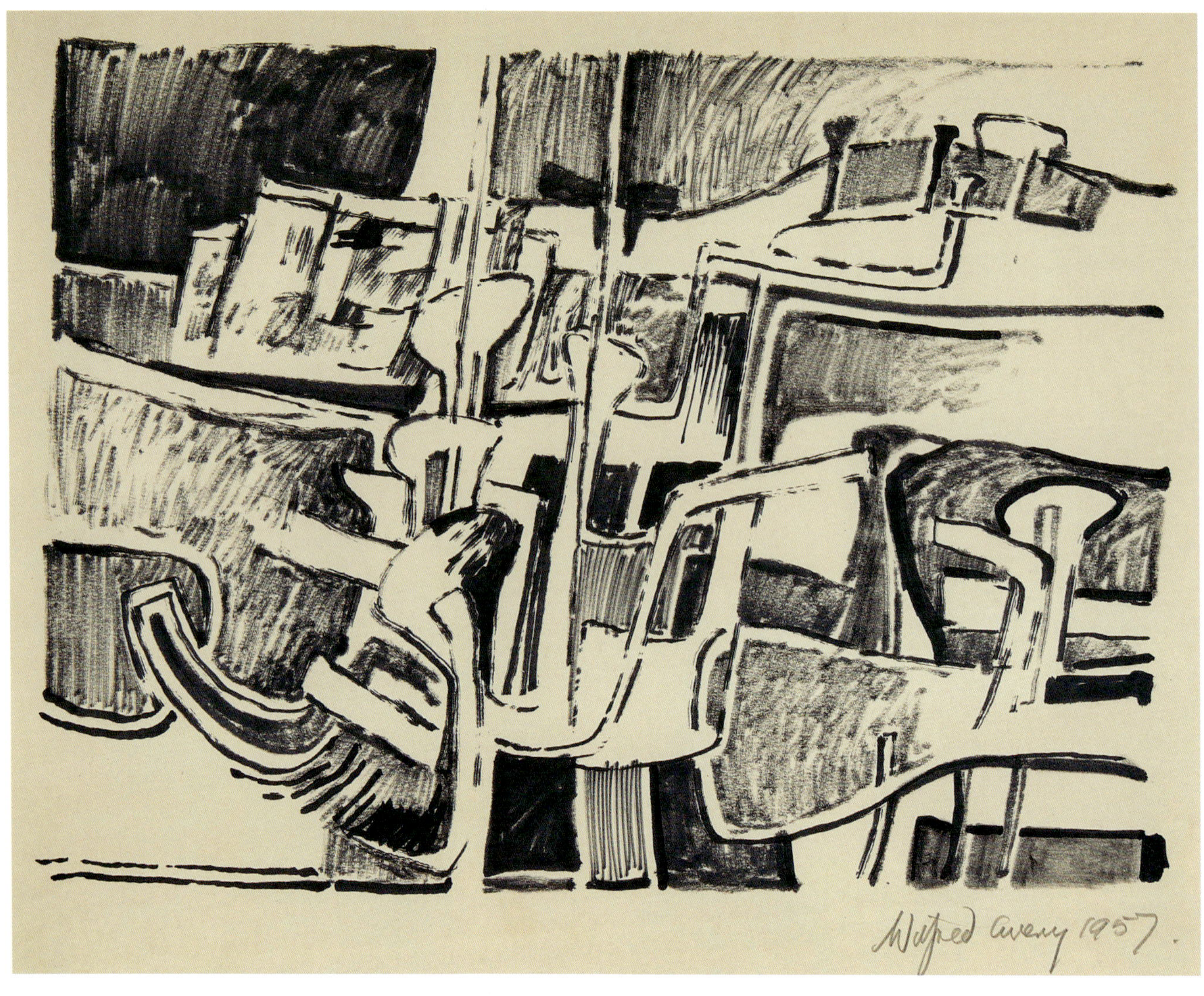

ABOVE
3:9 Coast Forms 2
1957
33 x 40 cm
Flomaster pen on paper
(Towner Eastbourne)

OPPOSITE
3:10 Summer Figure
1960
168 x 122 cm
Oil on hardboard
(Studio)

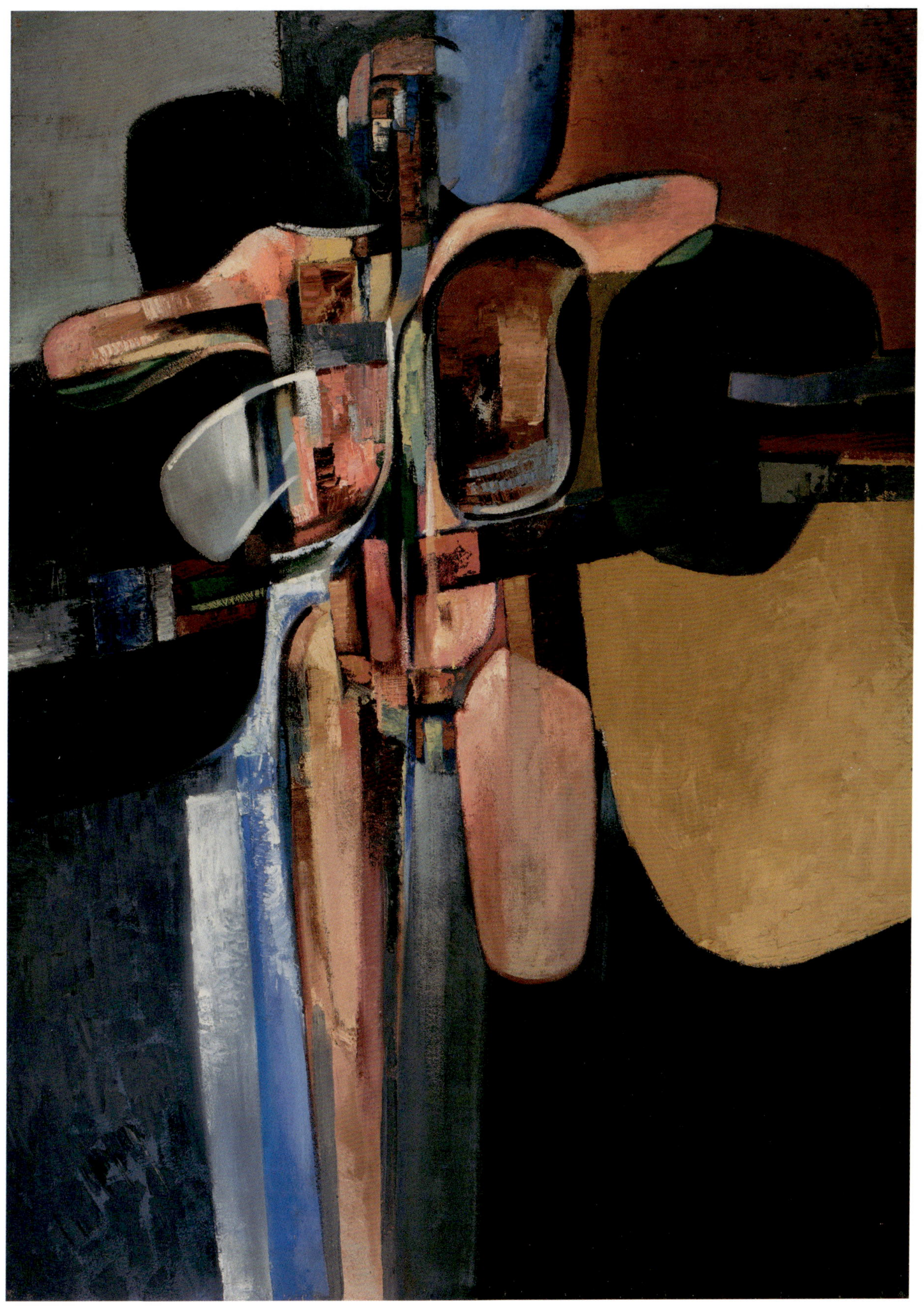

shifting sense of space and physicality in his flat, semi-geometric terms.

Wilfred's experimentation into Cubism reached its climax at the end of the decade with the enormous *Summer Figure* (1960). The work was shown only once, in his solo show, *The Evolving Image*, at the newly opened Woodlands Art Gallery in Blackheath, from 5 May to 7 June 1977.

Summer Figure is a real show in the mastery and multiplicity of Wilfred's paint application. Here, colour has been palette-knifed on to the hardboard in blocky sections; thick impasto coupled with smooth brushwork. In parts, sand has been mixed into the paint to create extra texture, a technique Wilfred shared with Braque and that he used until 1961. There is a confidence and joy in the use of colour; a Klee-like division and colouration to the figure's face. Flesh tones add a sense of naturalism to something just teetering on the edge of abstraction.

Summer Figure shows, for the first time, evidence of the artist in full control, whose application of paint tells us exactly where and how to look. Our eye is directed right to the centre of the cruciform composition, the same quartered pictorial structure first seen in the background of *Fountains Abbey (Late Afternoon)*, painted earlier the same year, and previous to that in *Coast Forms* 2. The work's background is mainly made up of curved forms (floating orbs of colour that offer the eye some respite from the painted complexity of the body), but it is the orthogonals that do most of the work here. They draw the eye into the crux of the figure, giving him a centre of gravity and rooting him via that elegant leg of his into real physical space. Two semi-horizontal lines, one running across his stomach and the other his bent arms, lead our eye constantly into the centre. Unseen hands gesture inwards, opening up the body for us to take a closer look.

Although a Cubist fragmentation is evident here, each disparate shape (not new by any means; instead, recycled tree tops, trunks, cliff edges and fields) has been brought in tight to form a single body. *Summer Figure* is a taut, unpickable knot. Unity. This is Wilfred's linchpin.

A year after painting *Summer Figure*, Wilfred put this discovery into words, 'What I searched for was something unified and total...'[15] This word, unity, first really visualised in *Summer Figure*, became increasingly important in later work. The collision of separate objects — the merging of trees, cliffs, ocean, roads — we will see all of this happening in Wilfred's later work. But he was doing more than simply trying to unify his work on a visual level:

> *The imaginative leap in the mind — say Einstein's sudden grasp of Relativity; Rembrandt's plunge into depth; Turner's vision of the envelope of light that reveals things to us; — these are all comings together of many diverse ideas and thoughts. What puts them together; what takes them forward is the unconscious mind with its wonderful sense of wholeness; its 'putting it all together' quality; it is here that the strands fuse and the sudden unknown truth is revealed.*[16]

This sense of unity between all things would come to be central in Wilfred's later practice. Painting was not a separate activity for him, set apart from the rest of life — it was *everything*. Wilfred lived synonymously with his art. And so this emphasis on unification can be seen to mark him not only wanting to unify the painted figure (collecting it up, like so many scattered building blocks), but to do the same with his own sense of self. It was less than a decade since Wilfred had suffered his huge nervous breakdown, and here we find him bringing himself back together; a post-Cubist reconstruction of his very identity.

● ● ●

Summer Figure set the path for Wilfred's largest work yet. The monumental *Figures on a Beach* (1960) is a strange drapery of nude bodies, set in front of that classic stepped cliff coastline. The work marked both a beginning and an end for the artist. 'The feeling of confidence that I had gained from the last series of paintings made me ready to take a more radical step forward,' he wrote. 'I wanted to leave behind the formative influences (late Braque etc.) and develop into a world of my own.'[17] The flesh tones of the bodies depicted would be some of the last in his practice as he consolidated his palette, moving away from anything directly

NEXT PAGE
3:11 *Figures on a Beach*
1960
244 x 152.5 cm
Oil on hardboard
(Studio)

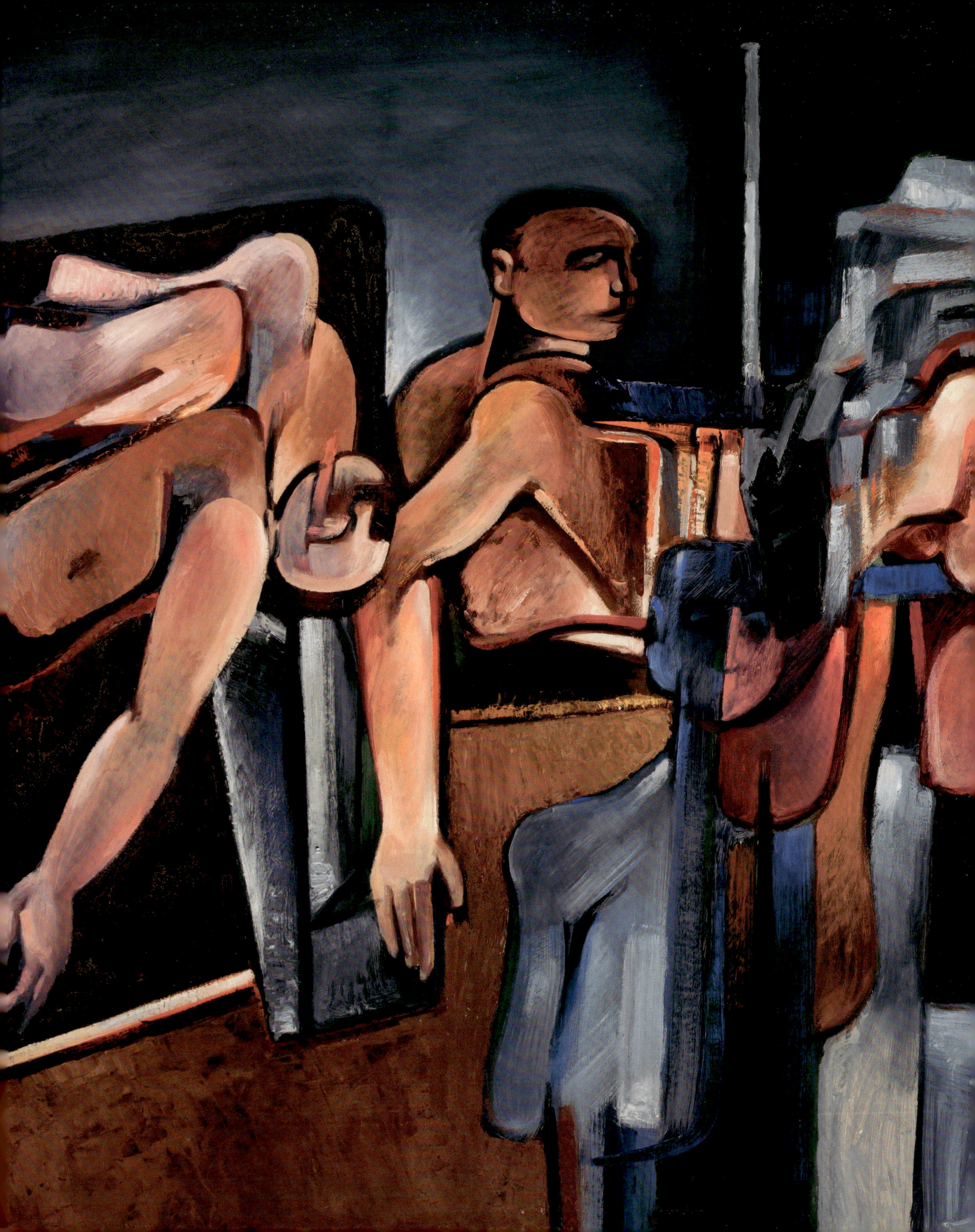

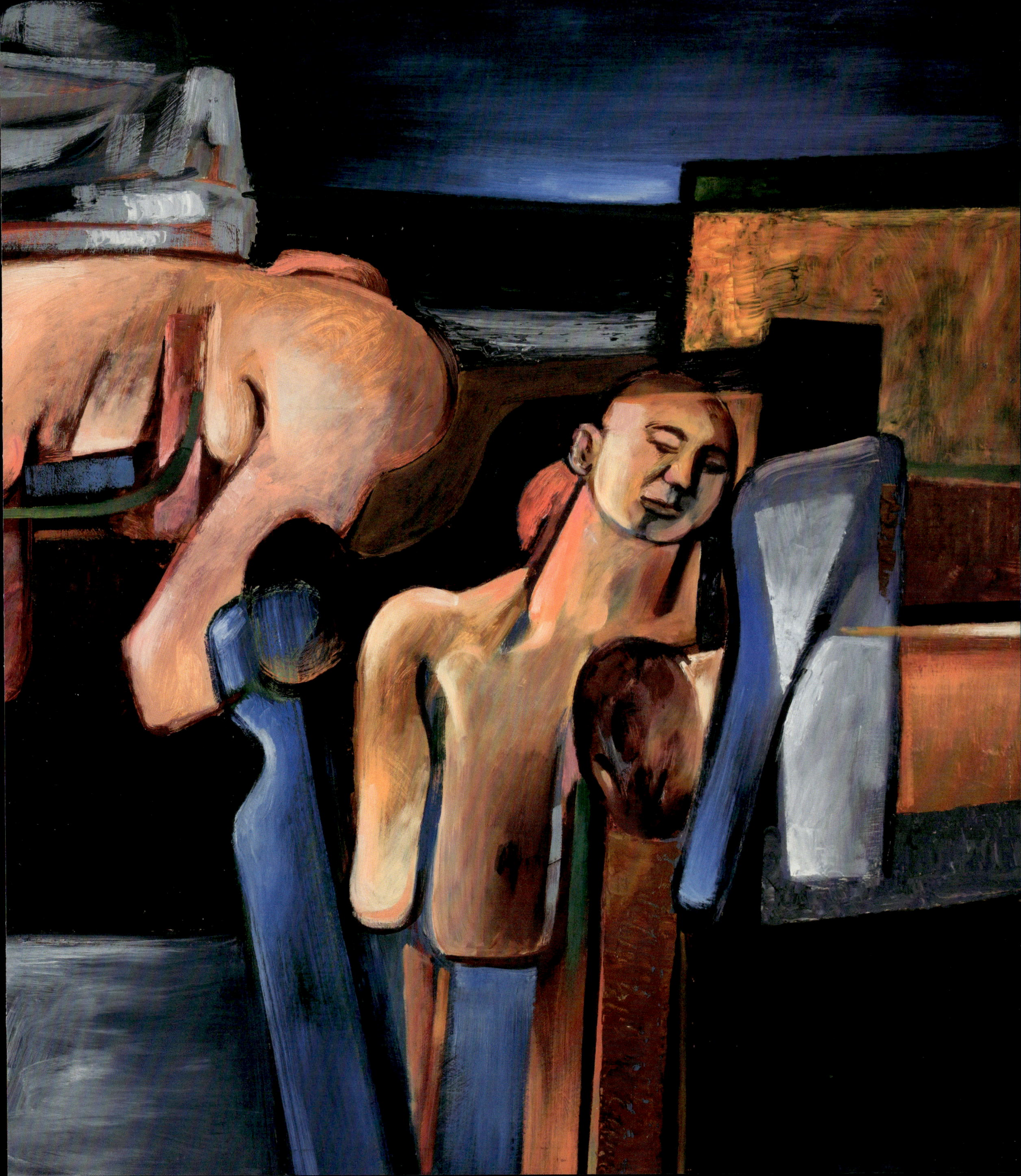

representational. The work also shows him now fully distancing himself from the formal fragmentation of Cubism and moving towards a fragmentation looser and more organic. As we will come to in Chapter 4, this turning point was triggered by an association with the British-Egyptian artist Adrien de Menasce, and the subsequent nurturing of Wilfred's interest in Jungian psychoanalysis.

Wilfred executed the work quickly, after only a rough sketch on the hardboard. And certainly there is an urgency, a sense of compulsion about it. He was unsatisfied with the finished piece, referring to it in 1999 as 'a crude and violent statement'.[18] And so in 1962, fed up with it taking up so much space in his studio, he entered it into a mixed show with the London Group, at the Art Federation Galleries on Suffolk Street. It looked ungainly and awkward hung high on the wall, placed between works by John Piper and Quentin Blake, and was declared by one critic as the ugliest picture in the show. Although Wilfred would go on to claim that he agreed with this statement at the time, the experience must have taken a direct hit to his confidence. Some artistic ability was, however, recognised by his acquaintance Brian Sewell, who later told him that he would have bought *Figures on a Beach* had it not been so expensive.

Although Wilfred was consistently critical of *Figures on a Beach*, unlike so much of his other work, he never went as far as to destroy it. It travelled with him from studio to studio, surviving seven house moves and even a flood. Being such a perfectionist in every other part of his practice, it does make one wonder if he was really as displeased as he claimed. The work's weighted figures certainly come from the same lineage as those in Picasso's *Guernica* (1937). A family trait is particularly evident in the heavy, hanging arms of the draped figure to the far left. And are they also related to William Blake's moping giants? Wilfred may have shaken these early visionary influences from his mind, but his hand certainly retained them. Not a bad family to be part of.

Figures on a Beach does, however, remain a tricky painting. It is compositionally uncomfortable, weighty and lumbering. By this point we are used to Wilfred's work directing our eye, but here we have become stuck. There is nothing light; we are earthbound and sluggish. The centre of the painting is particularly difficult to look at. That slumped torso, ungainly and imbalanced, is more slab of meat than human body. In what can perhaps be described as 'organic cubism', the figures appear more mutilated than fragmented. The painting contains the same sense of surreal unease as Giorgio de Chirico's *The Uncertainty of the Poet* (1913). Marble or flesh, we remain unsure.

Figures on a Beach is not a comfortable painting, but it is a pivotal work in Wilfred's career trajectory. In its jarring appearance (those naked hefts laid heavy amongst the composition's complex spatial arrangement), we witness an artist just on the cusp of something; a new style in its foetal state. Is this why it appears unfinished? Is it another example of Wilfred's work being more thought process than anything complete?

Nearly thirty years later, over the course of which the work of Carl Jung took an increasingly important role in his life, Wilfred would interpret *Figures on a Beach* in archetypal terms, with each figure representing different aspects of the human psyche:

> *Every figure in the work is seen at a different level of consciousness and with different archetypal inferences. The large figure on the left is the collapsed ideal or classical figure and is a direct reference to the work made before this — the 'Summer Figure' of 1960... On the beach is a 'primitive' figure, a 'foetal' figure, a 'shadow' figure and every embryonic figure in between. In the centre is a large 'sexual' figure. The dark feminine that will draw the various figures under her mantle and bring them into a whole.*[19]

In this strangely satisfying analysis, Wilfred's direct reference to *Summer Figure* in this essay highlights one of the ways in which he considered his work: however abstracted, however tense and tight or loose and broken up, Wilfred continued to use the same body. By the time that he painted *Figures on a Beach*, this body, Cubist and fragmented in *Summer Figure*, has fallen, limp, to one side. It has become softer, more malleable, a far cry from the rigid formalities of his 1950s undressing boys. Where, it leads us to ask, will Wilfred take the body next?

BRAQUE'S BIRD (1999)

Seeing a number of the 'Atelier Paintings' by Braque at the exhibition in London of his late work, I was immediately reminded of the great effect they had on me when I first experienced them over thirty years ago.

It is however, only now that I see how important they are and what a wonderful invention the bird flying through the spaces of the pictures is and how brave it was of Braque to have allowed it to appear.

We didn't really understand it at the time. Many people, I remember, thought it rather fanciful. Braque was associated with the great tactile tradition of French Still-Life Painting; with a sense of earthy form and rich texture that seemed inappropriate with a flying bird.

There were other smaller images of the bird that affected me even more. 'Le Nid', for example, where a small ochre shape floating against a deep blue becomes the 'nest' traversed by the stylised wings of the bird.

But the bird is of course a way of lifting us up and away from the materialism that had so preoccupied the first half of the century. It is a symbol of 'SPIRIT'. It is the Holy Ghost, as it were. What it really does as it weaves its way in and out of the complex spaces of the paintings is to show us that, despite Braque's thrilling analysis and reduction of form, there remains a space that still eludes him.

This is the space created by Braque's own subjectivity. The bird is in fact the artist's 'aura' moving through the work and reminding us of the subjective process in our perception of matter. It is the rebirth of spirituality in Western Art. It is Braque's recognition that we move in a dimension where the parameters are a mystery beyond our understanding.

This became my way forward as a painter. Every image that I now make is in a way Braque's bird. They come into being as forms dissolve and the after-image emerges; when the conscious mind has questions as far as possible the predictable and the unpredictable image emerges. Through the bird we are able, as D. H. Lawrence once said we would have to do, to 'put the imagination back into the centre of Life.'

Wilfred Avery, Brighton, March 1999

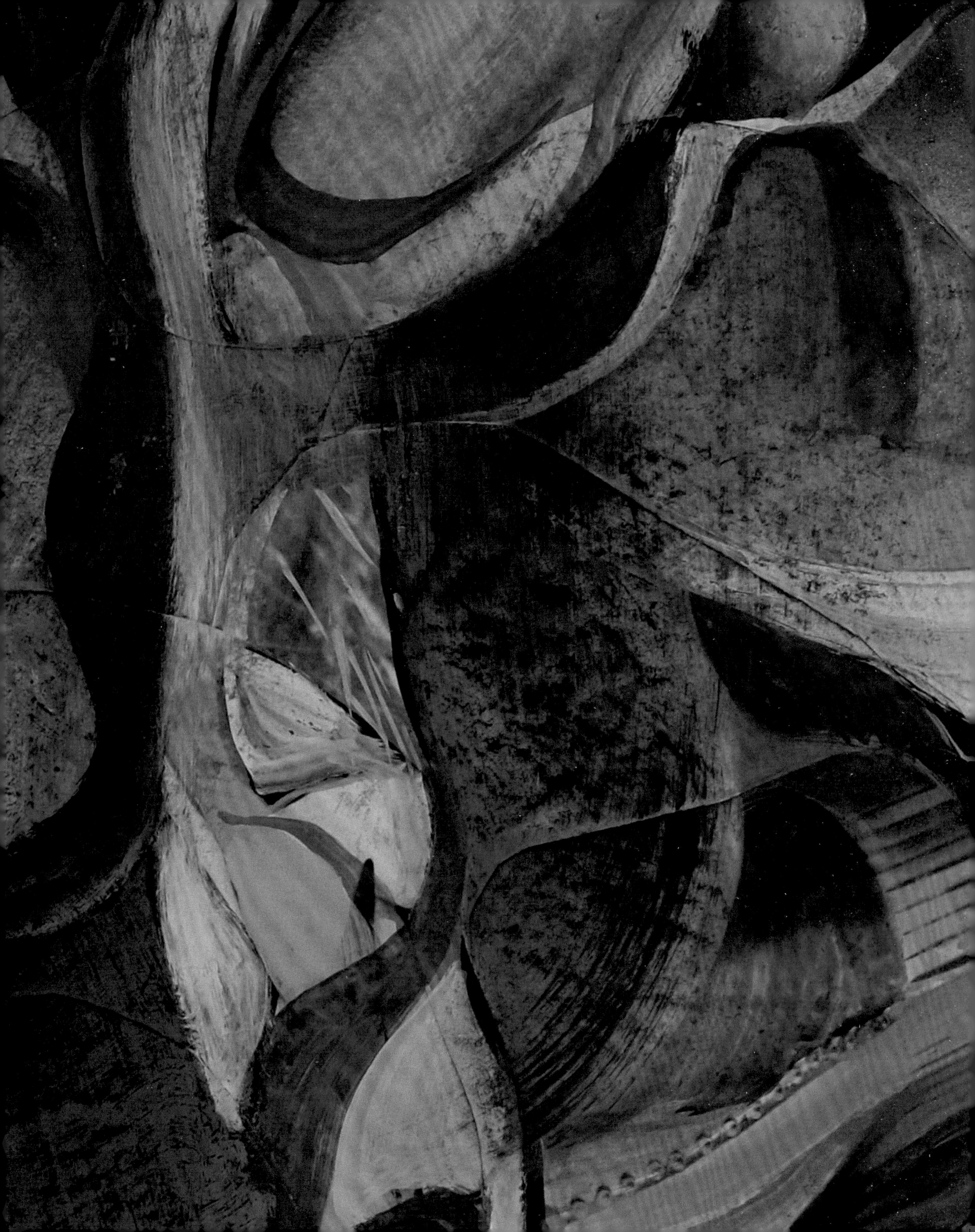

4 THE UNPREDICTABLE IMAGE

What one wanted more than anything else to do was to arrive at the image that lay beneath all the others; to have been so involved in one's work that one was no longer conscious of its destiny: to work so that the final form and shape could not have been imagined or predicted. Strangely enough, however, the final work seemed oddly familiar. One had glimpsed mysteriously the sense of the 'whole' in which we are all involved.[20]

STYLISTICALLY, WILFRED WOULD never again sit so comfortably with the trends of his time as he had while showing at Lessore's Beaux Arts Gallery. His influences, however, continued to remain true to the cultural identity of the period in which he was working.

Wilfred's work from 1960 onwards is indisputably a product of the Long Sixties. This era of social, cultural and technological progress spanned the years 1955 to 1973. It was coupled with the astrological move from the Piscean into the Age of Aquarius, thought to bring with it aspirations of utopia and a shedding of old rules and traditions. Space travel, astrology, psychoanalysis, liberated attitudes towards sex and the body; these all make themselves apparent in both Wilfred's work and art theory of the same period. For the artist it was also a time of increased social and political engagement, and one in which he became deeply influenced by Jungian psychoanalysis. Wilfred painted alone, the door to his studio closed. Nevertheless, it is clear that even in his isolation, his mind was directly focused on the zeitgeist.

Planetary shapes begin to appear in Wilfred's work from 1969 onwards;

a reflection of the ongoing influence of Paul Nash, perhaps, but more likely the beginning of a lifelong fascination with the birth of space travel. Titles, even right up until the end of the 1990s, continue to reference the event: *Double Space Figures, Space Walk* (both 1966), *Solaris* (1970), *Moonwalk* (1984) and *Galaxy* (1997). For Wilfred, space travel was more than a physical journey. He believed it instead to be a psychoanalytic leap into new and previously unperceived realities. This is encapsulated in an essay written at the end of the decade, just twelve days before the moonwalk. 'Somewhere at the edge of our Memory,' he wrote, 'lies another dimension.'[21] Wilfred referred to this 'other dimension' as a half-world, lying somewhere beyond our day-to-day vision. This was — and still is — a place that can also be reached through other means: via meditation, spirituality — or psychedelic drugs, to which it feels important to say that Wilfred was vehemently opposed. He had no need of them; he was there already. The transcendental states that his work of the period hints at were sourced entirely alone.

Given this influx of new ideas, it is no wonder that the early 1960s were an uncomfortable creative period for Wilfred; their translation on to canvas could hardly have been a smooth process. The enormous *Summer Figure* and *Figures on a Beach* were immediately followed by a drastic drop in scale and colour. Wilfred's work grappled and shrank. They were 'dark, struggling canvases' he wrote in 1969, 'long since destroyed, in which I sought in vain for a humble way forward; a way that would not lift me but would lift the paintings themselves and give them their own life'.[22] The use of the word 'struggle' gives us a sense not just of the difficulty of making this work but again of the passivity of the artist. It seems that there was no conscious knowledge of what was coming. In the same essay Wilfred refers to himself as 'stumbling' on this new style. Here we see once again the importance of chance, of serendipity in his practice.

❙ THE INFLUENCE OF ADRIEN DE MENASCE

In 1961 Wilfred met the British-Egyptian artist, Adrien de Menasce. It would be hard to overstate the importance of this friendship, an association that would have a profound influence on his practice and development of his work.

Adrien was born into a distinguished Jewish family in Alexandria, but lost both his wealth and home during the 1956 Suez Crisis. Cramming all of his worldly possessions into three Louis Vuitton suitcases and a hatbox, he fled first to Zurich and then in 1961 to London. It was here in London that he met and began a romantic relationship with Wilfred's brother Sam. Adrien went on to live with Sam in Knight's House for the next thirty-five years until his death in 1995, and over this time became an incredibly close friend to Wilfred. In fact, with Adrien in both his and Sam's lives, Wilfred's exclusive creative community was complete.

If Wilfred's *Figures on a Beach* is the manifestation of one of his transformations in style, it was a transformation that directly coincided with this new creative relationship. Wilfred had flirted with psychoanalytic theory over the later years of the previous decade, but having now met Adrien, who had undergone Jungian analysis in Zurich with the Swiss psychologist Jolande Jacobi, it began to take a pivotal place in his life and practice. This Jungian influence was two-fold; not only allowing Wilfred's work to develop, but giving him a new language with which to discuss it.

Adrien's influence on Wilfred can be summed up in three words: *the unpredictable image*. The term was used by both artists to describe the end result of a creative process increasingly influenced by the unconscious mind (a practice, no less, that connects both to a great heritage of twentieth-century creatives).

In the early 1960s, Wilfred began referring to himself as a passive participant in the making of his work, emphasising the importance of following an idea without being either too self-conscious or too self-aware about technique. This new attitude can best be encapsulated in one wonderfully light-hearted comment of his, 'the joy of painting is to be surprised!'[23]

From this point onwards, he began all his oil paintings in the same way. Rather than starting immediately, he would stand the empty canvas on an easel in the studio, working beside it on other things, letting his thoughts come and go until the urge to begin something new became almost irresistible. And even then, he would wait, certain that the longer he did so the more powerful the final image would become. When he could wait no longer, he would begin with the same mark each time — a cupped little 'u' shape like the lip of a vase or a bowl (the result of a quick wrist flick on to the blank canvas). From this initial mark, the image would begin to emerge.

> ... one started in from a meaningful but unrelated mark and worked as unconsciously as possible until an image began to occur; to rise to consciousness as it were. Then one tried to hold this image only to find the deeper rhythm coming up again and transforming the image even more. So one worked on, holding and surrendering consciousness to unconsciousness until the vein was worked out: until the conversation seemed at an end and there was nothing more to be said.[24]

In 1964, while spending the summer in the riviera town of Cagnes-sur-Mer in southeast France, Wilfred stopped using an easel altogether. He would move his colour right off the flat plane of the canvas and around the sides of the stretcher.

In his essay 'Approaching the Unconscious', Carl Jung touches upon the derivation of the word 'invent' – from the Latin *invenire*, 'to find'. Hence to invent (and without doubt the process of creating a painting is a process of invention) is to find something by seeking it.[25] In Jungian terms, Wilfred's creative process was one of pure invention, one in which he dipped into his unconscious mind to find the image.

Each one of Wilfred's oils from this period onwards highlights this exploratory process. Evidence of transformation can be found in the shadows and hints of forms decided against and painted over; each painting proof of this process of passive discovery rather than of predetermination, of intuition over rationality. Paintings were built up layer by layer – stronger and more basic colours would work as the ground, shining through as layers of different consistencies were added over the top. This could take months or, more likely, far longer. Wilfred's process was not a matter of continuous work, rather one of beginning and setting down, then beginning again. He was able to mix the exact same tones (even on paintings he had not looked at for twenty-five years) by intuition alone. In the early 1990s he pushed himself even further, experimenting with a new technique in which he would attempt to fall into a trance-like state while making drawings. This condition, he felt, allowed him to switch off his rational mind and bring him even closer to the 'half-world' he had so long been seeking.

Wilfred's interest in the unconscious combined with an increasingly passive creative technique ties his work to the Surrealist practice of Automatism – the process of creating art without conscious thought, as a means of accessing material from the unconscious mind. But although his work retained a Surrealist aesthetic (most evident in his 'Sixties Figures' series, discussed in Chapter 7), he soon began to object to any close association with the theories behind the movement.

The Jungian psychoanalyst Aniela Jaffé, in her essay 'Symbolism in the Visual Arts' (1964), wrote, 'It is consciousness that holds the key to the unconscious ... only in the *interplay* of consciousness and the unconscious can the unconscious prove its value...' The pivotal importance of the conscious mind as *the way into* the unconscious jars with Surrealist theory – its artists often looking solely inwards for their imagery. For the same reason, Wilfred's work never became fully abstract. He wanted to use the unconscious in a conscious way, to find a way of tying the two together in his work. '... in merely abstract paintings,' Jaffé continues, 'the world of the known has completely vanished. Nothing is left to form a bridge to the unknown.'[26] All of Wilfred's work is bound, or more to the point is *balanced* by reality:

> *My interest in Jungian Psychology was leading me to the conclusion that everything is subjective; that material and physical phenomena are not separate or opposite but the same. I wanted to find a way in which I could express this quality. What I want to do is to paint with both eyes open yet with a mind freed from the idea that what I see is ever more than what I want to see. I try to find in the world about me a reflection of the inner story that is constantly guiding and forming my way of looking and so make manifest a subjective view of the cosmos in which I, as a microcosm of it, am at the centre.*[27]

Given his escalating interest in the unconscious, it is no wonder that Wilfred also lists the Metaphysical painter Giorgio de Chirico (a seminal predecessor to the Surrealists), as an influence. Their work shares the same thinly-layered, luminescent surface quality, rich colours that seem to glow from an unknown source. In 1919, de Chirico alluded to '... the unknown that is hidden in the depth'[28] of a Metaphysical artwork, a quote that could just as easily describe Jungian theories on the unconscious. Like de Chirico, Wilfred made images that encouraged his audience to look deeper. Both artists were preoccupied with something just beyond the empirical. This is again described in Jungian terms by Jaffé:

> *Every object has two aspects: The common aspect, which is the one we generally see and which is seen by everyone, and the ghostly and metaphysical aspect, which only rare individuals see at moments of clairvoyance and metaphysical meditation. A work of art must relate to something that does not appear in its visible form.*[29] ●

4:1 *Little Cowarch*
1962
25.5 x 30.5 cm
Oil on canvas
(*Studio*)

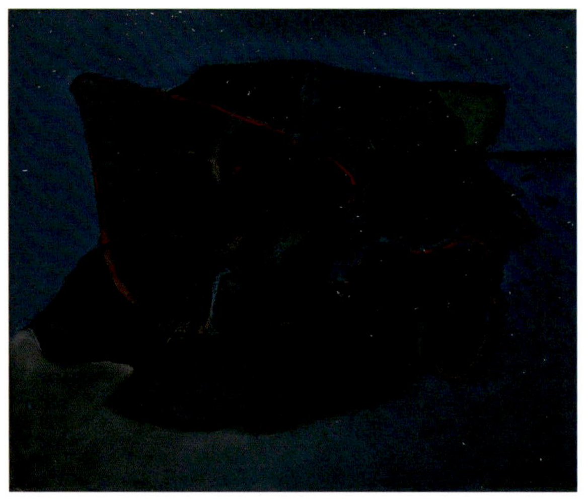

4:2 Cowarch 1
1962
41 x 51 cm
Flomaster pen and crayon
on paper
(*Studio*)

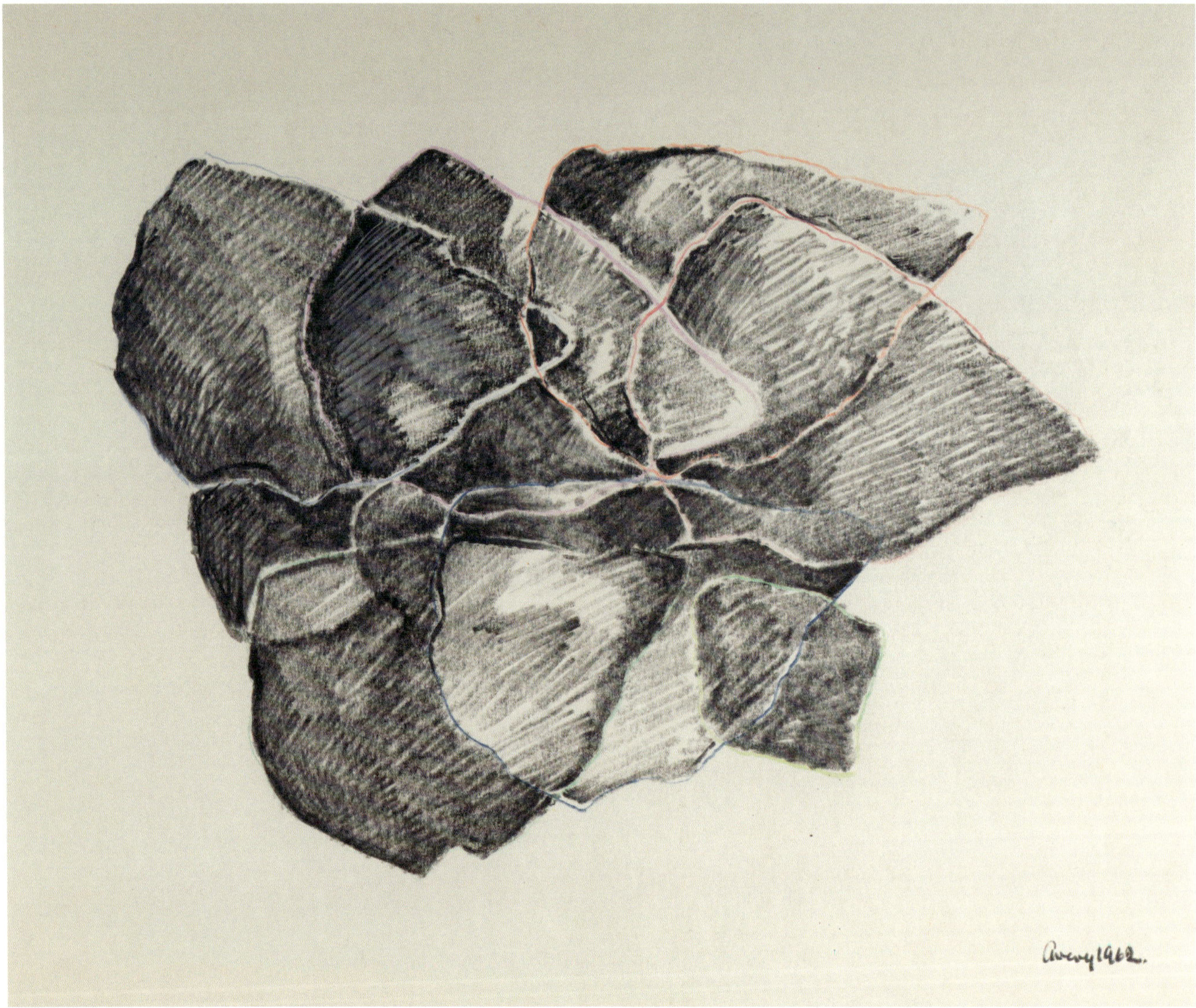

This was a brutal period of self-censorship, and few works remain in existence. But one in particular shows us the hard-won culmination of this year of trial and error. The tiny *Little Cowarch* (1962) is named after a vast and rambling Welsh mountainside. It is a multifaceted, abstracted form. Abstracted to a point, that is; rather than the particulated little orb appearing in a completely abstract space, Wilfred has tied it down. A thread of paint at each side holds it to the edges of the canvas, stopping it tumbling away and giving us a sense of its physicality in a realistic space (though the same threads must have snapped in *Origins*, painted later the same year and taut as an inflated balloon).

Little Cowarch's uncomfortable energy is exacerbated by its diminished size. There is a full weight to it, as if Wilfred has managed to condense the entire mountainous landscape right on to the small canvas. It is the visual equivalent of squeezing one's hand into a tight fist.

The muddied body of *Little Cowarch* has been delineated in vivid reds, purples and deep green, a fusion of the dour palette of Wilfred's work of the early 1950s and the brightness he discovered towards the end of the decade. Thick outlines are reminiscent of the division of an agricultural landscape, making the work as a whole almost self-referential. In *Cowarch 1* (1962), one of a series of Flomaster drawings made in tandem with the painting, the same divisions have been picked out in coloured gouache.

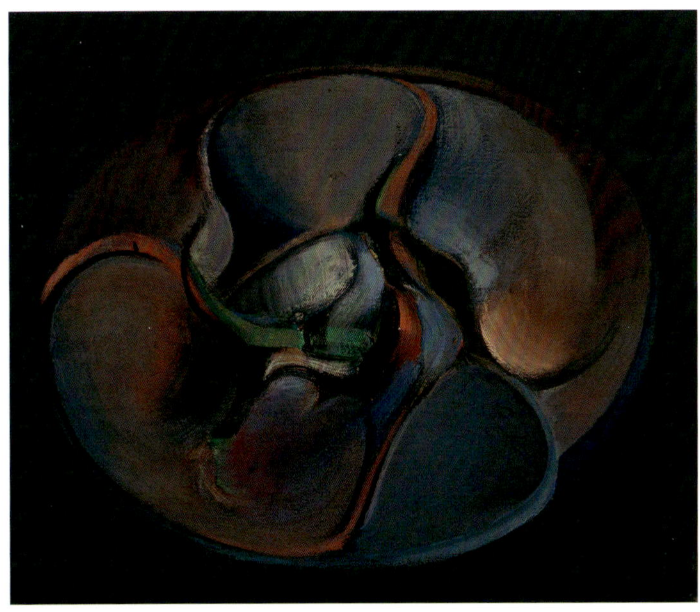

4:3 *Origins*
1962
25.5 x 31.5 cm
Oil on canvas
(*Studio*)

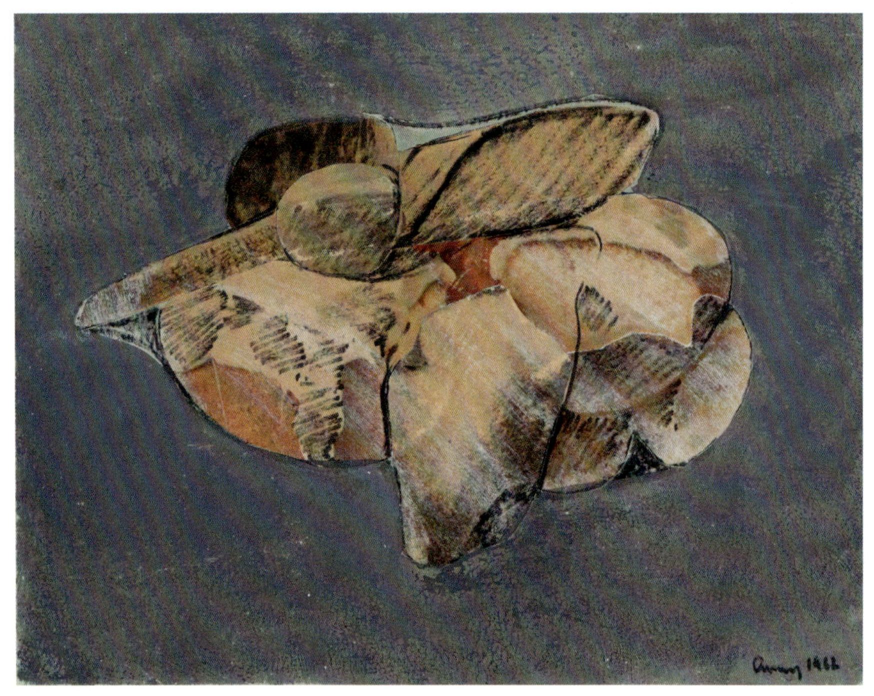

ABOVE
4:4 Prototype
1962
20.5 x 25.5 cm
Collage-gouache
(Studio)

OPPOSITE
4:5 Mandala
1962
62 x 53.5 cm
Collage-gouache
(South Molton Museum)

Wilfred began experimenting with collage in the same year, and both pieces prophesy later work made using shapes cut from maps of the British Isles. The fittingly named *Prototype* (1962) — soft shapes in subdued pastels that have been slotted together over a dark blue background — was the first of a series of what he termed 'collage-gouache'. One might imagine it hollow inside, it appears so light on the page; a perfectly balanced shape as much extra-terrestrial (or at least, something outside of our known existence) as some strange fungus we might stumble across in a forest, spread between the roots of an ancient tree. The form is dynamic and somehow fleeting, as if Wilfred had caught it mid-air; an encapsulation of the moment just before the unsettled shape whisks itself off, leaving us with nothing but that blue gouache background, felt pen signature to bottom right. The sense of purpose evident in the image takes no heed of its viewer, showcasing a dynamism that after this would never leave Wilfred's work. Shaded areas have been hashed out in his favoured Flomaster pen; we can see the exact speed and force with which he made each mark. The artist, here, is as present as the work we have in front of us.

Mandala (1962) is another early collage, and Wilfred's largest. Rendered in exquisite detail, it appears almost three-dimensional, levitating, luminous and humming. An object from an alternate universe, or is it some kind of a creature, curled up but waking? There is certainly something alive about it — at any moment it might rise, stretch out, unravel.

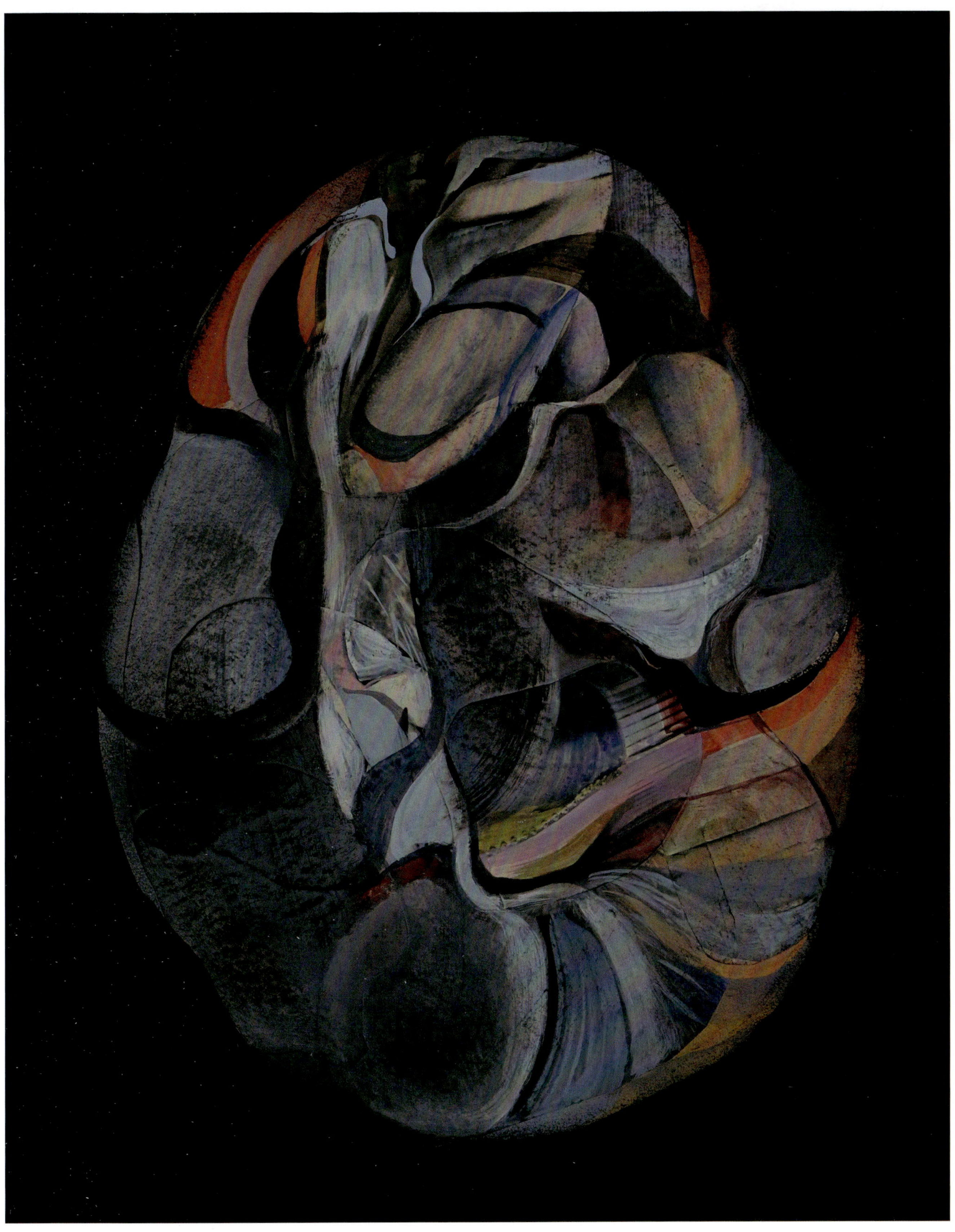

NOTES ON PAINTING 1961

The Enigma fascinates because it contains the past and the future as well as the present. It is ever-changing and there is a point where memory, reason and imagination seem equally present that involves me most in what I do. To lose myself in this balance is to discover who I am.

In my reaction away from cubism I looked for forms and forces which seemed more concerned with the particular. I had become tired of the universal look of Picasso's nudes or the faceless models of Matisse. The generalised, over-rational look of things appalled me and I felt 'left-out' by it all. What I searched for was something unified and total; not put together by man's will but already existing, mysterious, momentary and full of the changing impermanence of life.

This led me towards realism and towards those painters, Rembrandt, Goya, Rouault, for whom the image is of paramount importance. I went back to the turning point at the end of the nineteenth-century, to the late water-colours of Cézanne. Here was so much that had been missed. I struggled with the image and I struggled to loosen the formal grip.

On the one hand I seemed to be defeated by imagery born out of an objective tradition in studying Nature, and on the other by the insistent demands for pictorial architecture that my respect for the European tradition gave me.

I looked towards the landscape and began to find in my subjective awareness of its scarred and aged face a parallel for the presence and essence of things. I discovered through it a point at which the forces of life both psychological and environmental seemed to meet.

It may seem strange to speak of psychology in reference to a landscape but in my subjective urges towards its forms I found my apprehension of it most alive and, following this awareness, discovered a dynamic energy that expresses itself in the most minute of forms.

As these patterns of thought evolved cross-references occurred that seemed enigmatic. I could not look at a cliff without seeing the patterns of a wave nor study a road without feeling the turn of the beach beyond. Planes and symbols began to lose or share their identity. I became interested in the space that existed between the planes; a space that exists because of the tensions rather than the harmonies inherent in my looking at things.

So I arrived at a point where I wished to acknowledge the presence of Man in Nature, for in studying nature I had only discovered myself.

Figures seemed to take on the same qualities of impermanence and often the image of landscape and figure merged into one. I became interested in a strange mixture of acceptances and energies, in an image which already existed in the paint mark as I made it and yet transcended it, giving a pattern that echoed a thousandfold.

Is it a world born out of the fusion of objective and subjective vision that I am discovering? I am not sure but for me this world of half-truths is in fact the true world. It is at this point where Memory, Reason and Imagination cross one another that I look for the image of Man in our time.

Wilfred Avery, 21 Fairfax Road, London NW6, 1961

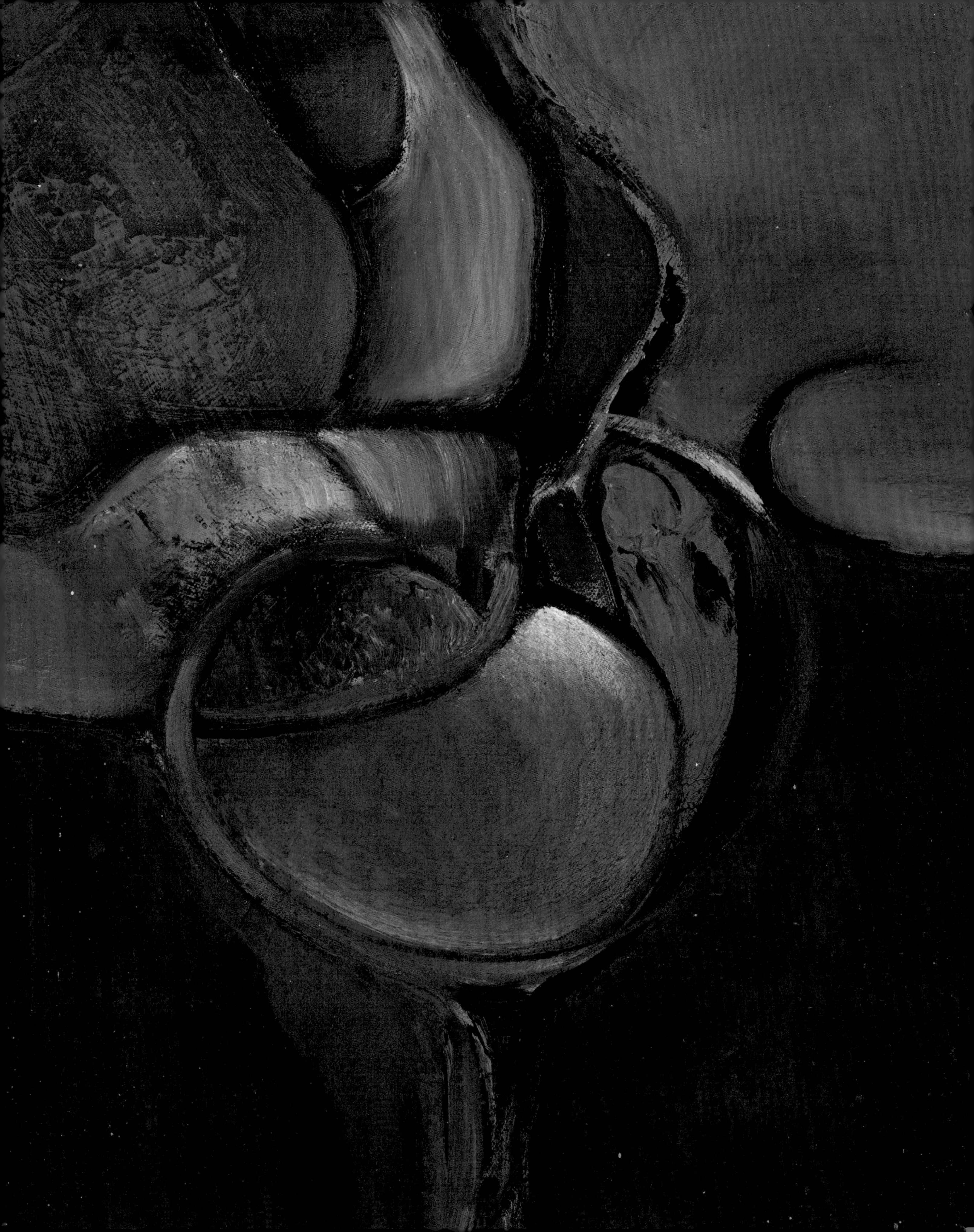

5 FRANCE AND THE ATELIER: COMING FACE TO FACE WITH ABSTRACT EXPRESSIONISM

IN 1963, WITH the advice of Paul Nash still in his mind, Wilfred moved to Paris. The opportunity to relocate came via Patty and Garry Thorne, close friends who persuaded him to spend a year with them on sabbatical in France. On his arrival, the Thornes secured him a studio at 6 Rue Pierre Curie through their friends, the American-Russian painter Zuka and her husband, *L'Express* cartoonist Louis Mittelberg. Wilfred spent the following summer with the Thornes and their three young children in a villa in Cagnes-sur-Mer.

Wilfred spoke good French, and was drawn to Paris as the home of the Cubist and Surrealist movements that had been such a strong influence in his early work. For the first time as an adult, he attended serious art classes — two a week at an académie, all that he could afford. Here he was taught briefly by both Braque and Giacometti. Braque instilled in Wilfred the importance of using instinct over intellect in his practice, advice that chimed perfectly with his burgeoning Jungian beliefs. Wilfred's académie experience in part made up for any lack in formal training, and would have a great effect on his practice long after he had moved back to England.

Prefigured in 1962 with *Origins*, *Prototype* and the 'Cowarch' series, the move to Paris snowballed a period of immense change in Wilfred's work. He had been distancing himself from the figurative since 1957, but it is evident in his French work that it was not until 1963 that he had made a clean break. And judging by the titles of his works in this period, it seems that he was also conscious of this — *Prototype*, *Origins* and *Genesis (The Source)*. But what exactly did this new beginning encompass for Wilfred?

Organic and abstracted shapes in all the colours of an oil spill; works that are miniature but all encompassing. Take *Mondial* (1964), a word that means 'relating to, affecting, or involving the whole world'. A small work, yes, but mighty.

As we have already seen in *Little Cowarch*, although Wilfred was toying with abstraction more closely than ever before at this point, his practice never became fully abstract. In all his work from the early 1960s, he takes us almost to the point of full abstraction — as close as possible — *just* before pulling us back. Take the bodily bloom of *Genesis (The Source)* (1963), for example — do you see lungs, the digestive system? Notice the dark vertical line just to the left of the stalk; a shadow cast on the wall. This is abstraction sitting firmly within physical reality.

Wilfred's French works and those made directly after he had returned to London in the autumn of 1964 are evidence of him reaching inside himself in more ways than one. Into the subconscious, undoubtedly — we know this is taking pivotal importance right now. But he has also grasped hold of something far less conceptual: shapes from deep inside the body. These are forms reminiscent of vital organs, of tumorous growths, slippery slick and pulsating. The inside coming out, all of it. Prefiguring a series of anatomical drawings made in 1965, *Mondial* is a thick lump heavy on the canvas, the colour of cooked liver. Was it placed there by the hands of *Summer Figure*, ever reaching inside its own open torso?

• • •

To hell with Design; to hell with taste; to hell with pleasing textures and 'plastic' form.[30]

In Paris, and really for the first and only time in his life, Wilfred found himself thrown into a circle of artists. From around 1900, the city had been unparalleled as the centre for creative expression, buoyant on the dizzying successes of the Impressionists and Post-Impressionists of the previous century. Artists of all nationalities had gravitated to Montmartre and Montparnasse, the cross-fertilisation of their ideas spawning movements like Fauvism, Cubism, Expressionism, Symbolism and

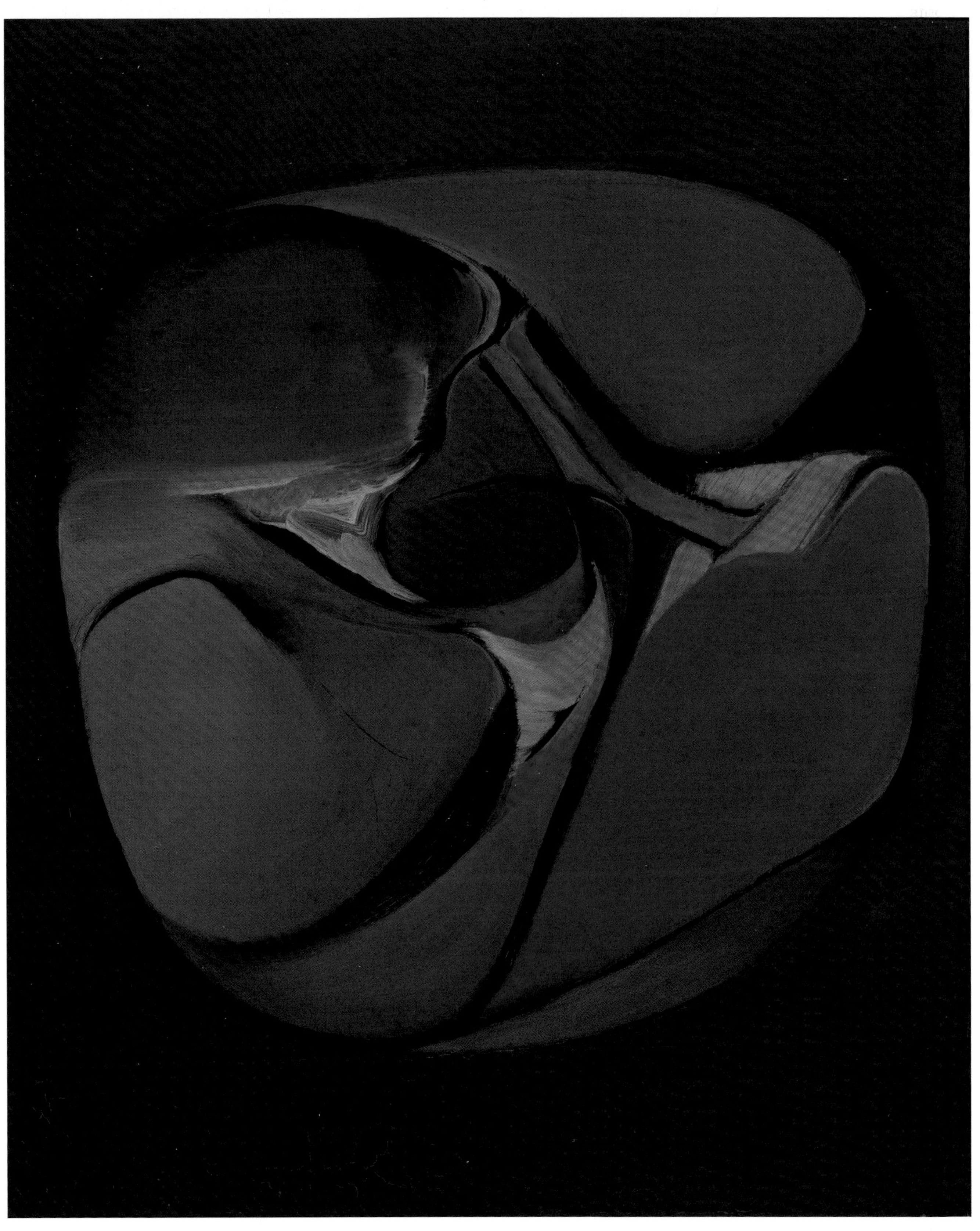

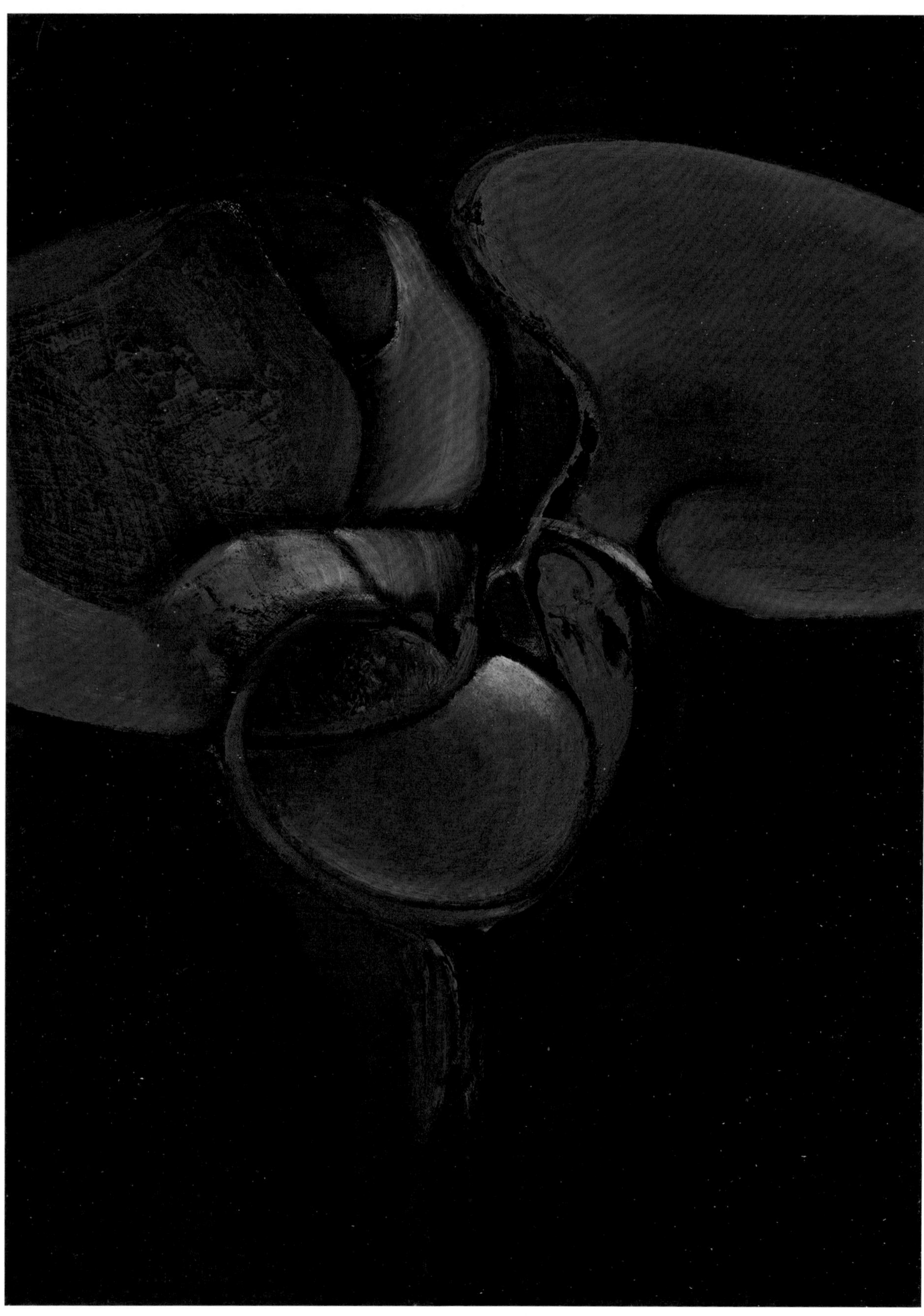

Surrealism. But from around 1950, the city's dominance ceded to the rise of the New York School. And so, despite travelling to Paris in order to experience for himself the European avant-garde, it was actually American Abstract Expressionism that Wilfred came face to face with on the continent.

Wilfred was already familiar with Abstract Expressionism. Its growing dominance in London coincided with his ongoing lack of commercial recognition in the city, and he soon began to lay the blame on it, referring to the movement as consciously *excluding* his own work. It is perhaps unexpected then that while in Paris he became close to the American Abstract Expressionist Joan Mitchell, a long-standing friend of Zuka. But it was only by this close contact with the rhythmic lines and layered colour fields of her work that he became fully confident he did not want to push his own in the same direction.

His dismissal of the movement was far from passive. Instead, in just the same way as he had done with the Kitchen Sink School in the late 1950s, Wilfred defined and strengthened his own practice against it. And while he made no attempts to show his work whilst in France, it was here that he was able to confront the taste for Abstract Expressionism, and by positioning his own work against it and decisively rejecting it, move it forward.

OPPOSITE
5:2 *Genesis (The Source)*
1963
41.5 x 30 cm
Oil on canvas
(Studio)

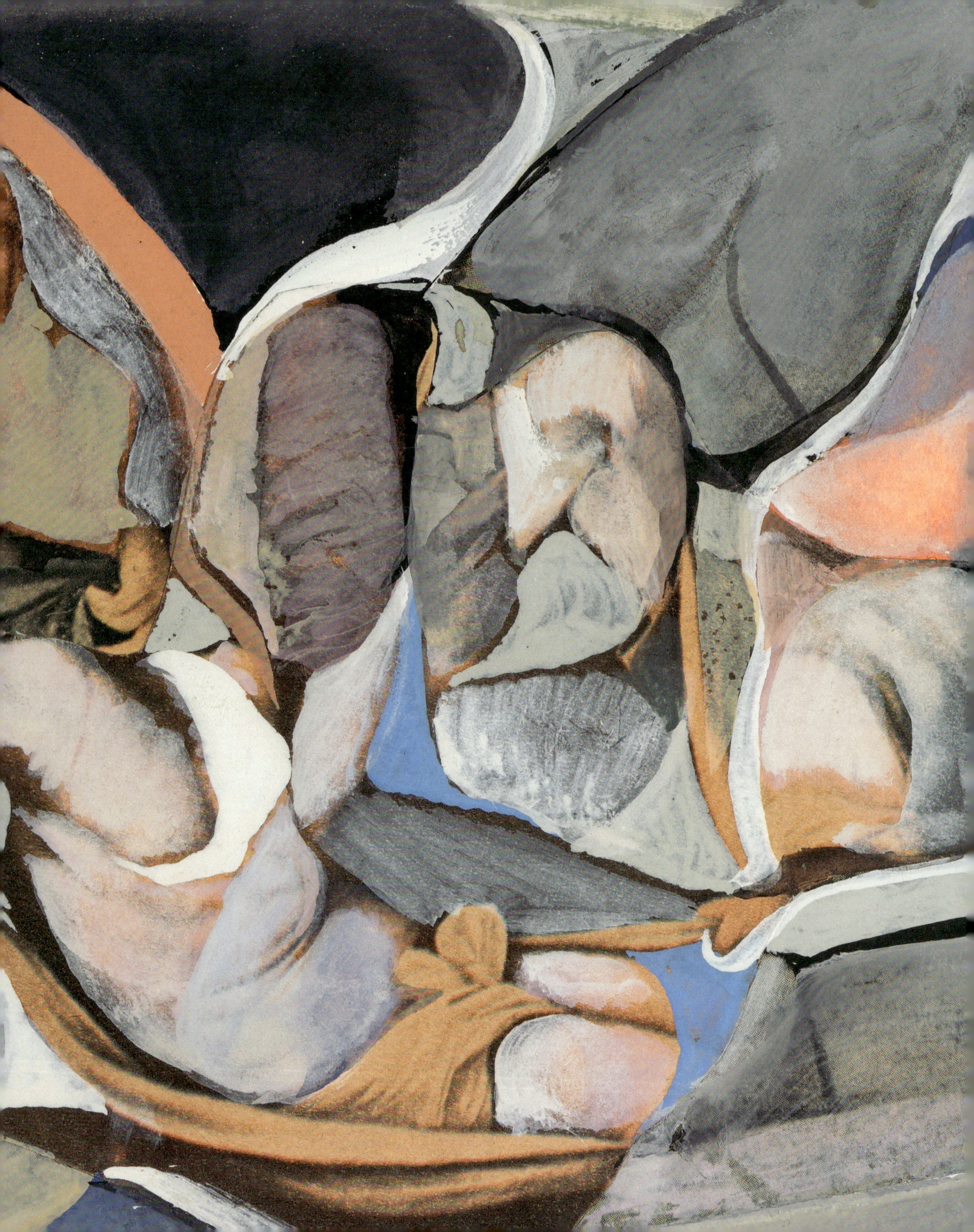

6 QUEER COLLAGE

COLLAGE IS A powerful artform. It is a medium that allows both the construction of new worlds and identities, and the disruption and subversion of traditional ones. It encourages experimentation and Wilfred used it for exactly this; his collages as a means to a painted end. The bound bodies of his mid-1960s work are synonymous with the 'Sixties Figures' oil series, made between 1965 and 1969, strongly influenced by Adrien and painted between 1965 and 1969.

Wilfred perfected his collage technique in Cagnes-sur-Mer in the summer of 1964. The process always began upside-down. He would tear pictures from newspapers and magazines and lay them out side by side, attempting to dissociate himself from the original images and looking instead for the pages he felt were drawn to one another in a non-figurative sense. Some force, he explained, would then take over his hand on the scissors, cutting out shapes that followed no outlines or preconceived ideas, the process simply happening without his conscious mind being aware. Shapes were combined to create irregular formations on a painted background, overlayed with colour washes and sometimes the dry scribble of a Flomaster pen.

When Wilfred began working in the medium it was not easy to access the male body without rousing suspicion. He was far from the only person to experience this issue. Without a legal space in which to exist, 1960s gay culture adopted the disguise of sport to survive and flourish. A proliferation of magazines like *Health and Strength* and *Man's World* were filled with unabashed homoerotic photographs of male physical perfection, and could be bought publicly in newsagents, having been published under the guise of 'health and fitness'. And although Wilfred was not using these beefcake magazines in his own practice, he was essentially working to the same effect. From 1965 he began using newspaper photographs of athletes and footballers in his college-gouaches, idealised bodies that would feature heavily in his later practice. Using a body already in the public sphere was a far less loaded act; it had already been 'ok-ed' by the general (read heterosexual) public. Wilfred's collages were never outrightly erotic (although certainly some are incredibly suggestive), but we find him here yet again skating close to the zeitgeist, his work feeding into what we can now translate as a queer art practice.

In *Double Space Figures* (1966), a pair of legs sits wide open, straddling one of two horizontal lines. The figure seems to have been caught just at the moment it topples from its perch. And below, a couple – all muscle and not much else – are embroiled in some mock wrestle. Here they pull together, apart, together again. The tension between them is alluded to in two swooping triangles of blue (the back and forth moving our eye endlessly from one side to the other). Both forms bring to mind Bacon's grappling *Two Figures* (1953); the overpowering animal of it. *Space Walk* has the same tilting, keeling feel. Arms restrained, two figures wobble precariously on trapped feet. There is something of St Sebastian in the right-hand form, of victim objectified. It is interesting to note here, too, that huge sense of space the horizon line produces, the graded wash deepening in colour at its furthest point.

BELOW LEFT
6:1 *Double Space Figures*
1966
43 x 34.5 cm
Collage-gouache on antique paper
(*Studio*)

BELOW RIGHT
6:2 *Space Walk*
1966
34.5 x 43 cm
Collage-gouache on antique paper
(*Studio*)

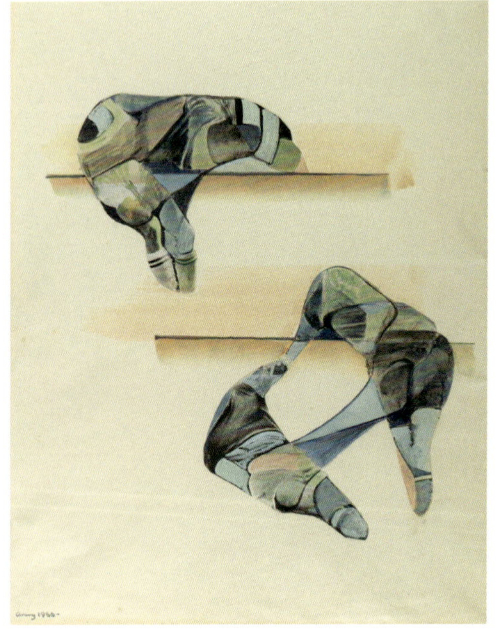

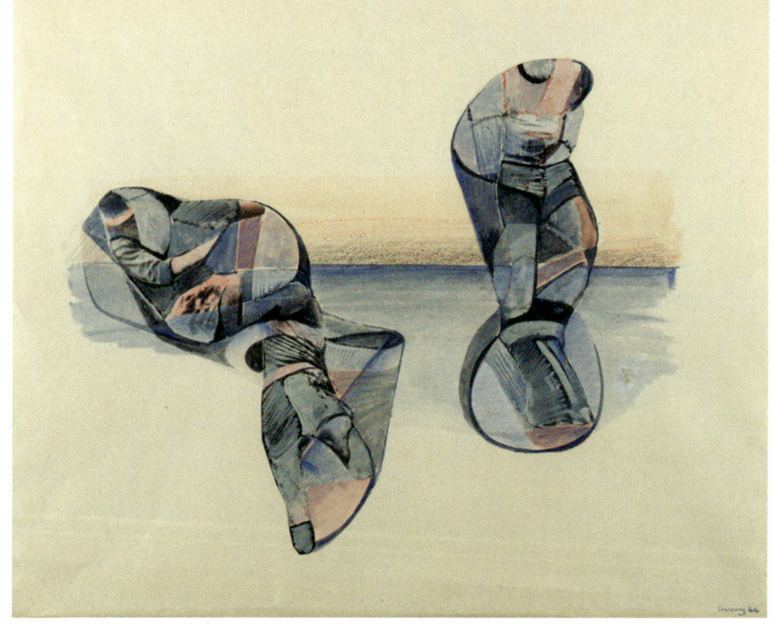

Wilfred continued to use this incredibly simplistic method (for what is simpler than a single line?) to powerful effect; a means to explore the space he was continually trying to expand.

Deposition (1965) occupies another overtly heterosexual space. The work brings to mind the floating orbs Wilfred had begun to construct on paper and canvas in the first two years of the 1960s, but this time comprising a fragmented composition of Christ being brought down from the cross. The torso is weighty, arms, hands and bodies bent double, hold him tight, strain with the physicality of him.

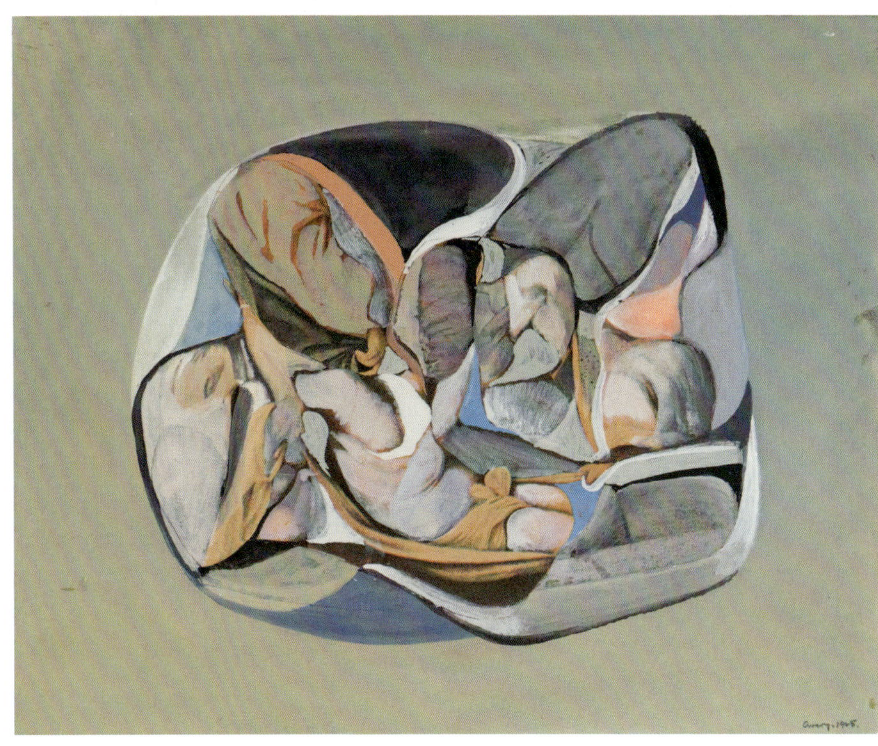

6:3 Deposition
1965
23 x 28.5 cm
Collage-gouache
(*Studio*)

A comparison of Wilfred's collages with Adrien's 1962 'Secret Museum' series really clarifies the stimulating intellectual and creative relationship they shared in this period. Although similar in subject matter and shape, Adrien's series — tangled athletes and footballers pasted on to white card — is far more outwardly explicit than any of Wilfred's collages. In one, torsos and legs are grouped together to form an erect penis. Even the name of his series alludes to its explicit nature, to the obligatory furtive nature of 1960s gay desire.

Nowhere is it more evident than in the work of this period that Wilfred is continuing to use his practice to better understand his position in the world. Just as he was doing in oil in the very early 1960s, his collages fragment and reconstruct the body. Here we see Wilfred dismembering and reconfiguring these sportsmen — symbols of cis-straight hypermasculinity — into configurations of same-sex physical intimacy. It would be amiss to ignore that this new subject matter coincides with his continuing reformulation of his sexual identity.

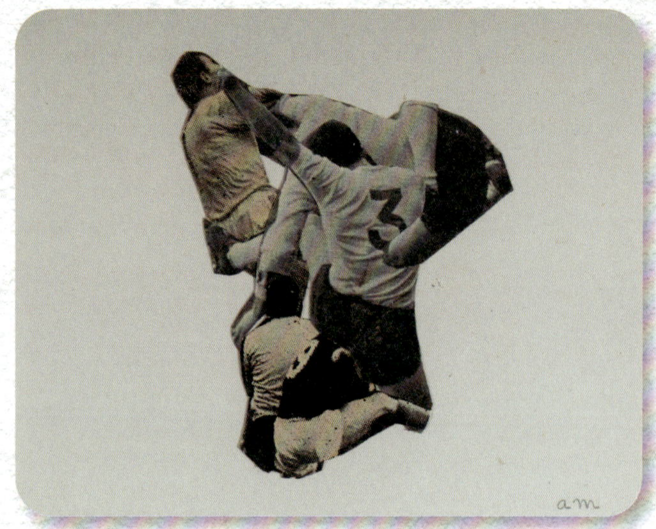
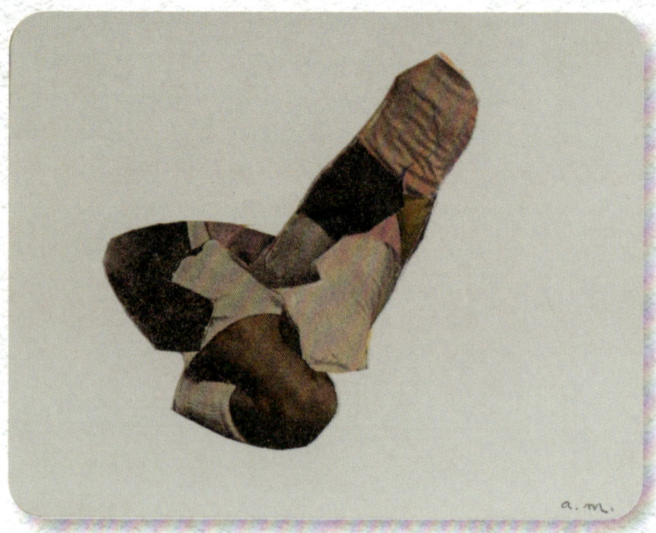

PAINTINGS 1965–1969

Today I have finished three years' work. When I started painting in this studio I realised that I was beginning a period of deep research and invention. What I did not realise was that four whole years were to pass before the twenty canvases that I began then would be finished.

These canvases certainly bear the scars of that struggle. Layer upon layer of paint has thickened the surface as I have constantly fought to deepen the image. I felt I wanted to pull together the bases of my work. I wanted to crystallise the many thoughts and ideas that had been forming during the previous years.

It has not been easy. Perhaps I should say here and now that the fulfilment of these ideas would never have been possible without the help, encouragement and support of my friend Raymond Crossley. He has lived with me during the greater part of this time and has borne a great deal of the strain and agony of creation with me.

It has not only been a physical strain, though hours of re-working and lack of money has caused this; it has been

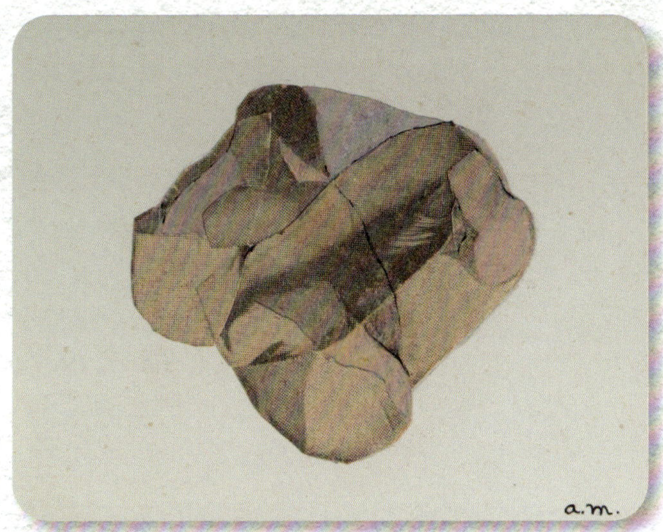

6:4 Adrien de Menasce, *Untitled*
6:5 Adrien de Menasce, *Untitled*
6:6 Adrien de Menasce, *Untitled*
1962
11.5 x 9 cm
Collage mounted on Winsor & Newton
Fashion Plate Board
(Private collection)

an emotional strain too. Holding on to a few images day in and day out; keeping the idea alive and daring more and more to cross the threshold of a new world has been very demanding.

For being able to make the paintings however I have been thankful. I can only hope that after so many years of struggle rewards are not too far off. I have fought as resolutely as I can for a new and meaningful view of Man. My work looks very unfashionable at the moment but I must believe that the times will move towards me. I hope they will.

The work in the galleries these days is pathetically shallow and full of ill-digested American influences. It would be terrible if the great tradition of European painting was really doomed. It has been my faith that that line continues and that these years of dedicated work is an attempt to extend once again that tradition.

Wilfred Avery, 70 Kensington Gardens Square, London W2, 30th June 1969

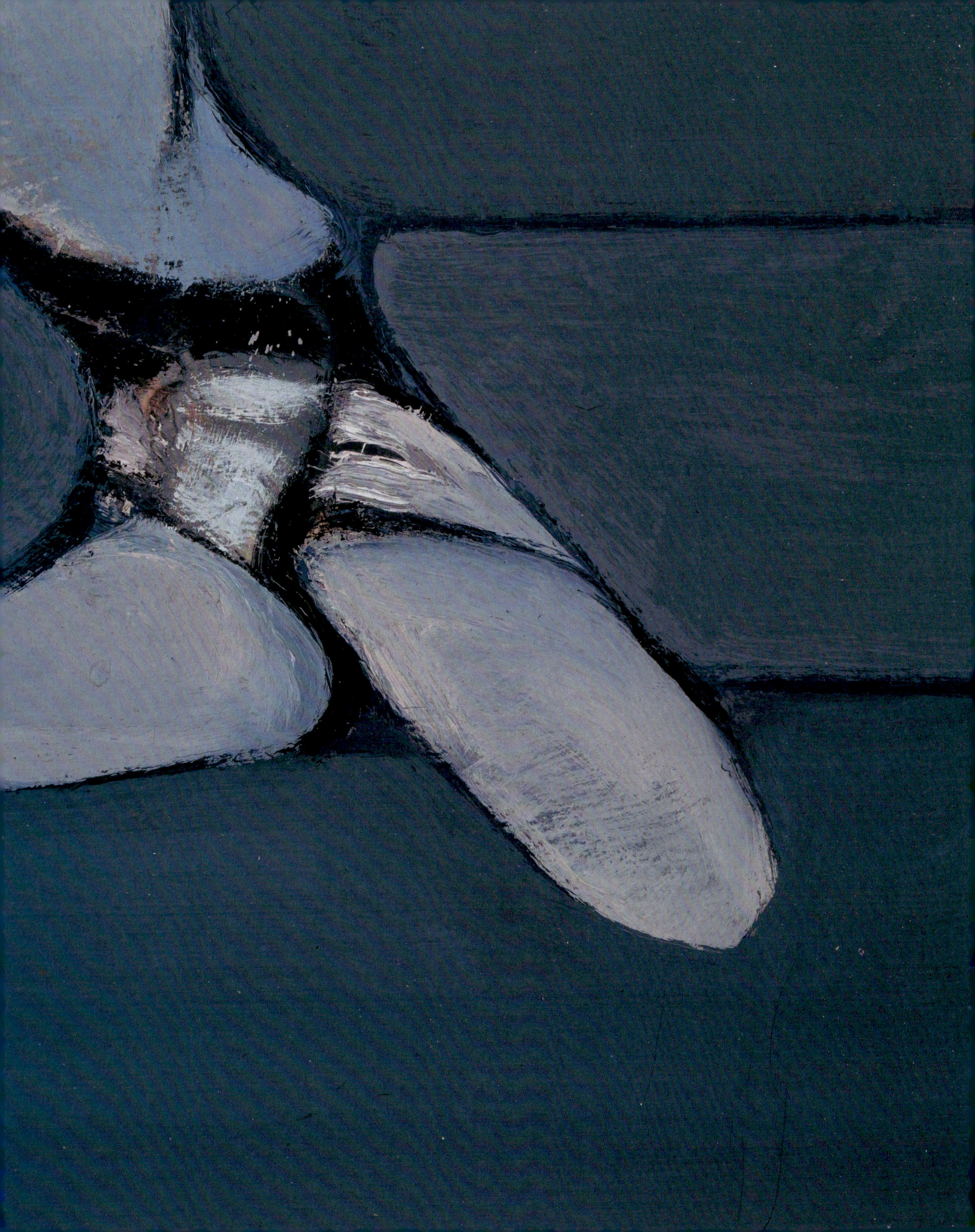

7 LOVE, SEX AND THE BODY: THE FIGURE EMERGES

The rawest nerve today is sexuality. Man seems only truly physical now when the nerves are bare and the flesh is strained.[31]

ON HIS RETURN from France, Wilfred moved to Kensington in West London, temporarily lodging with and then living in the flat below his friend Jack Humphries, at 70 Kensington Gardens Square. He found a job teaching part-time at Queen's Manor Primary School in Fulham. Wilfred's flat was small, but by placing a large mirror above the dining room mantelpiece, he made himself a workable studio. The extra light and illusion of space allowed him the perspective to work on a number of large oils, including and most importantly his 'Sixties Figures' oil series (1965–9).

The twenty works without doubt encapsulate the climax of the artist's experimentation with the figure, and mark the real sea change back to the human form. This refocus is also evident in Wilfred's drawings. Although not directly preliminary, an exploratory series of Flomaster anatomical drawings was made in 1965. Disembodied tangles of sinew and muscle, the richly textured *Anatomy 1* and *Anatomy 6* reveal a fascination with the human body that links Wilfred's drawing practice directly back to the beautifully rendered anatomical studies found in early Renaissance Italy.

But although Wilfred always referred to the paintings as his 'Sixties Figures', they are hardly figures in any traditional sense. Here, instead, we find strange and strangulated limbs; *shibari*-bound shapes that balance

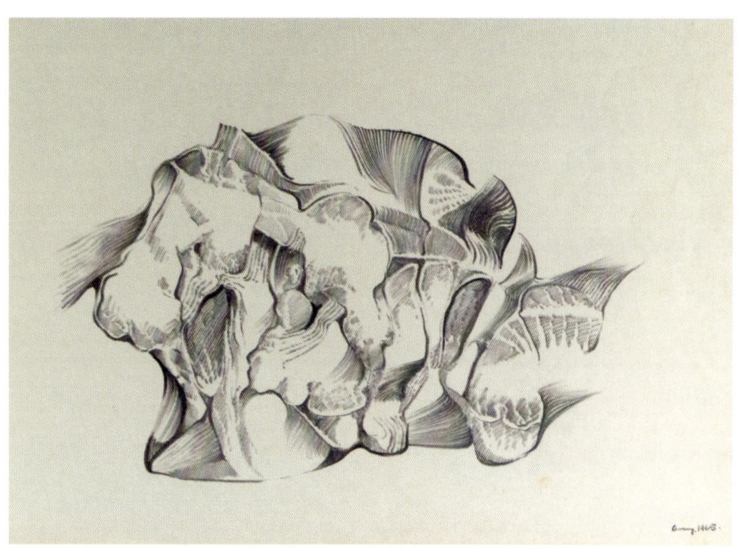

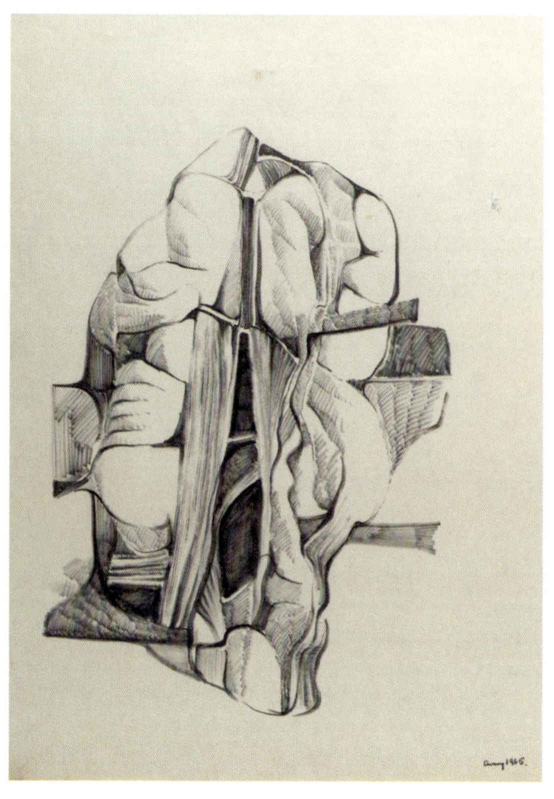

themselves unsettlingly between the human form and something totally other. Understated colour tones have replaced any obvious vibrancy of previous work. Wilfred's forms became increasingly enigmatic, malleable and shifting, and gone, too, is the flat 'shop-window' picture plane; here, now, a new and abstract sense of depth. (Finally, breathing space.)

Wilfred considered the 'Sixties Figures' his first truly original series, but it is absolute visual proof of the profound effect of his meeting with Adrien de Menasce. Both were working at the time in a muted palette, a geometry of organic and twisted limbs appearing in both painting and collage. This aesthetic similarity is also evidence of the Jungian direction both artists were moving in. 'I allowed my subconscious to help create the forms,' Wilfred wrote. 'My interest in Jung's idea of the unconscious begins to dominate.'[32]

In Adrien's *Heaven is Green Too* (1965), three sets of disembodied limbs drape themselves lazily across the canvas, folding over, in front of and behind a trio of horizontal lines. Wilfred's own experimentations with the line came fully into play at the same time, but to a markedly different effect. They provide a lightness rather than a weight. On comparing his

Regent (1965–9) with Adrien's *Warhorse* (1966–81), we find Wilfred's form elegant, almost floating in front of the tripartite background, whilst Adrien's situates itself firmly on the ground.

Over his career, Wilfred used the line to varied effect. The horizontal line lends each work a formal structure, directing us, as ever, to exactly what Wilfred wants us to focus on. It also acts as a divide, alluding to the different

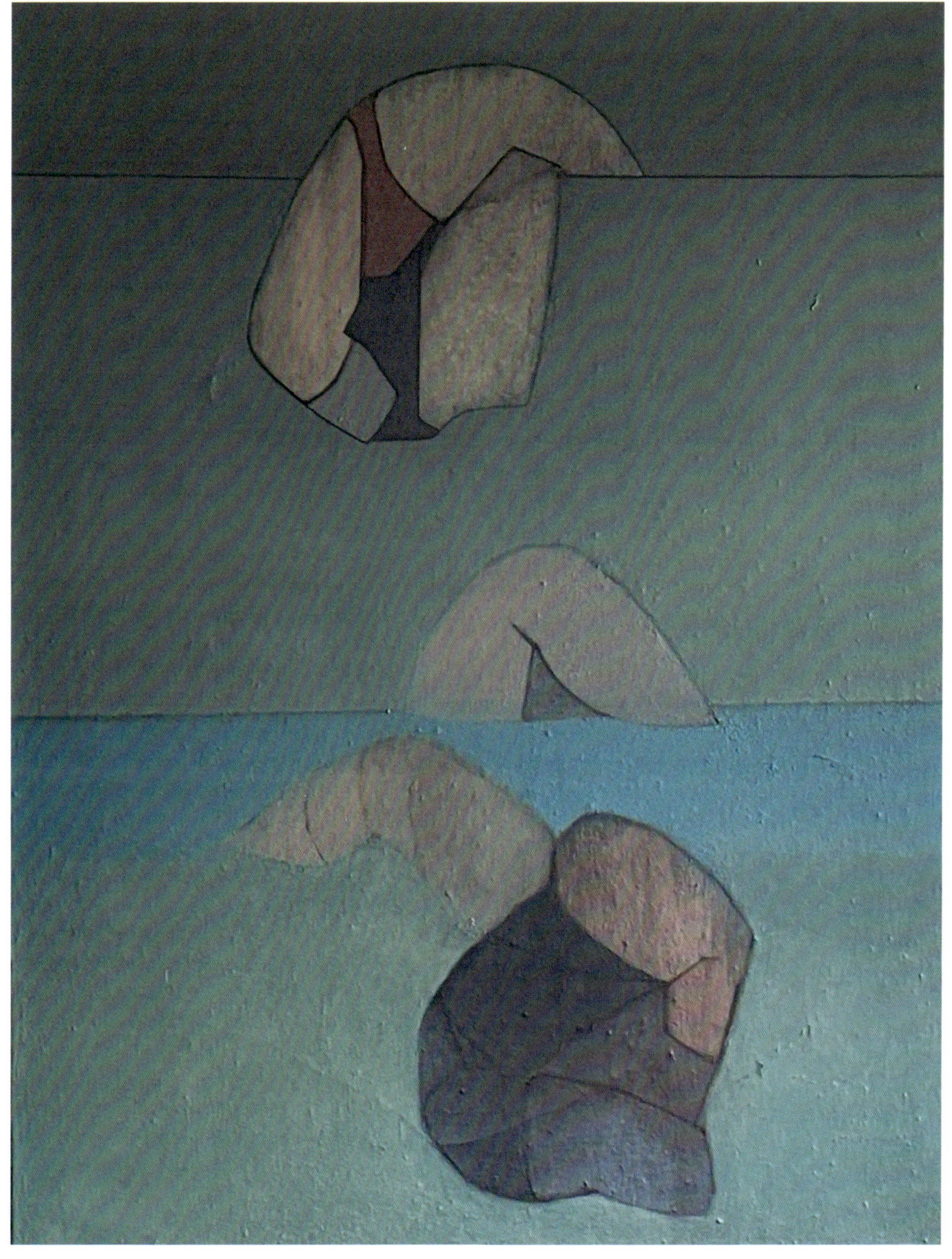

7:3 Adrien de Menasce,
Heaven is Green Too
1965
80 x 50 cm
Oil on canvas
(*Private collection*)

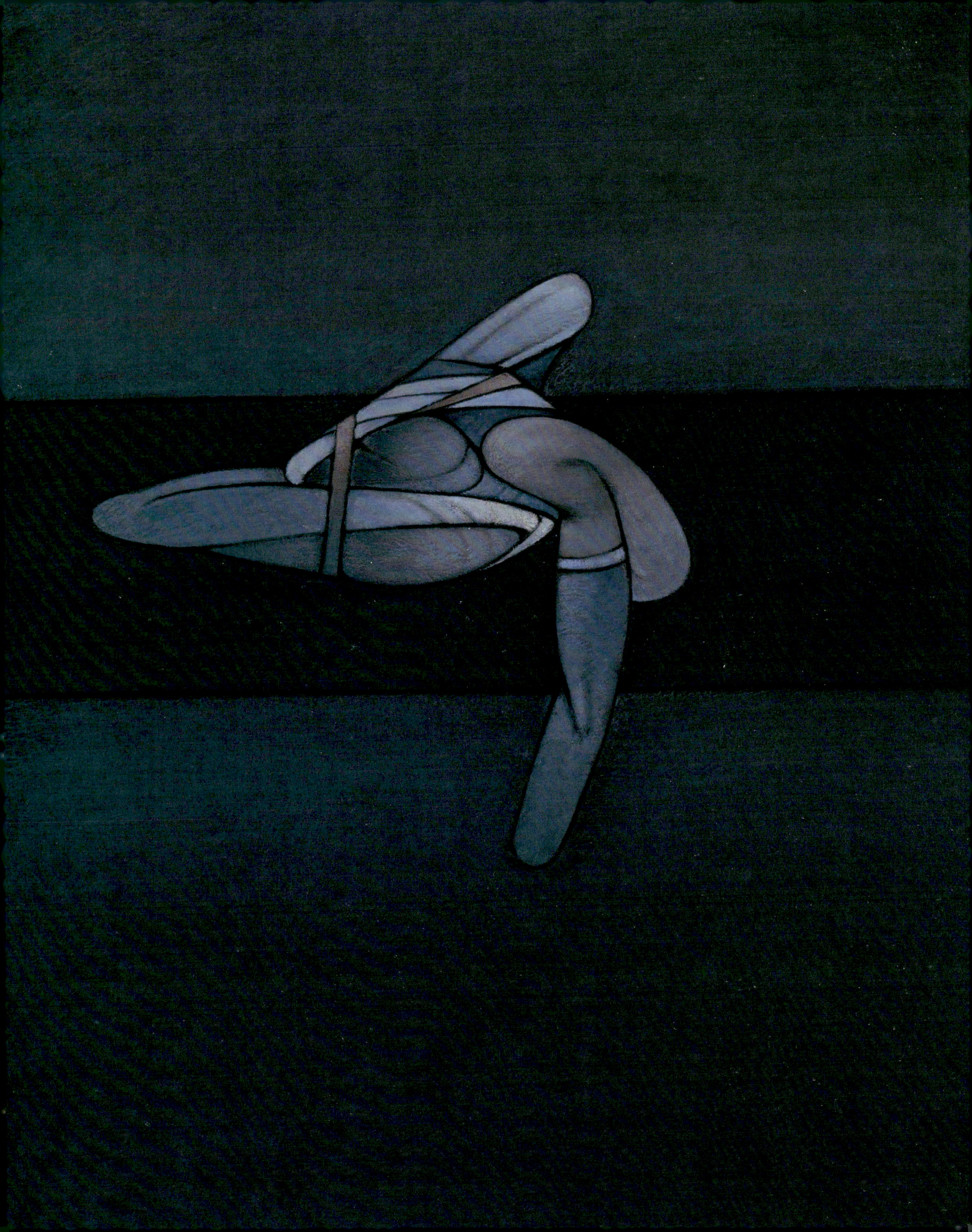

realities the artist is exploring; the division of mental as well as physical space, and between the conscious and the subconscious. And on top of this (and in its most simple translation), it acts as a horizon line, a way of creating space on a two-dimensional surface (Wilfred's use of the horizontal line will be explored in greater depth within the context of his 1970s works in Chapter 8).

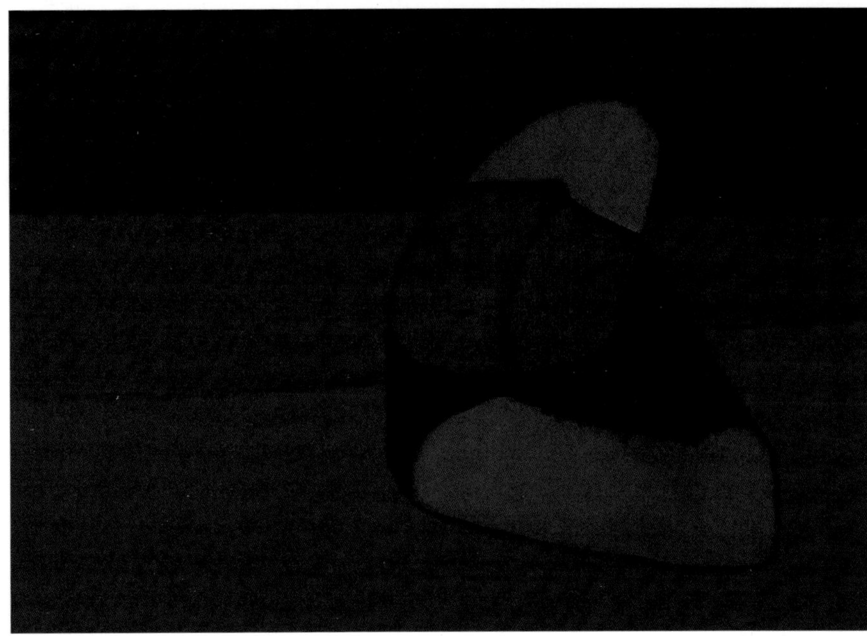

7:5 **Adrien de Menasce,** **Warhorse**
1966–81
39 x 55 cm
Oil on canvas
(Studio)

The French philosopher Catherine Malabou describes plasticity as an object having the ability to become something else whilst also retaining the possibility of resuming its original form.[33] By placing their constrained figures on top of these off-kilter striped backgrounds, Wilfred and Adrien accentuate the plasticity in each of their works. Note in all the push and pull of each opposing plane, the interplay of form and surrounding space. We get the feeling that the forms have been restrained against their will, and that this is a forced rather than submissive restraint, each taut as a coiled spring. Plasticity, you see, also indicates a capacity to explode, to come apart.

As an aside, Malabou's description could just as well be used to encapsulate the mutability of the mind. Thought and image; all of it shapeshifting.

Wilfred was certain these were the paintings that would make his name. But were they exhibited? Only twice. The first time the series was shown was just a year after its completion, at the recently opened Archer Gallery on Grafton Street, Mayfair. Here Wilfred exhibited thirty-seven works, including five from 'Sixties Figures' (*Eros, Oracle, Vigil, Talisman* and *Double Elevation*) in his 1970 solo show, *Exhibition of Paintings and Collages by Wilfred Avery*. As was so often the case, he felt very out of place and sold nothing. Seven years later, five from the series (*Doge, Eros, Pharos, Oracle* and *Penitent*) were exhibited as part of a semi-

OPPOSITE
7:4 **Regent**
1965–9
152.5 x 122 cm
Oil on canvas
(Studio)

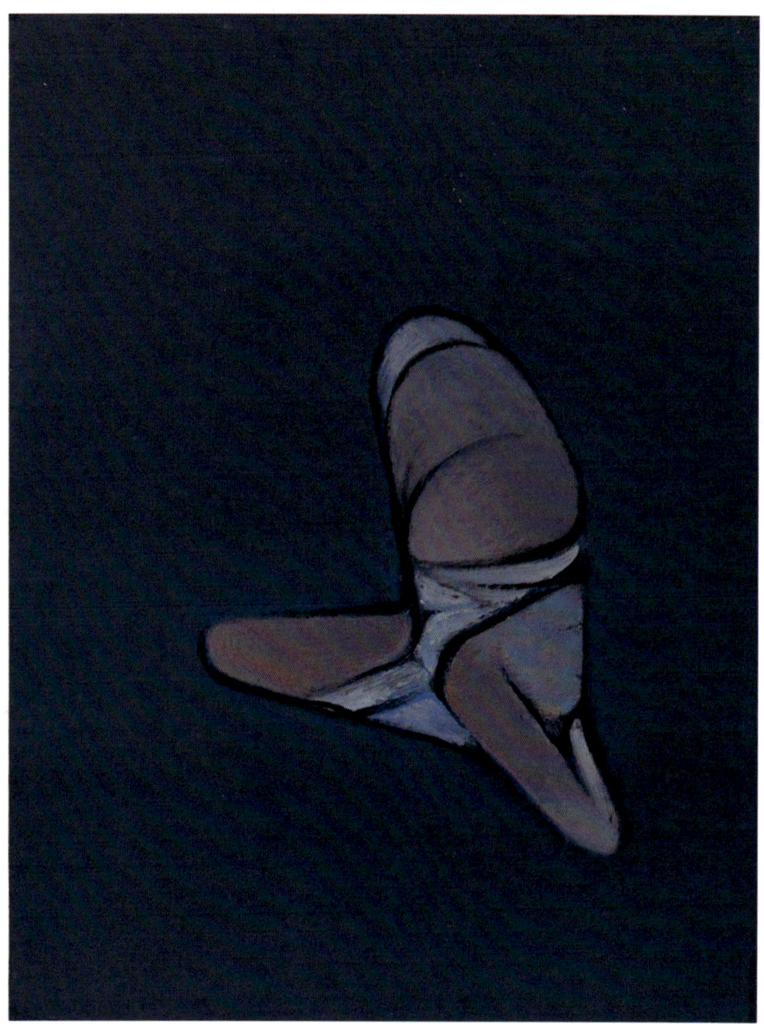

retrospective, *The Evolving Image*, at Woodlands Gallery in Blackheath. Twelve works, primarily landscapes, sold. The 'Sixties Figures' have never been shown as a complete series.

• • •

By 1969 Wilfred had distanced himself from Surrealism completely, but his 'Sixties Figures' retained a strong aesthetic influence. The series plays upon a number of Surrealist objectives – the subversive, erotic and fetishistic; the movement's macho (and often masochistic) themes more than hinted at. A shoulder, the creased flesh of a torso as it twists backwards, a leg bent at the knee; each shape as inherently suggestive as Man Ray's *Anatomies* (1925) or Lee Miller's *Nude Bent Forward* (c. 1930). Wilfred's phallic-like *Doge* is the most explicit of the series, and alludes, too, to the continued cross-pollination between his and Adrien's work; the same shape to be found in Adrien's 'Secret Museum' series.

Wilfred's contorted figures also bear similarity to Hans Bellmer's 1930s sculptural and photographic series 'La Poupée'. *Double Elevation* (1965–9), in particular, matches the corpulent, twisted torsos of Bellmer's dolls; rolls of flesh, restrained and uncomfortable. This fragmented and fetishised doll figure was repeated throughout Bellmer's oeuvre – the young body often recognisable only by her white socks and patent leather shoes. Once in Wilfred's hands, however, Bellmer's unsettling and often lumpen form has been slimmed out. Note *Nocturne* (1965–9), two bodies a tangle of clothes and flesh, limbs stretched, lithe and muscular. Must have been all that struggling.

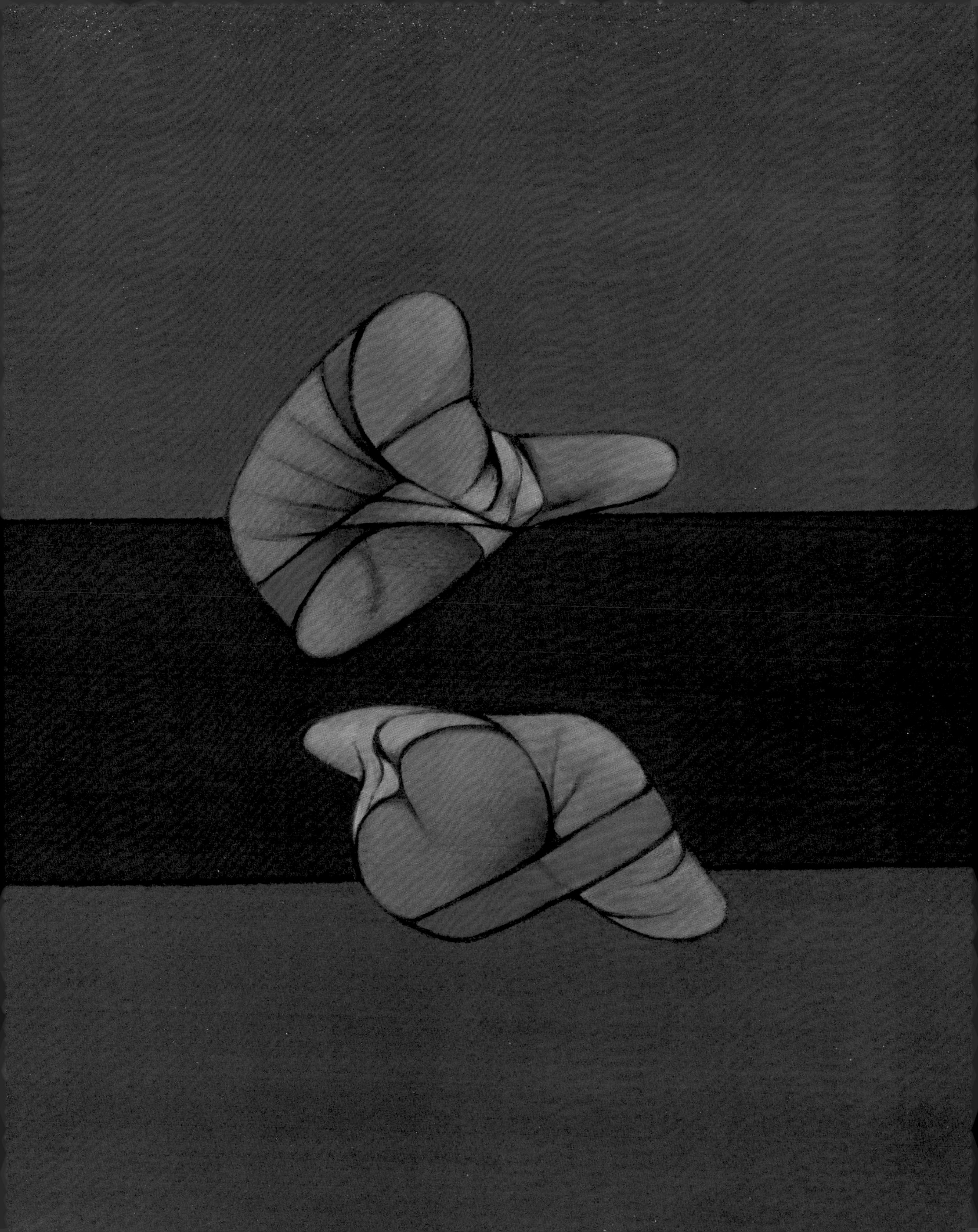

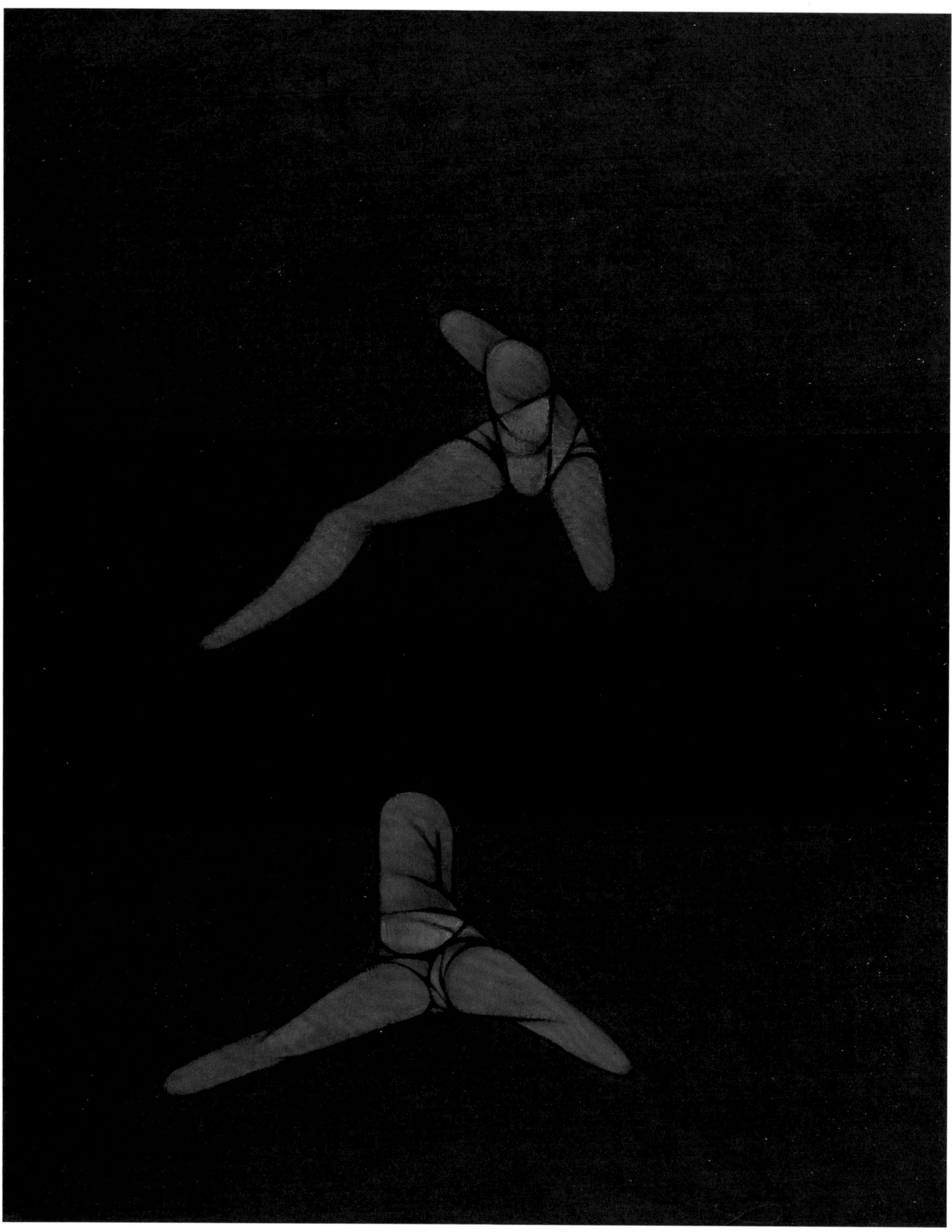

Using ball joints allowed Bellmer to maximise the unnatural articulation of each of his dolls, and gave him the freedom to dismantle and reassemble them in numerous disturbing combinations. Wilfred's 'Sixties Figures' also rotate around one particular axis. His centre of operations, though, was the crotch, clad, as ever, in white underpants. The gestural tri-limbed *Jester* (1965–9) sits splay-legged on a three-part background. Our eye is drawn immediately to the crux of the figure (seated as it is almost in the dead-centre of the canvas). The same with *Eros*, muscular thighs wide

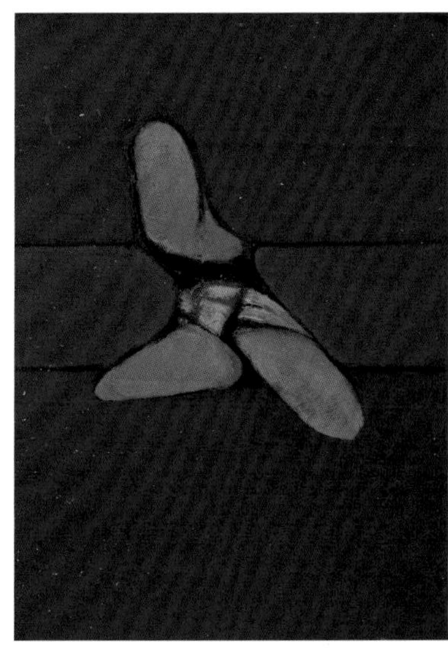

ABOVE
7:9 Jester
1965–9
26.5 x 19 cm
Oil on canvas
(Studio)

OPPOSITE
7:8 Nocturne
1965–9
101.5 x 81.5 cm
Oil on canvas
(Studio)

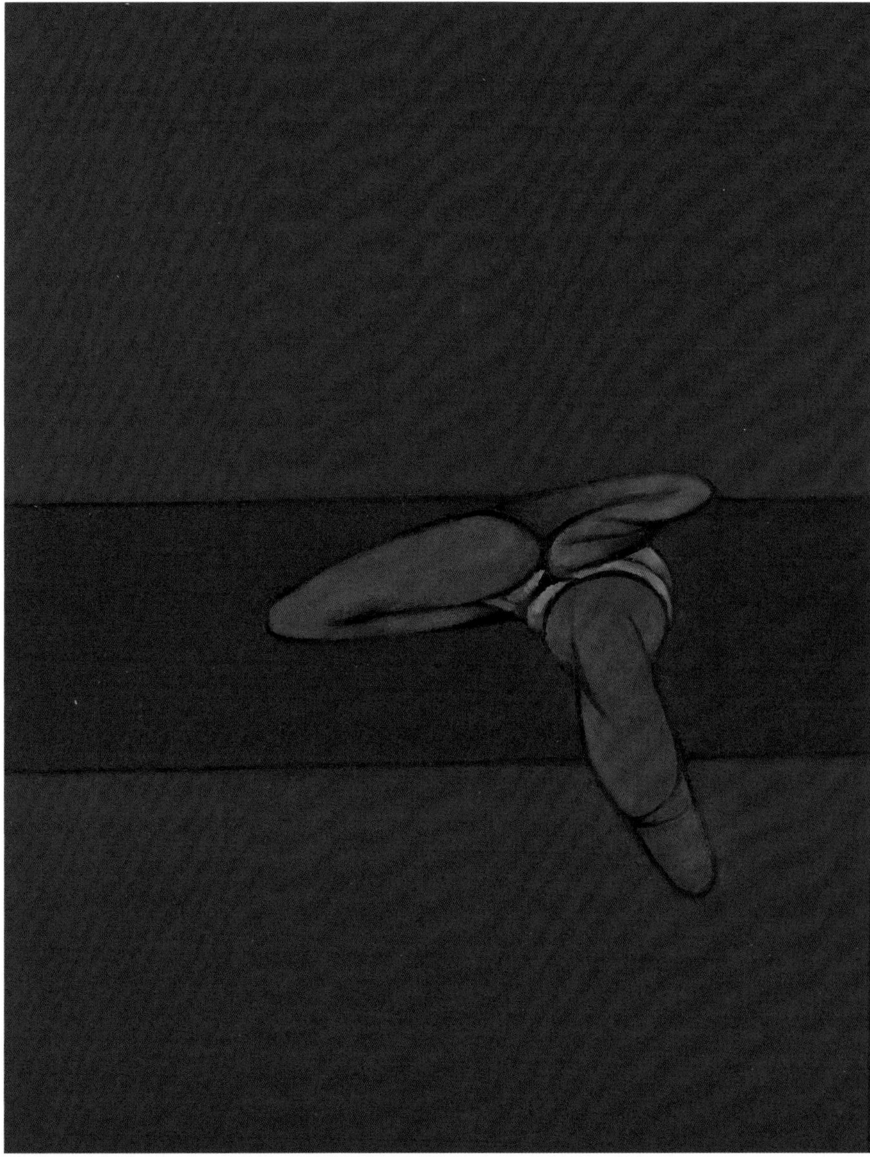

BELOW
7:10 Eros
1965–9
51 x 40.5 cm
Oil on canvas
(Brighton & Hove Museums)

open. Both feel painted as an invitation more than anything. Wilfred undoubtedly knew where he was leading our eye; was aware what these paintings alluded to.

Bellmer's dolls are uncomfortable to look at, mutilated torture victims strung up and abandoned or photographed from above, putting us in the shoes of the perpetrator. But Wilfred's 'Sixties Figures', though still psychologically unsettling, capture none of this sadism. Instead, they are imbued with a sense of sexual power; these are male bodies with a great and active energy.

This is most evident in *Regent, Serpentine* and *Talisman* (all 1965–9).

7:11 *Serpentine*
1965–9
122 x 152.5 cm
Oil on canvas
(Studio)

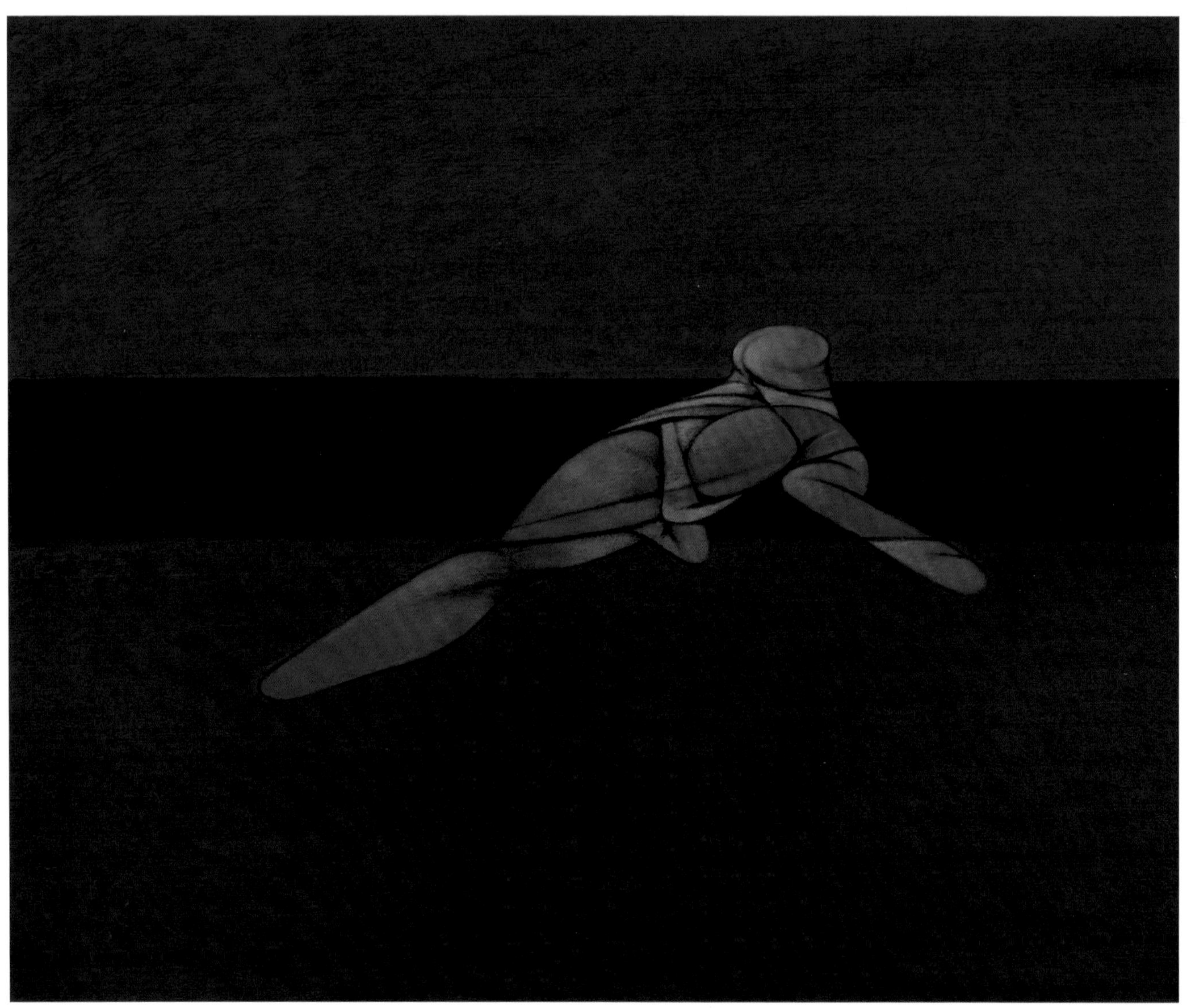

There is something luxurious — something feline, even — in their stretched compositions. The extended leg of *Serpentine* shows us the ligaments taut in the back of the knee; a full body yawn encapsulated. *Regent* is similar, though this time the lower leg hangs (note the sports sock, these continued to crop up in many of his works, a call-back to his collaged athlete days), fades almost into obscurity before coming to any sense of a foot. In fact, the entire figure is made up of legs, folded and stacked like piles of clean sheets and bound together with a near vertical strip which adds a perfect tension, a dynamic eroticism to the scene. But why so sensual — what must have changed for the artist over these last few years?

7:12 *Talisman*
1965–9
81 x 99 cm
Oil on canvas
(Private collection)

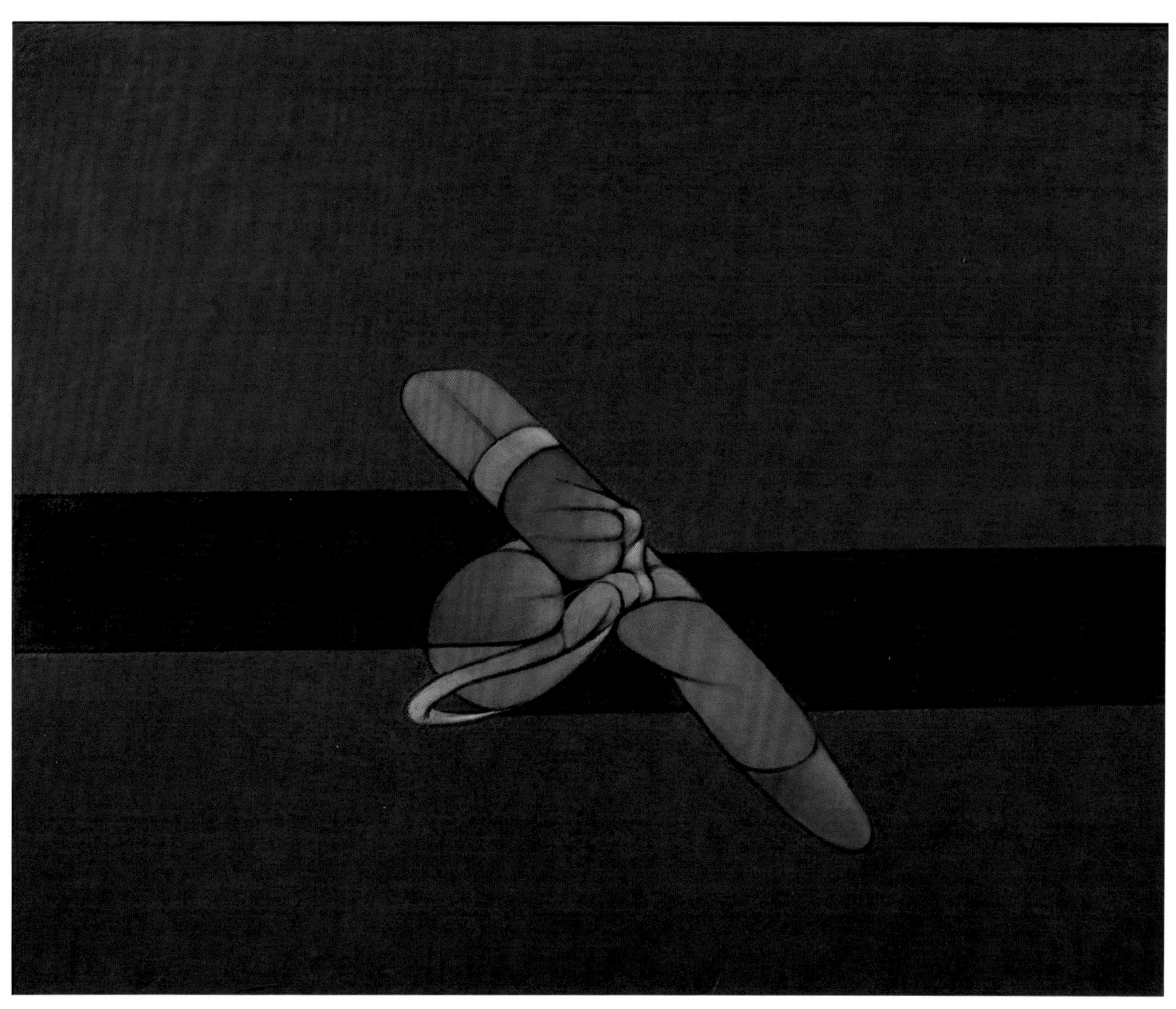

II A CHANCE ENCOUNTER

What a mysterious business painting is. One thing is certain — it is no good looking for a painting. It is like love, suddenly and unexpectedly it is there.[34]

Wilfred met Ray Crossley at the Salisbury Arms in St Martin's Lane in November 1966. Fairly fresh to London, Ray had only visited the pub a handful of times. And Wilfred, despite enjoying the artistic clientele and stimulating intellectual conversation found there, was overall weary of the scene and had resolved to make it his last visit.

Jung termed it synchronicity, these deeply meaningful coincidences that can so drastically alter the course of a life, and the pair's chance meeting marked the first of a series of them that would continue to play across their relationship. You see, although serendipity is like mist to most of us, to Wilfred and Ray it was something concrete.

Shortly after they first met, Wilfred found a small piece of thin rectangular card which 'emerged', he said, from the skirting board of his bedroom. It must have been hidden there for decades. In neat old-fashioned writing (the black ink faded to brown), the following handwritten lines:

> K
> No — *in my opinion true love can be*
> *felt but once*

Over the next fifty years the couple would often find single playing cards wherever they went. In 1973 Wilfred wrote, 'There are endless examples I could give of surprising "signs" and "events". As they grow more numerous they are less surprising. I accept more and more the rich field of psychic touch that begins to enter one's mind as one accepts and becomes receptive to the interaction of the spirit and matter.'[35]

And through all of its varied ups and downs, Wilfred and Ray retained a firm belief that their life together was what they came to term 'meant'. Their relationship was 'meant' to such an extent, in fact, that it had been prophesied years earlier by one Mrs Bentley, a Yorkshire medium that Ray's mother had taken to visiting in the late 1950s and early 1960s. It was during one of these sessions that Mrs Bentley said, 'I am getting a young man. It could be your son and he is with an older man who will be good for him.

W. Is his name Will or William? I'm not sure but you'll know because when you meet him, he will have fur all around here [stroking her shoulders and neck] and when you see him, you'll remember what I said and you'll laugh.'

The day after their second date, to the musical *Jorrocks (The Happiest Man Alive)* at the New Theatre, Wilfred invited Ray to move in with him, a decision that seemed to surprise them both equally. In his characteristic sharp-tongued manner, Wilfred told Ray a few weeks later that if he had known that he was a solicitor at the beginning, he never would have pursued a relationship. And moreover, his first thought on Ray was, 'What am I doing with this little git?' Ray, however, had come to an almost immediate conclusion that Wilfred needed him, and that he needed to be needed. The next time he visited, Wilfred had replaced his single bed with a double.

Ray had been living with his mother in Brentwood, Essex, since returning from a year in Sicily a few months earlier. Before moving in together, Wilfred felt he wanted to meet her, and it was during an overnight visit to Brentwood, shortly after this second date, that the prophecy came true. After showing Wilfred to his room, Mrs Crossley remembered that she had sent all the eiderdowns off to be cleaned. If he felt cold in the night, she told him, he could find something in the wardrobe to put on. When she took him a cup of tea the next morning, she nearly dropped it laughing. Wilfred *had* felt cold, and found himself a fur coat. Mrs Crossley discovered him, as prophesied, all wrapped up in fur.

Ray had not introduced Wilfred as his new partner, rather as the man he would be sharing a house with so that he could be closer to his work in London. We can only imagine that after that morning he really had to say no more. Likewise, without the need of any formal discussion, all of Wilfred's family accepted Ray without hesitation. They stayed together for the next fifty years. Wilfred's lifelong dedication to his work is a testament to the strength of this relationship.

Ray's influence on the 'Sixties Figures' was twofold. Firstly, their moving in together minimised the financial pressures that had hounded Wilfred throughout his adult life. In 1968, with Ray's support, he was able to give up his teaching position at Queen's Manor Primary School. Despite the unusual freedom the job allowed – the headmistress, Annie Burns, let him use the school's art studios for his own work – Wilfred had come to realise that he was no longer happy teaching, even part-time. He wanted to devote himself fully to painting. Secondly, through being in a committed relationship, Wilfred gained a newfound confidence in his sexuality, something that directly translated into his work. Gone are the quietly avoidant figures undressing, hidden away in their darkened rooms.

Here instead we find the figure splay-legged, its sexuality centralised and unavoidable. Although each form is clothed, there is an awareness or, more to the point, a learned knowledge, of the naked form. We should not make light of the practicality of having a nude and willing body in such close contact. Wilfred never used Ray as a life model in any formal sense, but familiarity with another undoubtedly had a marked effect on the artist's more figurative works. ●

7:13 Detail: Regent
1965-9
152.5 x 122 cm
Oil on canvas
(Studio)

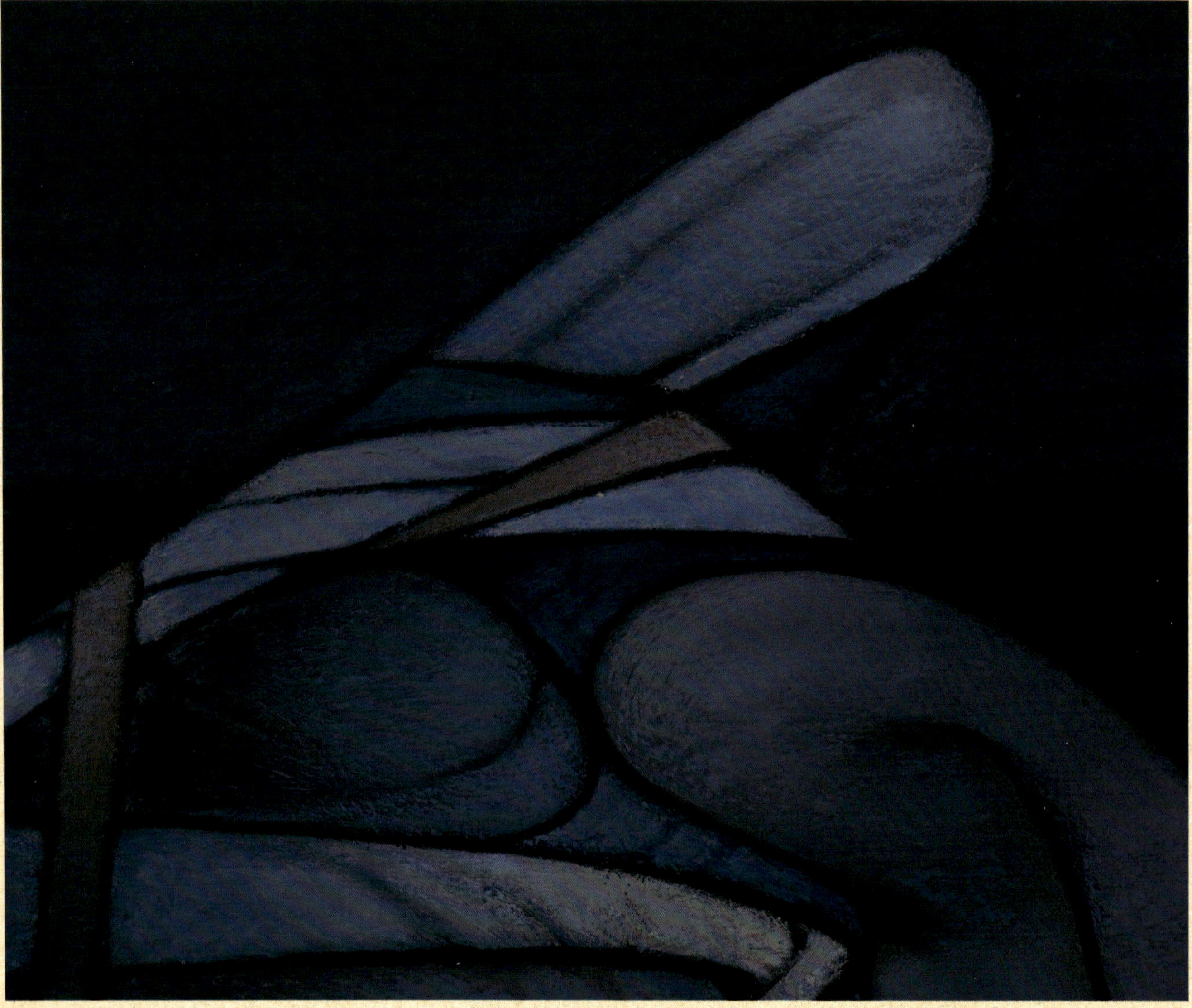

Wilfred's newfound sexual confidence mirrored the cultural landscape of the 1960s, further proof of an awareness — if not a conscious following — of the zeitgeist. It is interesting to note, however, that not once in his career thus far had Wilfred depicted the male body in the public sphere. Either the body is hidden inside or, as in the 'Sixties Figures', totally outside the landscape that we ourselves exist in. Although the 'Sixties Figures' series is a far cry from Wilfred's early work, there remains a sense here that it continues to mirror, in part, the still hostile environment of 1960s Britain.

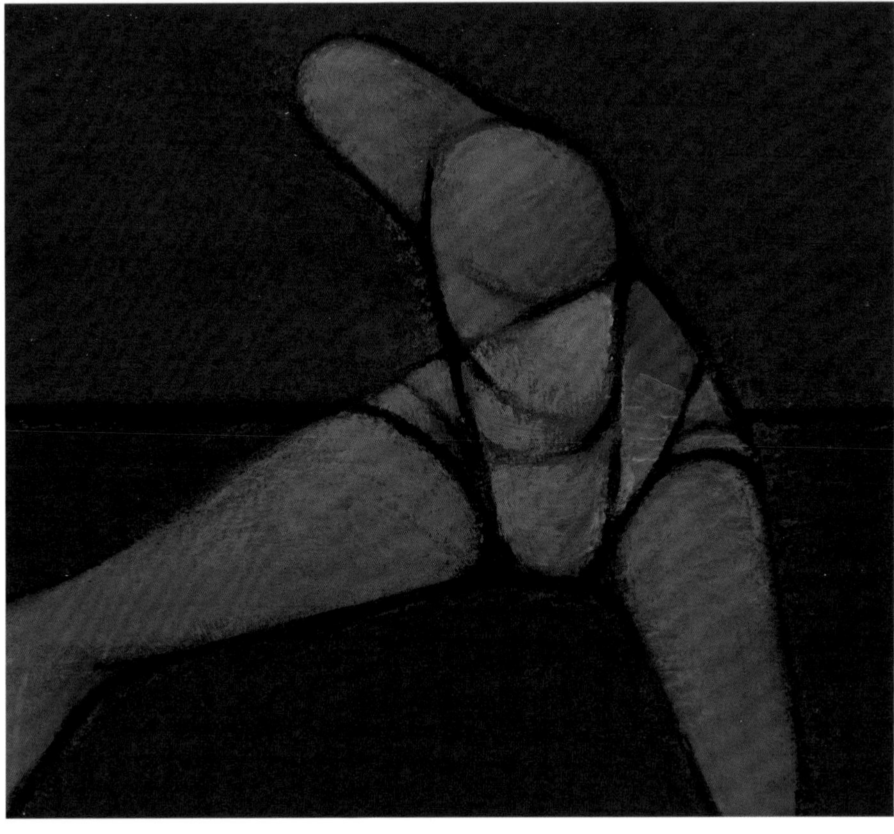

7:14 Detail: Nocturne
1965-9
101.5 x 81.5 cm
Oil on canvas
(Studio)

Wilfred worked on the twenty paintings almost daily, often making changes to more than one at the same time. In this period, he neither started any new work, nor retouched another. The series changed drastically. Look closely, and you will discover highly worked surfaces, evidence of half a decade's struggle and effort. It is concentrated, even obsessive work; an intense consideration making itself apparent in each brushstroke. In *Regent*, various underpainted curved shapes show themselves beneath the layers. The added texture, both intentional and through the multitude of changes and reconsiderations made over the course of painting, gives a depth to each piece, a sense of the three-dimensional on a strictly two-dimensional surface.

After five years, and a move to Montague House in southwest London's Blackheath in the summer of 1969, the twenty paintings were simultaneously finished, despite Wilfred's insistence that he had not set any meaningful time frame.

PLACE – THE MODERN CONSCIOUSNESS

We live in a world of disillusioned materialism. All around us the patterns of life and society that depended on an objective idea of physical achievement seem to grow more and more diffuse.

Our explorers no longer find the source of the Nile or some remote corner of the Amazon, they throw the whole world into perspective by setting off on highly sophisticated journeys to another planet. In doing so they give us a new awareness of 'place', a new consciousness of where we are and what we are doing.

Some young people still search for causes to champion; the undeveloped countries, racial equality, sexual tolerance or a bomb-less peace but one has the nagging suspicion that at heart the outward aspirations of any particular group lack real conviction.

There are those who prefer to 'drop out' believing that the present orientation of society is fundamentally lacking. They seek new affirmations of human awareness in communes and 'love-ins' and shared experiences. Perhaps they have got to a point and are in a way prophets of changes that will sooner or later come.

But the real problem lies in the projection of the human image by the overwhelming and ill-digested mass media that constantly assails us. Whenever new group manifestations occur they are immediately analysed, assessed, commented on and disseminated as further 'types' of human beings that we might choose to be.

It is all of course to no avail. I remember trying around 1959–1961 to make paint images of figures that had conviction but try as I might to find a 'wholeness' to which I could relate my 'man', I ended up fragmenting him in order to avoid the generalisations that seemed inevitably to occur. I wanted to make him particular – I wanted to avoid making him abstract.

It was not until I surrendered the concept of an idea or ideal of Man and began to work with the canvas as a virgin space for human activity where I would discover whatever image wished to occur that I began slowly to create a human paraphrase that really convinced me.

So our modern consciousness, it seems to me, needs more and more to discover our awareness of place. We need to establish more truly than man has done before not what we would like to be or be seen to be or choose to be but more precisely what we are.

This is no easy task. It requires a new faith in and evaluation of the role of the individual in society. We have to begin to learn to live with ourselves without the mask, as it were. We have to learn that our most substantial contribution to the group lies in the exploration of our own psyches. Our link with our fellow man lies in the most intimate of actions. We must believe that it is our first, and at this moment our urgent, responsibility to be not Christians, Socialists, Humanists, hippies, drop-outs or saints but to be deeply and truly ourselves.

This means in terms of art that the story we must tell is essentially autobiographic. The true revelation of the artist's personality in depth is his sole preoccupation. Thus my work reveals the myths, the memories and the experiences that have made me. No one will have quite the same unconscious concerns as those that reveal themselves in my work. No one will have the same sexual interests or sensual responses. Nor will they inherit quite the same cultural knowledge (the country philosophy of my own parents for example) or be familiar with the same sights and scenes that have helped me to form the myth of my own particular identity.

But this search for individual reality is the first step for Man in a move towards a heightening of the human condition. Society will change because we change. People will be able to touch each other because we have made *ourselves touchable. The circle will be joined in a new unity of human consciousness not because we declare ourselves to be a particular group sharing an agreed or projected concept of Man but because we have made our existence as individuals valid in terms of truthfulness to ourselves; not in another ideal world or Heaven but here and now in this particular place.*

Wilfred Avery, Montague House, Dartmouth Hill SE10, 20th November 1969

• • •

SPACE

Space in picture making is talked about a great deal these days. Everyone uses the word but its meaning is very diffuse. When I was young we talked about the canvas space. Cézanne, it seemed, had turned all the planes towards the canvas surface and created a new space for pictorial architecture. Later Matisse had created a 'Byzantine' space. Nothing was more than the space it occupied. Illusion and magic were out and the wall space was the only permissible space for the painter.

So, the Americans came and tried, with bigger and bigger walls, to extend this space. They are still doing it as I write but these spaces seem dead and empty. The Rothkos and Motherwells hang, like yesterday's wallpapers in the back passages of the museums. It has become the tombstone of American materialism; a huge dead production line of physical remorse reminiscent of the worst of the neglected murals of Victorian England.

Picasso and Braque used only one aspect of Cézanne. The shallow space of Cubism is a prescribed world. It is a perfectible space rather like a room setting for a photograph or, like a shop window. Through it they discovered a world in which man and society meet and in which our dependence on each other is fully explored.

But there is no mystery in it and no death. Death, despite the 'Charnel House' of Picasso and the skulls and bones sitting like teapots on a table, is never really present in their works. They express a faith in the possible arrangement of man and his environment into a meaningful whole.

But we are interested in a more meaningful whole and wish to break this obsession with the canvas space. I am interested in the strange space of the late Cézannes, of Pisanello and Rembrandt and the early Surrealists.

One works with the unconscious, releasing it as much as possible through the reality of the canvas space where one is working. Through it one hopes to find a new space; a space neither 'plastic' nor 'illusionistic'. Perhaps the images one creates will belong to a bigger consciousness than oneself. One may manage in time to draw the curtain a little and glimpse the space that really interests us — the space that is yet unknown.

Wilfred Avery, 1969

III SEX AND ACTIVISM

Thank god for the hippies, for the pop groups and the underground press.
Thank God for anything which can make us once again proud of our feelings,
unashamed of our bodies, neglectful of possessions and full of faith in our spirit.[36]

An increased sexual confidence is mirrored not just in Wilfred's work of the later 1960s, but in his art critique and theory, too. In this, as ever, he aligns his attitudes to those of Carl Jung.

Wilfred shared Jung's view that both the male and female (the animus and anima archetypes) exist in every human. An early oil, *Standing Figure* (1959), painted two years before the similarly postured *Summer Figure* (and sharing its vibrant colour scheme) alludes to this belief. It is a hermaphroditic form, with both breasts and a penis. Dynamic struts of paint shooting out diagonals from the torso give a sense that we are somewhere mid-shift; that the body may transform again completely within the next instant. It is alive with a simmering energy, painted in the period just before the artist's work becomes known for the taut binds discussed in Chapter 7.

Although Wilfred often referred to his own female side, *Standing Figure* is a rare example of the depiction of anything remotely anatomically female in his own work. There are some early female Flomaster nudes, made in 1959, but by the end of the decade the female form was all but dropped in favour of increasingly sexualised depictions of the male body. A general dismissal of the fully female form gives further weight to the theory that Wilfred was using his practice, in part, to come to terms with his own sexuality.

And again, like Jung, who considered sexuality a vital part of the personality, Wilfred was outspoken about the power of the erotic force. This attitude also connects him (albeit perhaps unconsciously), to Neoplatonism, the school of thought inherent to the whole intellectual background of Renaissance Italy, and particularly prevalent in the art and poetry of Michelangelo. Neoplatonist theory connected the spiritual to the sensual: 'He who uses love properly certainly praises the beauty of the body, but through that contemplates the higher beauty of the soul,'[37] wrote the Florentine Humanist Marsilio Ficino in 1474. In 1969 Wilfred mirrored these words in writing: 'What a fool man is to think he can find his spirit without his body; to refuse the deep erotic force inside him and not see that this force alone will lead him to a greater truth.'[38]

For Wilfred, art was *crucially* important. Believing as he did that it had the power to elevate humanity, he became increasingly frustrated when his own work did not garner the attention that he believed it deserved. 'If the mystery of my life leads me in the way that I feel it does,' he wrote in 1975, 'then the time must surely come for my work to make its contribution to the movement for liberation and truth.'[39]

This philosophical convergence with the Renaissance ties in nicely to Wilfred's aptitude at drawing, his works on paper sharing the same fine-tuned lines as those of the Renaissance master draughtsmen. *Three Figures* (1979) is a stupendous and interconnected trio of bodies. They are embroiled in some kind of wrestle, attempting, it looks, to untangle themselves from their taut elasticated binds. The work is exemplary in showing Wilfred's skill in plasticity; the push-pull of it making it as aggressive as it is sexual.

An increasing preoccupation with sex and sexuality led Wilfred to an involvement with the Gay Liberation Movement, and in late 1974 Ray and he joined the Lewisham branch of the Campaign for Homosexual Equality (then based in St Lawrence's Church, Catford and later at the Lee Centre on Aislibie Road). Wilfred became an influential member of the branch, notably directing the consciousness-raising film, *David is Homosexual*, in 1976, with Dave Belton, another member of the group, acting as his cameraman. The film, now of cult status, is in the BFI archive. Inspired by this experience, in 1993

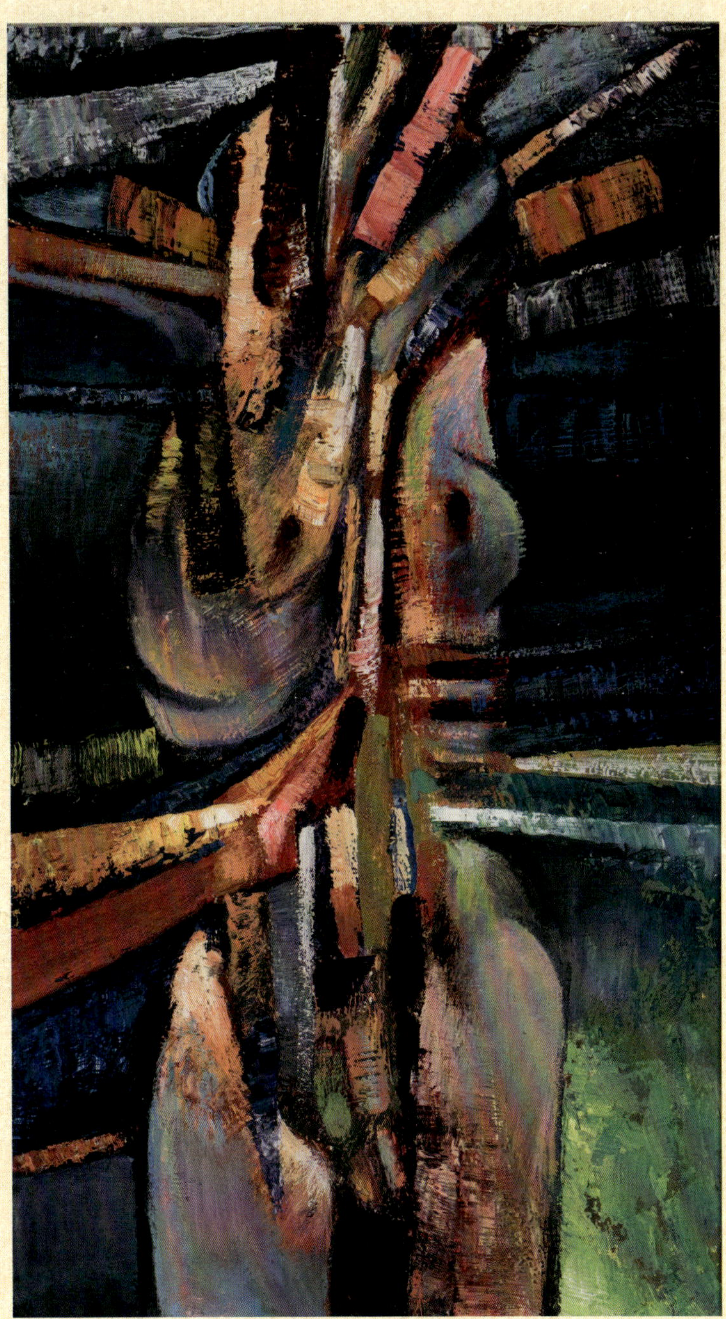

III:1 Standing Figure
1959
51 x 30.5 cm
Oil on hardboard
(*Studio*)

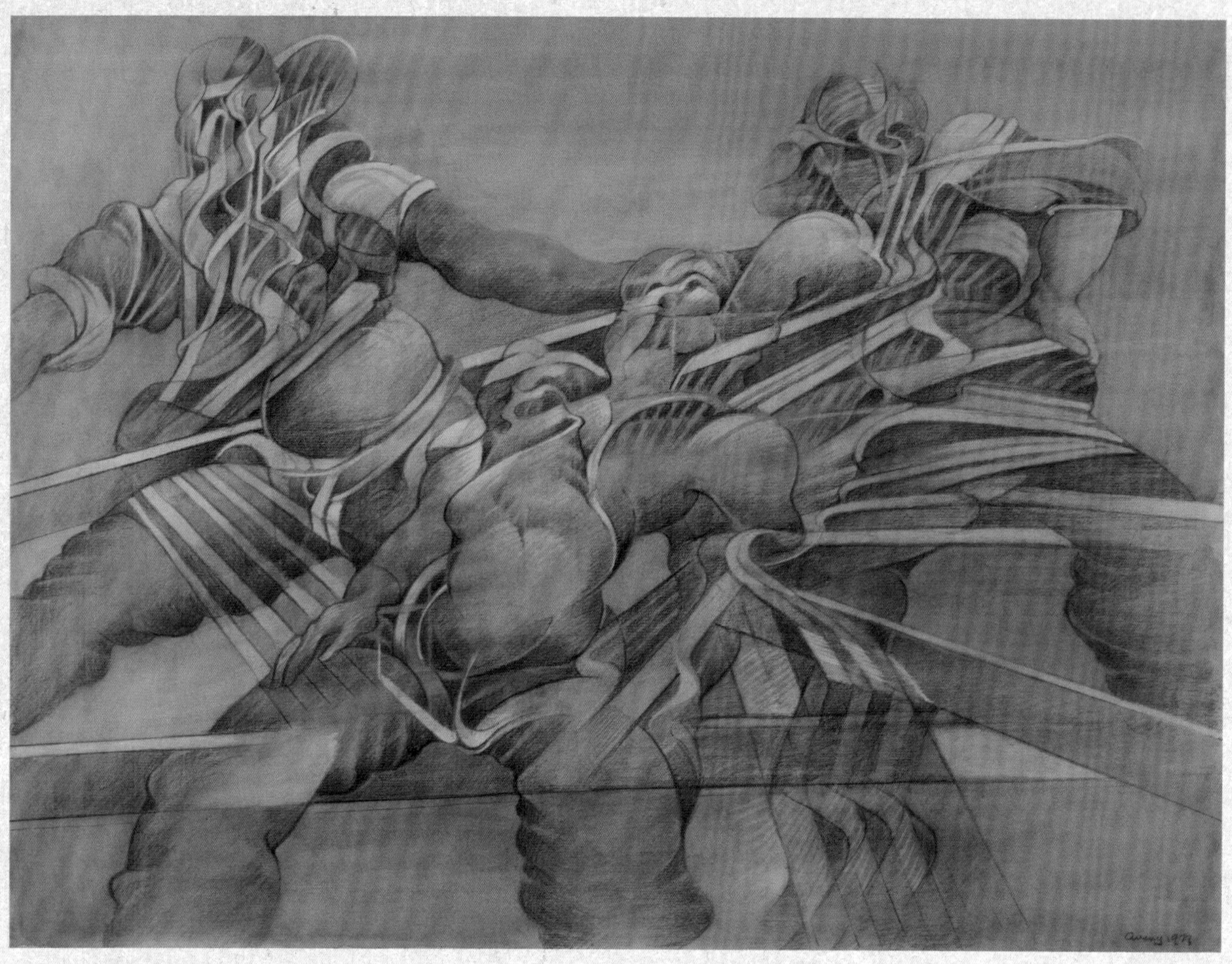

he bought a film camera and began to make recordings of his work. He showed the film to a small and select audience in his studio the following year, playing a recording over the top of it of Stravinsky's *Apollon Musagète*. Wilfred's involvement with the film was a pivotal part of his increased political and social engagement, something that came into play with his 'Sixties Figures', and is apparent over the duration of the 1970s.

> *My involvement with the Gay Liberation Movement is making me more and more aware of the oppression of homosexuals and more and more aware therefore of the oppression within myself. My work has always tried to be an honest expression of my own subjectivity and this oppression is therefore evident in what I do. I realise that I do have very big hang-ups about being homosexual and that this liberating process is needed in me as much as in society.*[40]

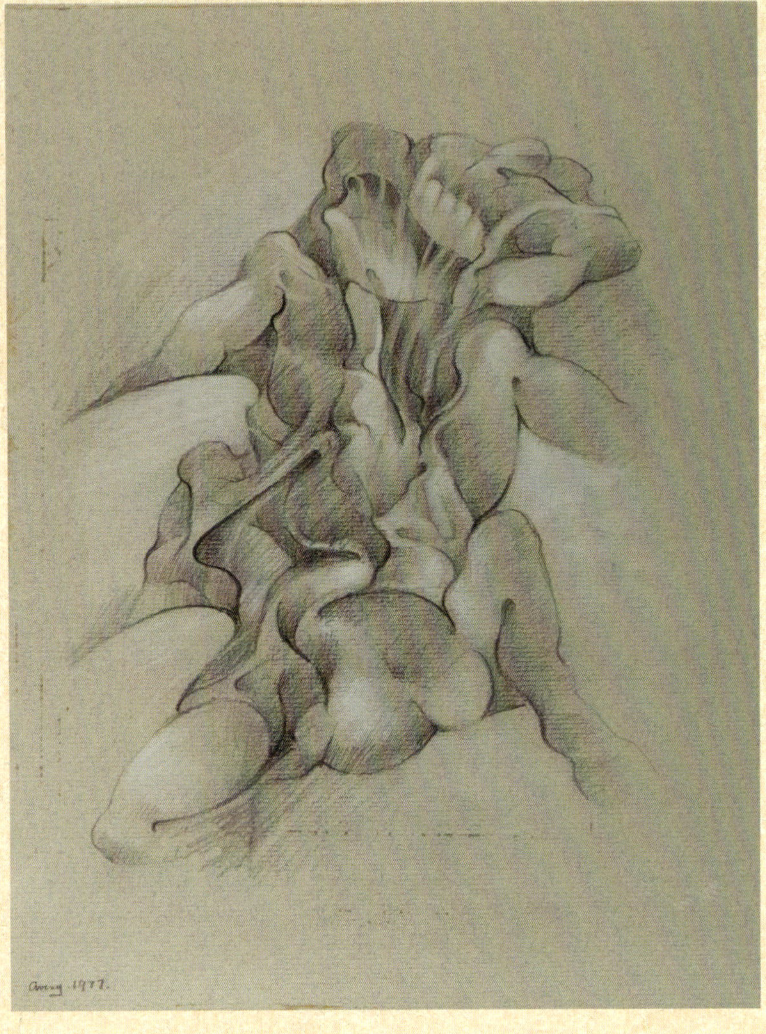

OPPOSITE

III:2 Three Figures
1979
47 x 66 cm
Pencil and gouache
(Private collection)

III:3 Hydra
1977
30.5 x 23.5 cm
Pencil and gouache
(Studio)

As Wilfred became more politically engaged, so did his work. It is important here to view the increasing homoeroticism in his practice not as a standalone aesthetic but rather as a political act against an inhospitable landscape. In June 1979, however, when Wilfred entered his drawing *Hydra* (1977) into a Gay Pride exhibition, held at London's Late Night Gallery, it was deemed by one critic as 'not gay enough'. The figure depicted is seen from above, and there is an upwards movement to its swirling mass of line and energy. Active pathways race to its very top, amassing together in place of a head (a direct message from groin to mind). When viewed in this light, it is difficult not to see this work as homoerotic. But the gay movement at this point in time could not afford to be subtle, and Wilfred's work was not deemed enough. Once again, it was difficult to know where he stood. ●

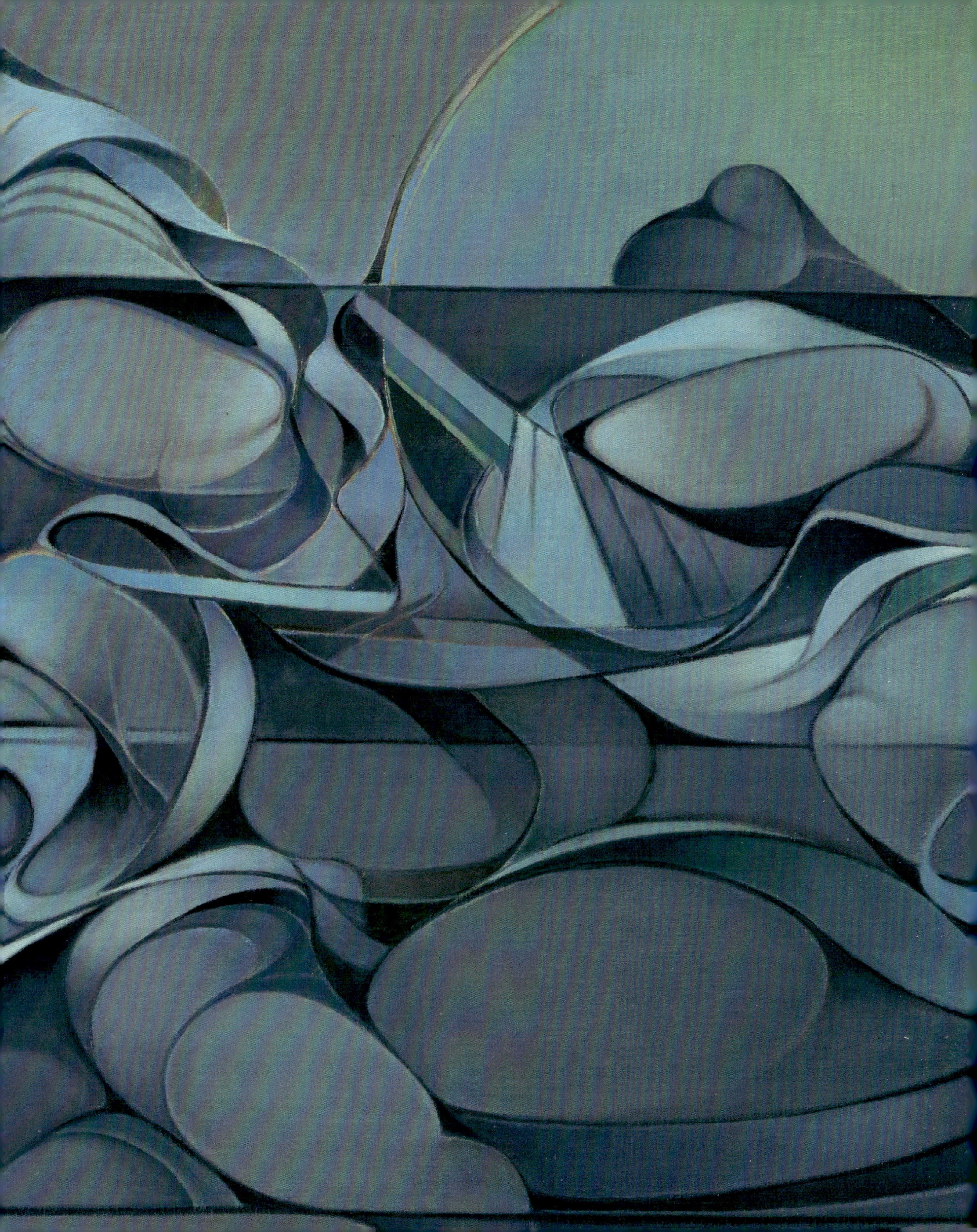

8 EMBODIED LANDSCAPES

LANDSCAPE HAD ALWAYS been important to Wilfred, and in the 1970s he began to focus on it with new confidence and fervour. But this was a far cry from work of the late 1950s. These are not gentle views. Works of psychogeography, they straddle the empirical and the unseen, balance themselves between the abstract and the figurative.

In the short essay of 1981, on his much-lauded Cézanne — in which he addresses the artist directly, Wilfred wrote, 'Your forms are strangely fluid — one feels that — solid as they seem, they would at any moment fall apart and reassemble into other forms.'[41] Wilfred may as well have been writing about his own work here. These later landscapes are studies in plasticity, embodiments of the ongoing struggle that we saw first in his 'Sixties Figures' series. They are strange and morphing islands, throbbing with energy and life. An ever-kinetic, rhythmic quality gives the sense that each work has its own pulse.

Neither remote nor isolated, each work is alive, *embodied*.

• • •

Between 1970 and 1972, whilst still living at Montague House in Blackheath, Wilfred completed a series of fifty collage-gouaches. We see, in the earliest of these, a return to an earthy colour palette after a fifteen-year hiatus. The works comprise varied shapes cut from magazines — some figural but others evidently sourced from a publication of interiors (you might notice casually arranged throws or the edging of an expensive rug).

The series is playful; tangled and tactile. *Solaris* (1970) is one of the earliest. A centralised glob has at points stretched itself right out, as if playing at mirroring those familiar horizontal lines it sits just in front of. It is both fabric and flesh, borrowing the organ-like shapes from work made almost a decade earlier.

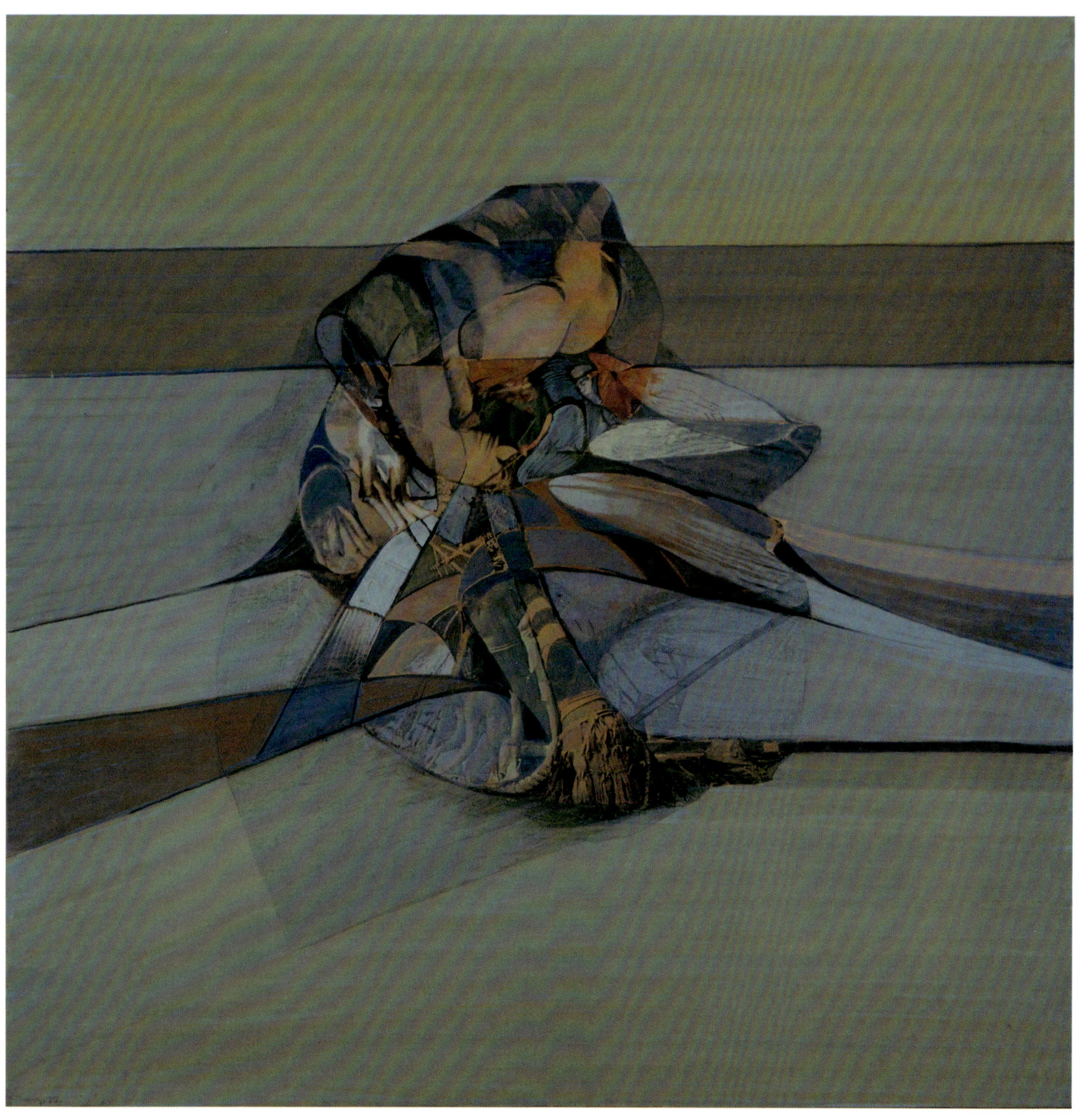

8:1 Solaris
1970
56 x 56 cm
Collage-gouache
(Studio)

Wilfred made *Leviathan* (1972) towards the very end of the series. It is not just due to its name that it brings to mind some enormous creature rising from the deep; at 51 x 63.5 cm, it is twice the size of many of Wilfred's collages. A domed head has broken the surface of the ocean, great rivulets of water cascading right off it. There are shapes reminiscent of fins and the sweeping arch of a tail. Ridged pleats bring to mind the neck of a blue

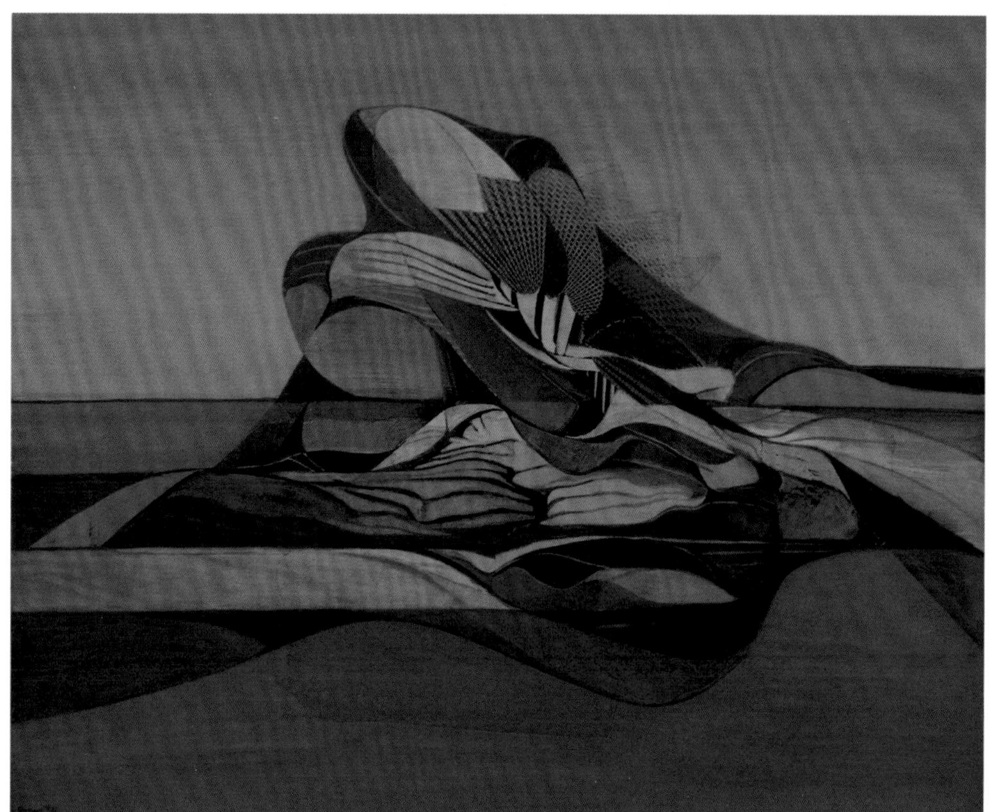

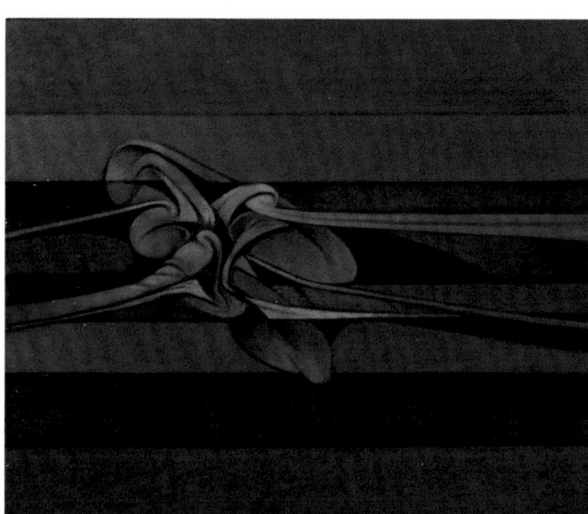

whale. The work as a whole has an upward thrust, a yearning power shared by the oil *Primavera* (1972–5), completed three years later. *Primavera* displays the same stringy elasticity found in the medium of collage-gouache. The oil gives no firm clue whether it is landscape or figure, yet (or perhaps, because of) it is strangely compelling; the audience invited not to view passively but to directly involve themselves with its tangled forms.

The oils that followed the series in collage-gouache became more complex, made using multiple canvases that often took the form of diptychs and triptychs. Although some works can still be broadly identifiable as either figure or landscape, far more often we find the two merged.

We can view this as the third part of Wilfred's visual journey with the body. At first the figure was deconstructed. It was then tied back together

8:4 Triptych
1973–5
Each canvas 61 x 46 cm
Oil on canvas
(Studio)

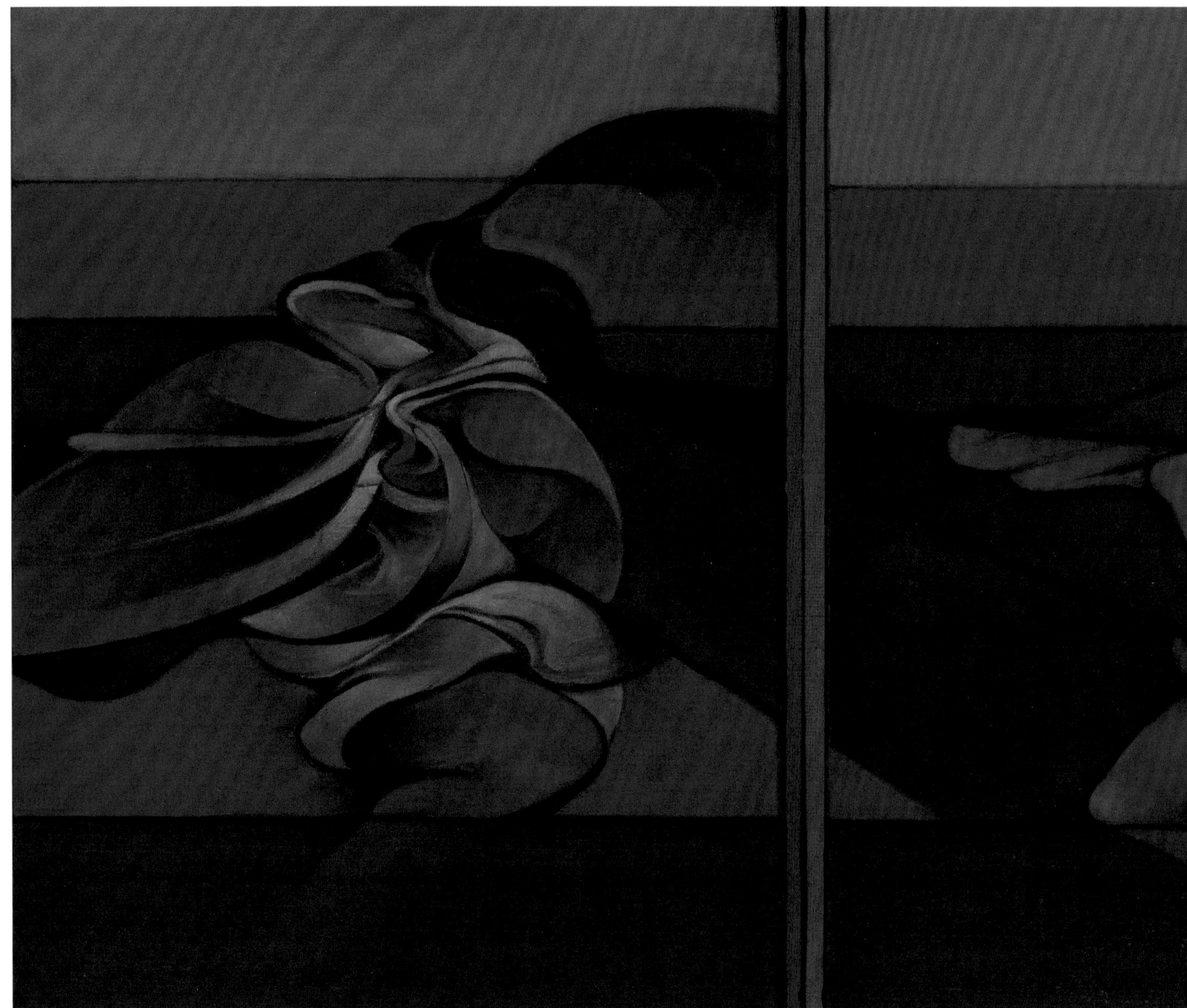

and here we see it unbound once again. The following oils each mark the pinnacle of explorations made over the 1970s.

Triptych (1973–5) is a true realisation of Wilfred's theme of embodied landscape, shown in all its astounding complexity. In a rare creative move away from the views of North Devon, the work was inspired by the North Sea. A semi-figural form has been depicted three times, from left to right and slowly unravelling around those rigid horizontals. The composition's

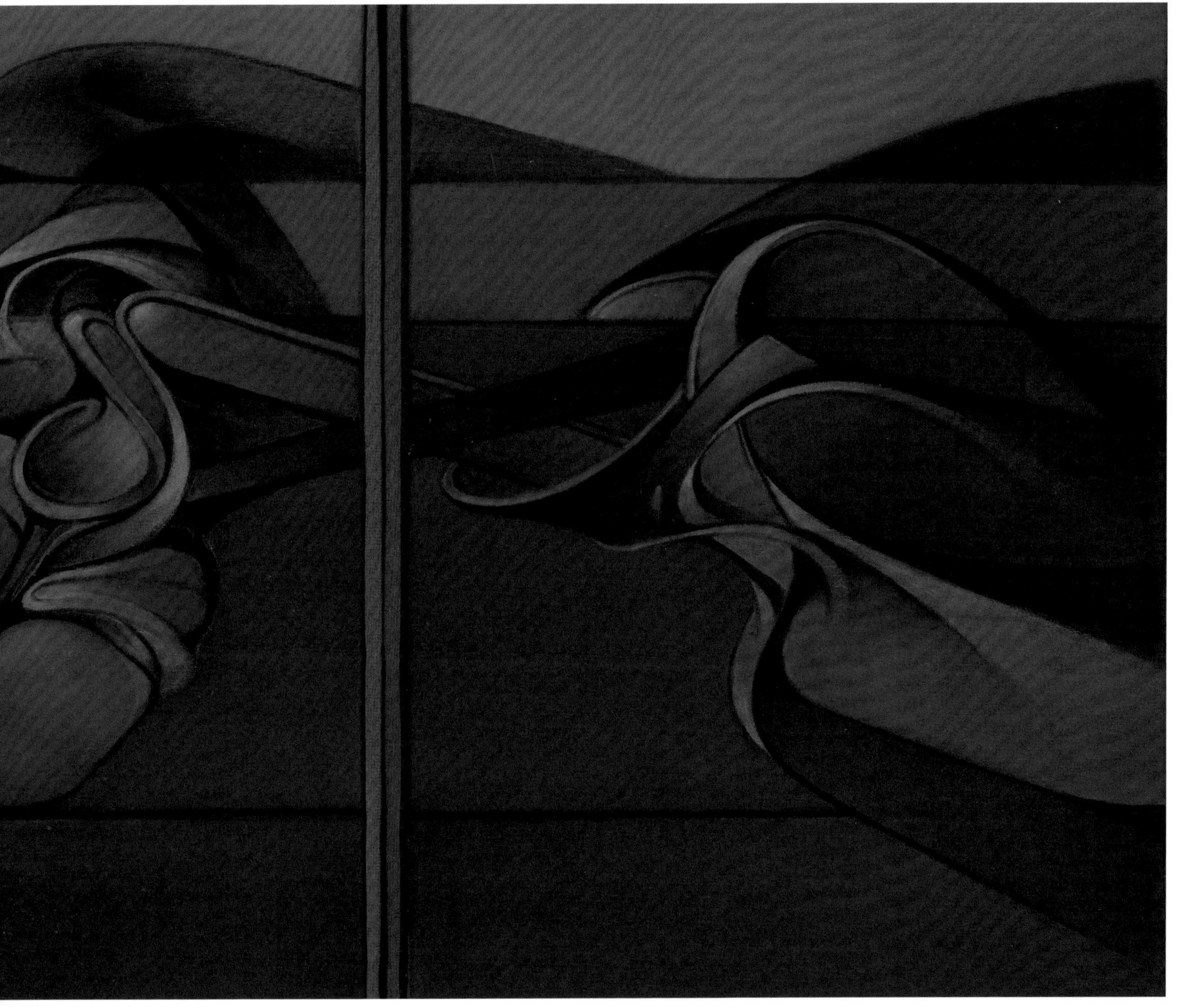

gentle curves are reminiscent of those found in the close Devon landscape of Wilfred's boyhood. These childhood hills in fact make up the entirety of the third body which falls, to the far right, as loose ribbon. A salmon pink undercoat glows through.

The same meandering ribbon is repeated four years later in *Composite* (1979). A body made up of nothing but loose tangles gives the impression of a figure falling backwards; those monstrous thighs at the lower edge of the work, a torso of tousled ribbon and flailing arms (one fold at the very top of the form to give the impression of a head). But most remarkable in this work is Wilfred's masterful use of foreshortening. The figure appears to be falling *into* something, marking the full fruition of the artist's career-

8:5 *Composite*
1979
81 x 100.5 cm
Oil on canvas
(Private collection)

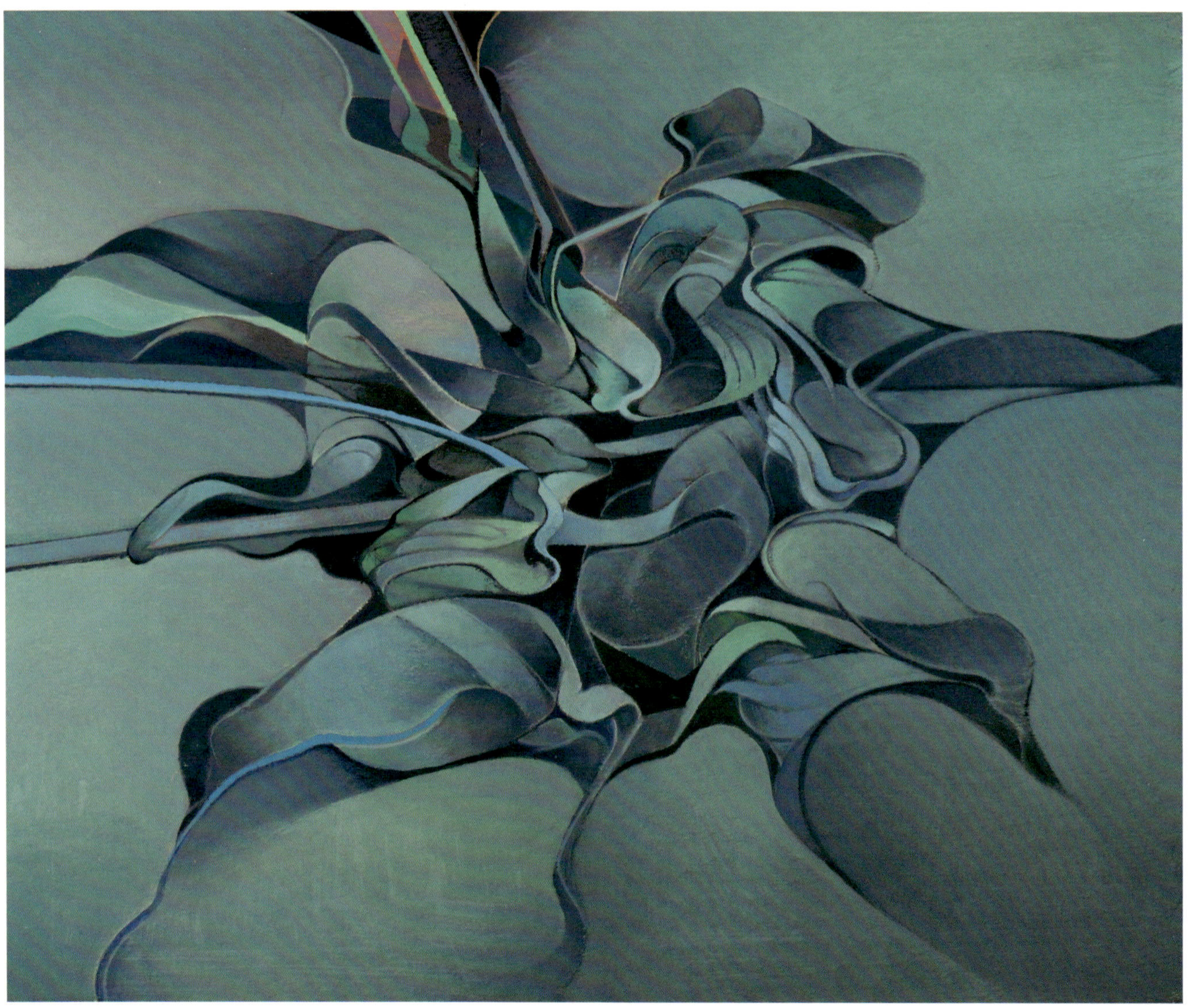

long preoccupation with finding a new sense of space: the three-dimensional depicted in two dimensions. In pencil and gouache, Wilfred has captured the exact moment of impact. The reverberations caused by the fall have caused offshoots from the body to reform as landscape. Hills to both sides. *Composite* is a work of incredible confidence, and prefigures the full synthesis between landscape and the figure that would comprise Wilfred's later practice.

Figure-Profligate (1975), a tiny work in pencil and gouache made four years earlier, holds a strikingly similar composition. Regardless of whether or not it was made specifically as a preliminary work, it clarifies that this particular form was already — and had long been — in Wilfred's mind. The same shape can be found in the *Double Figure* duo, a pair of gouaches that, although completed after *Composite*, were likely worked on at the same time. They share the same massive and Michelangelo-esque thighs.

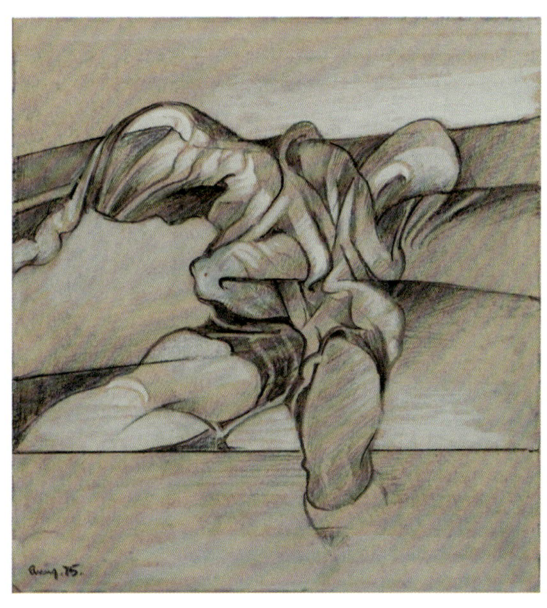

8:6 Figure-Profligate
1975
15 x 14.5 cm
Pencil and gouache
(Private collection)

The complexity in *Composite*'s composition was prefigured in *Trinity* (1974–5), painted as a private commission for collector Tony Moore. Tony first saw Wilfred's work in the mid-1960s after visiting their mutual friend and Wilfred's then-housemate Jack Humphries, in Kensington Gardens Square. Here, he came across a small work-in-progress set up on an easel in the dining room. Finding himself unable to forget it, almost a decade later he called up the London telephone directory and asked for a list of all W. Averys in the London area.

'Is this Wilfred Avery?' he asked, the first number on his list.

'Yes,' a voice replied.

'The painter?'

'Well, not many people think I am.'

Tony now owns the largest private collection of Wilfred's work, a loyal patronage that was pivotal to Wilfred's spirits and continued creative journey. On the artist's death in 2016, Tony discovered that Wilfred had left him that same small painting he had first seen fifty years before.

Just as in *Triptych*, *Trinity* details three versions of the abstracted body

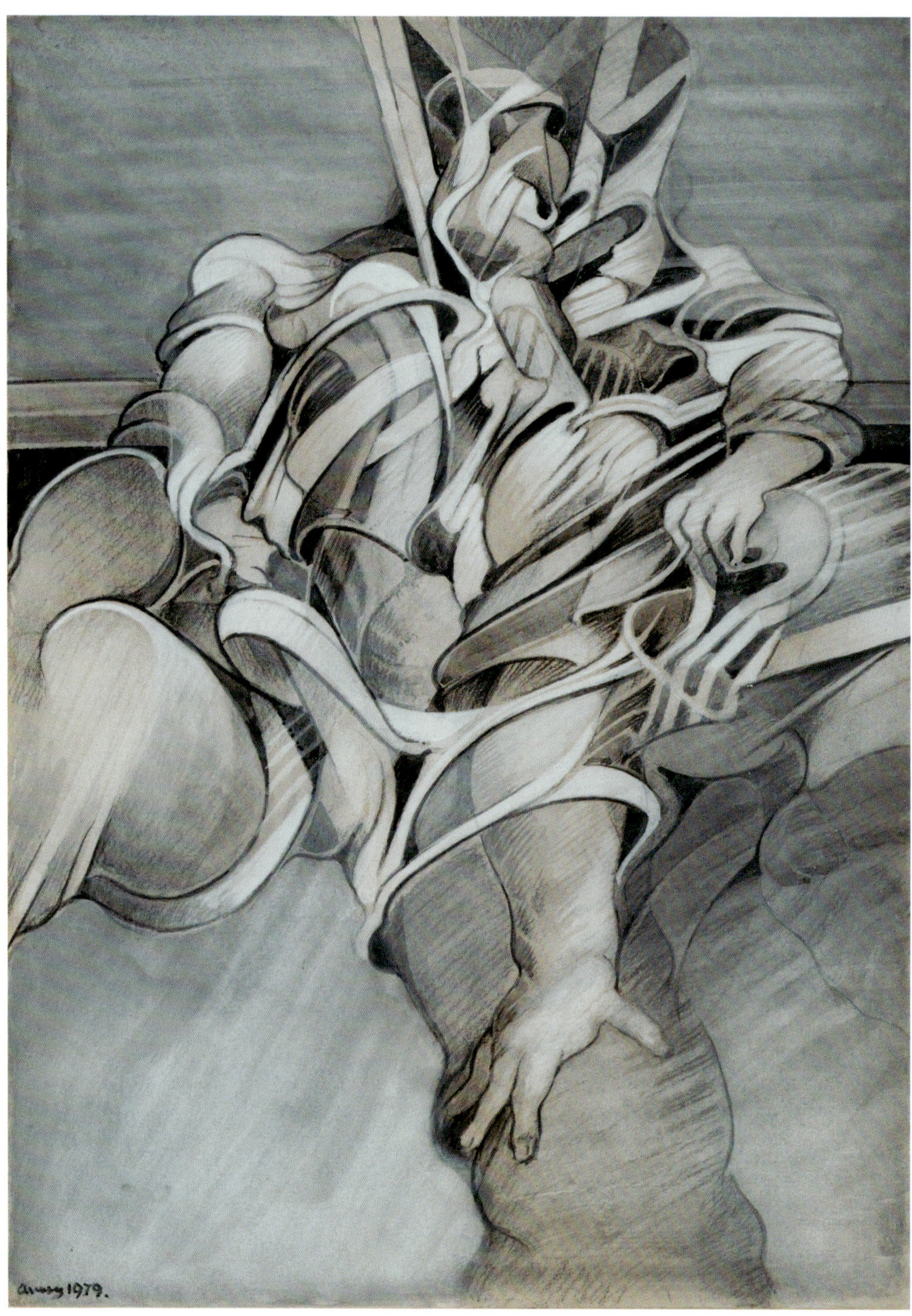

8:7 Double Figure No 1
1979
49.5 x 36.5 cm
Gouache on paper
(*Private collection*)

interlinking and unravelling to varying degrees. The human is only very subtly hinted at here, mainly in the depiction of legs bent at the knee and thighs emerging from bed sheets. The cool material draped over them looks to slide off at any moment; the knots as loose as those that hold together Christ's robe in Piero della Francesca's *Baptism*. The painting's

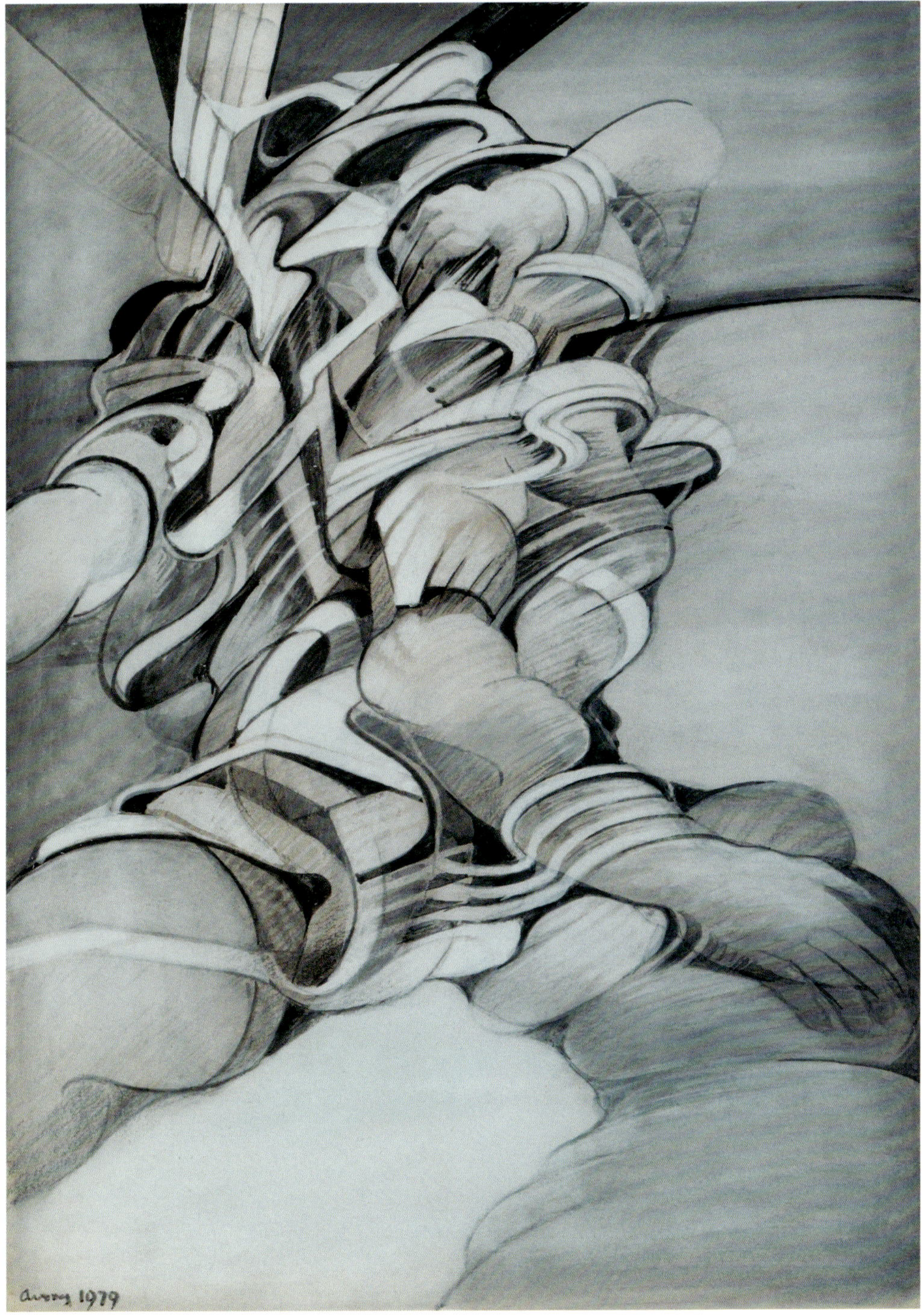

8:8 Double Figure No 2
1979
49.5 x 36.5 cm
Gouache on paper
(Private collection)

lazy hold is kept in check only by four lines, the background of the work quartered into horizontal compartments. Its lowest section hints at water — the simplistic magnification reminiscent of looking at an object through liquid. The expanded form falls out of sight, into space unbound by the constraints of the canvas. A great planet emerges huge over the horizon.

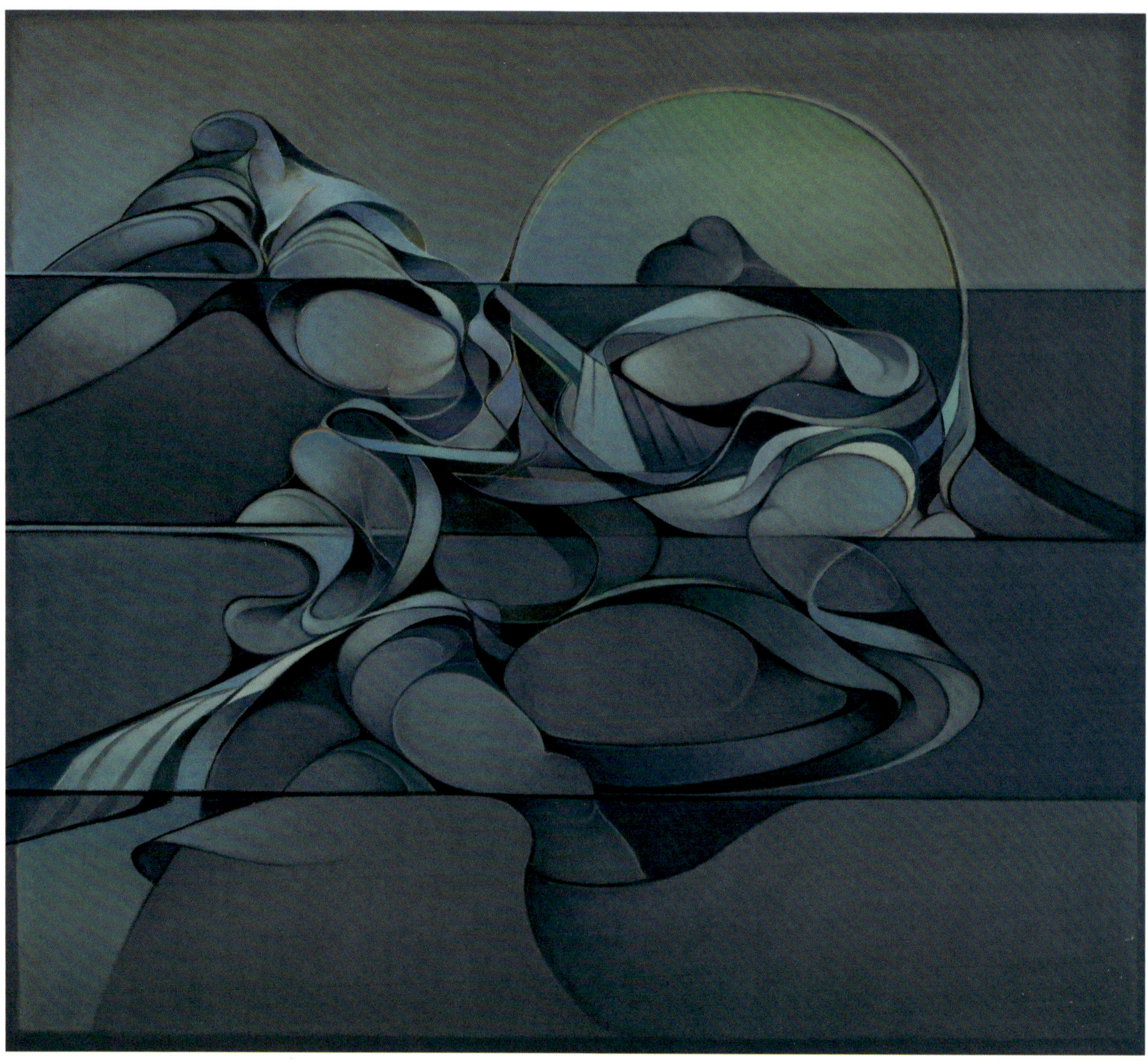

8:9 Trinity
1974–5
122 x 107 cm
Oil on canvas
(*Private collection*)

Since the moon landing in 1969, but most prevalent in the mid-1970s, this shape regularly appeared in Wilfred's work. The circle was often described by Jung as symbolising the self. In Western philosophy the circle is linked to the celestial sphere, and of course to eternity, and in the East it is an important symbol both in terms of contemplation and of wholeness. Whichever held true for Wilfred (and we can be all but certain he would have enjoyed these myriad translations of his work), we know that as much as an aesthetic decision, he was using this particular shape to dig deeper inside himself, to again bring his own fragmented self into Jungian synchronicity.

Two circles included in the small drawing *Moonwalk* (1984) bring to mind the planets Paul Nash used in many of his unexpected and semi-surreal compositions. To the furthest left the circle is just on the verge of becoming a yin and yang symbol; all sorts of unexpected forces continue to appear in Wilfred's work. And in *Syndrome* (1975), a pair of enormous spheres emerge from opposite corners of the diptych. Pushing into the centre, each circle interrupts the two figural forms who are in the process of unravelling themselves on to the canvas. There is a force here, a sense of the inevitable frozen in a moment of perfect balance. *Syndrome*, again, is both figure and landscape. Hidden in each tangled process are folded limbs, upper thighs, a rounded back. Landscape elements are most evident in the uppermost segment. Two islands sit on the horizon, the peaks of both reminiscent of the upward thrust of *Leviathan*.

At 183 x 244 cm *Meridians* (1970–75) is by far Wilfred's largest painting and one that he would pick back up and rework for the next thirty-five years (he was never quite certain it was finished). The work's original title was *Sunday AM* but changed when Wilfred, having lived in Blackheath since 1969, realised he was painting almost directly on the Greenwich Meridian. It is an astoundingly detailed painting. In impossibly subtle tonal variations, the work is made up of lines wrapping around, under and through. Bodies (revealing themselves as usual only by their bent legs and white striped sports socks pulled up to the knee) sprint across to canvas to the lower right. Is this an interplanetary sports match — moon as football? The horizon line has been used both to divide and reveal the organic twisted mounds that rise above its surface. Below, a hinted reflection makes it appear as if the whole work has been set on the edge of a deep, dark lake. Water, Jung once said, is the most common symbol for the unconscious.

Wilfred's use of the horizontal line is

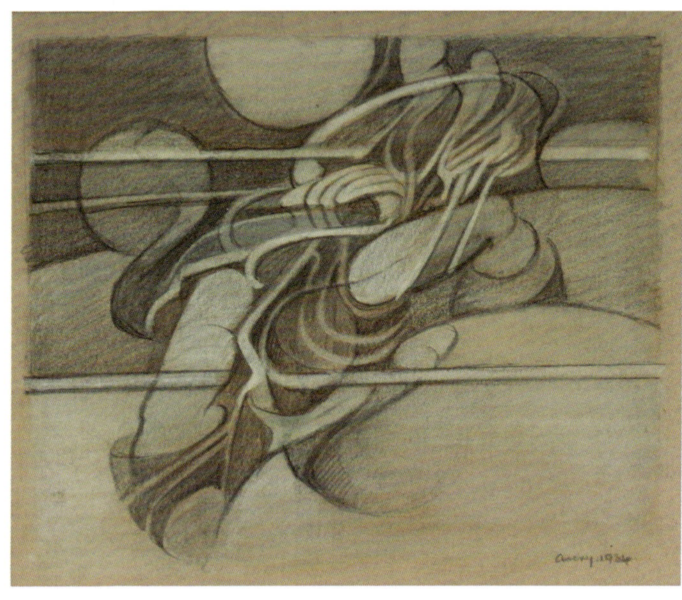

8:10 Moonwalk
1984
19.5 x 22 cm
Pencil and gouache on paper
(Studio)

prevalent in works of this period, but his reason for including it on the canvas changed. In the 1960s (most evident in his 'Sixties Figures' series) Wilfred used the horizontal largely as a technique to both direct and ground the eye, allowing for further complexity and kineticism elsewhere. Now, though, it transformed into a horizon line, synonymous not just with the physical but with a revitalised focus on the unseen world. As much as homing us in a physical space, Wilfred was now using the line as a way of both dividing and revealing the conscious and unconscious worlds. What we see day-to-day, he seems to be telling us, is not even half of it. And by translating the line in this way, we can go on to understand the upward thrust, seen in works like *Leviathan* and *Syndrome*, to be a pushing through of the unconscious into the conscious world. In 1970, at the very beginning of a decade of increasingly exploratory practice, Wilfred wrote:

> *My obsession has been to explore as far as is humanly possible, the full extent of personal awareness. Self-consciousness is the goal and when forms rise to the surface in my work I examine and explore them until they reveal themselves in the light of understanding. Beyond them or perhaps, between them, (interwoven with them), lie the forms that are beyond our understanding and which can only be accepted as part of the mystery to which we all belong.*[42]

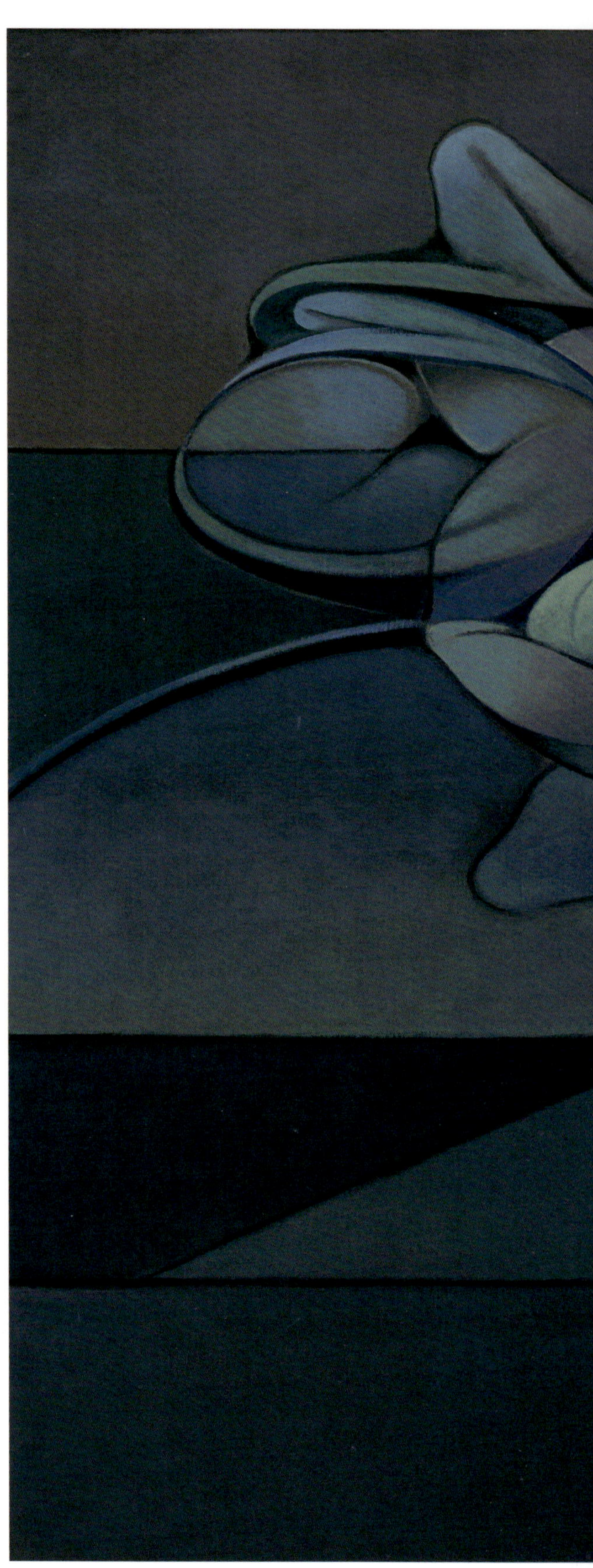

8:11 *Syndrome*
1975
Each canvas 91.5 x 61 cm
Oil on canvas
(Studio)

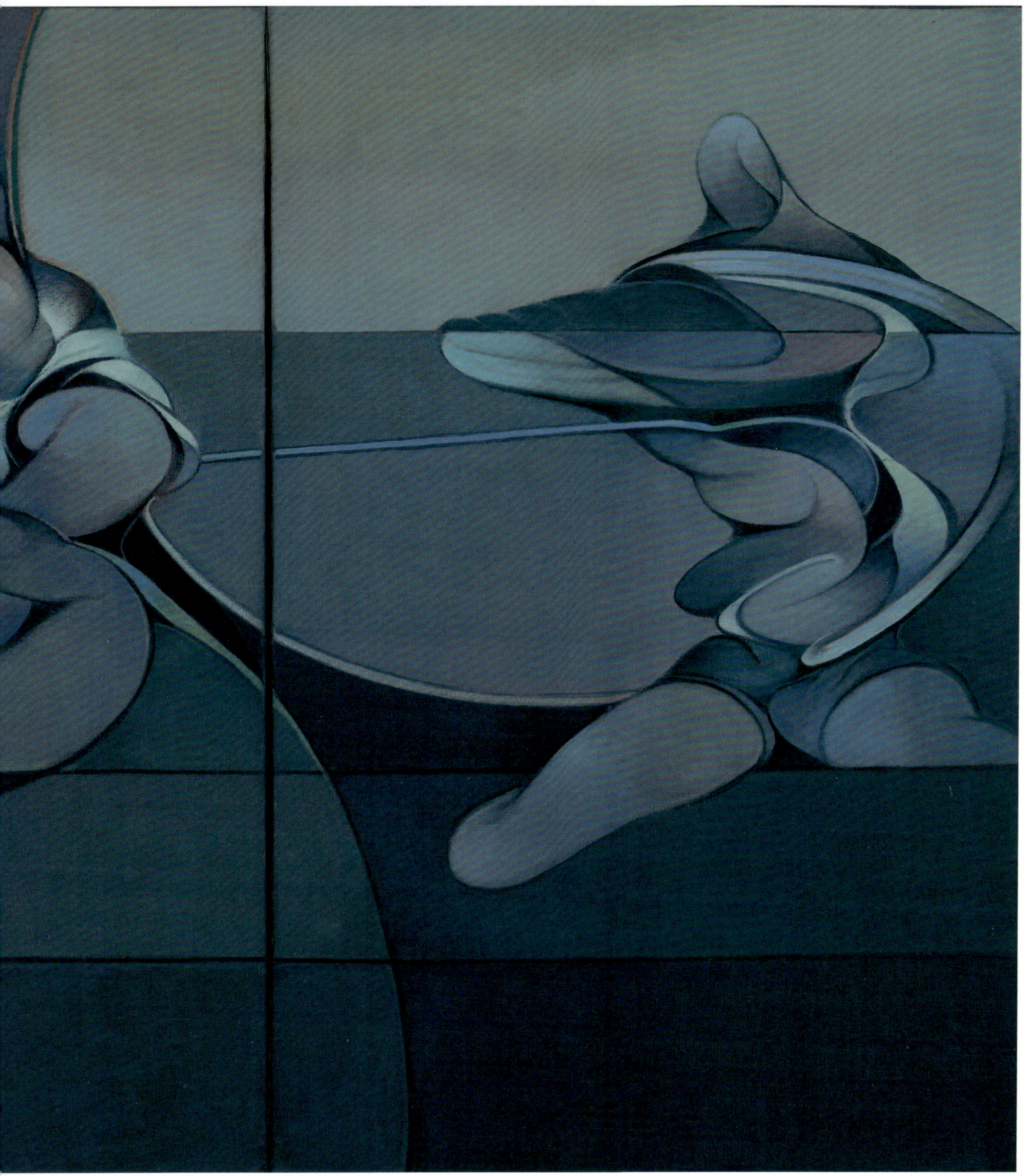

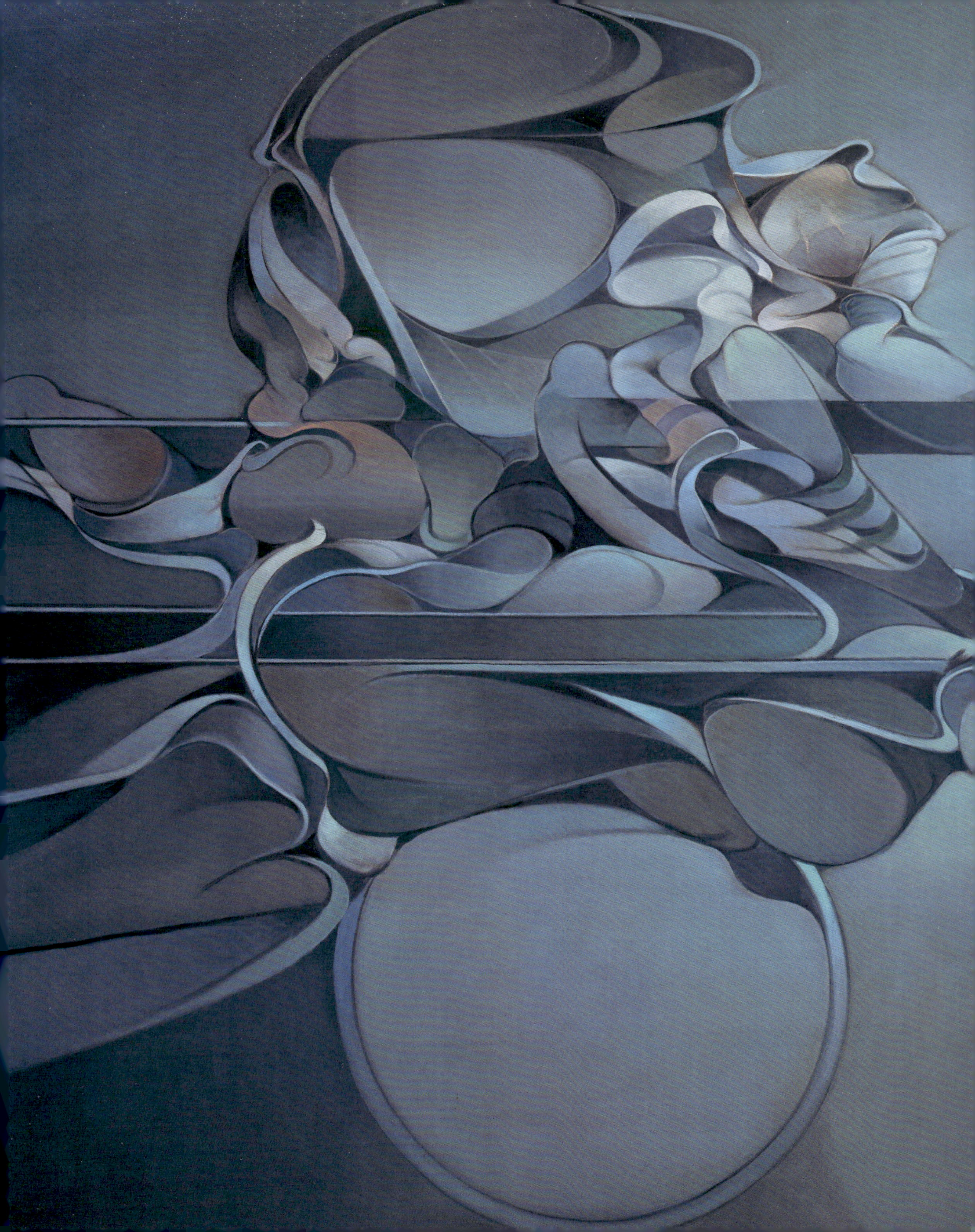

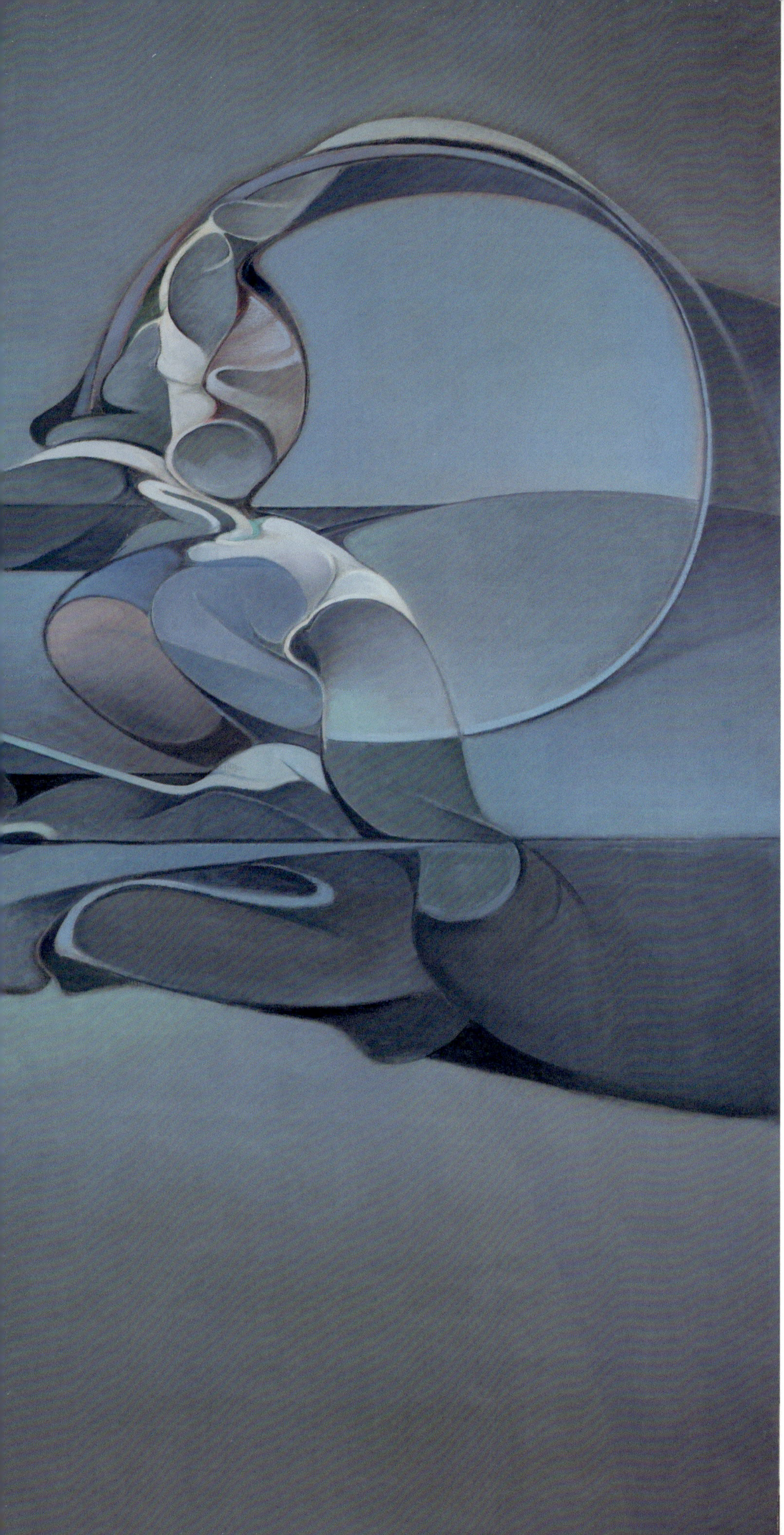

8:12 Meridians
1970–75
183 x 244 cm
Oil on canvas
(*Studio*)

For over a decade Wilfred had been using the term 'reveal' when writing about how he made his images, but it is only from this period onwards that he begins to depict exactly *what it is* that he is attempting to draw out (shapes bulbous and kicking make themselves apparent just under the surface).

This intention was well understood by the newly founded Open University arts magazine *Proteus*, when it published a short photo essay about Wilfred and his work in November 1977. The edition was themed around creativity and its relationship to consciousness. '... he believes that the subjective effect of the images are more important than their aesthetic properties', the essay begins. 'The enigmatic quality of his pictures reaches many layers of consciousness and it is perhaps the "after-image" that they carry which gives them their particular fashion and power.'[43]

Despite this dedication to revealing the unconscious in his work, Wilfred continued to draw from themes and images from his previous creative body. His landscapes went on hinting at work made in the 1950s; coastal views with the sea in the distance. *The Point* (1976–7), though formed of the same subterranean tumble synonymous with the rest of his 1970s work, references earlier work like *Landscape Near the Sea* and *Landscape with Cliffs*. Its vertical spread draws our eye upwards and out to the far landscape and onwards to the horizon. *Counterpoint* (1976), the title hardly arbitrary, meaning a balance between two opposites, is a coastline in a muted palette, the hills and sea interwoven with body parts. The colours reveal themselves slowly – an undercoat of pink glows through the cooler tones of blue that wash over the top of it. Striped horizontals give a strict structure to what might at first look like a dishevelled and fallen form. They tie the image together, making obedient those languorous limbs, those gentle hills.

This confidence in style and subject matter, however, was not to last for long, and the work that Wilfred made after this was evidence of his faltering for the first time on his creative path.

OPPOSITE
8:13 *The Point*
1976–7
106.5 x 91.5 cm
Oil on canvas
(*Studio*)

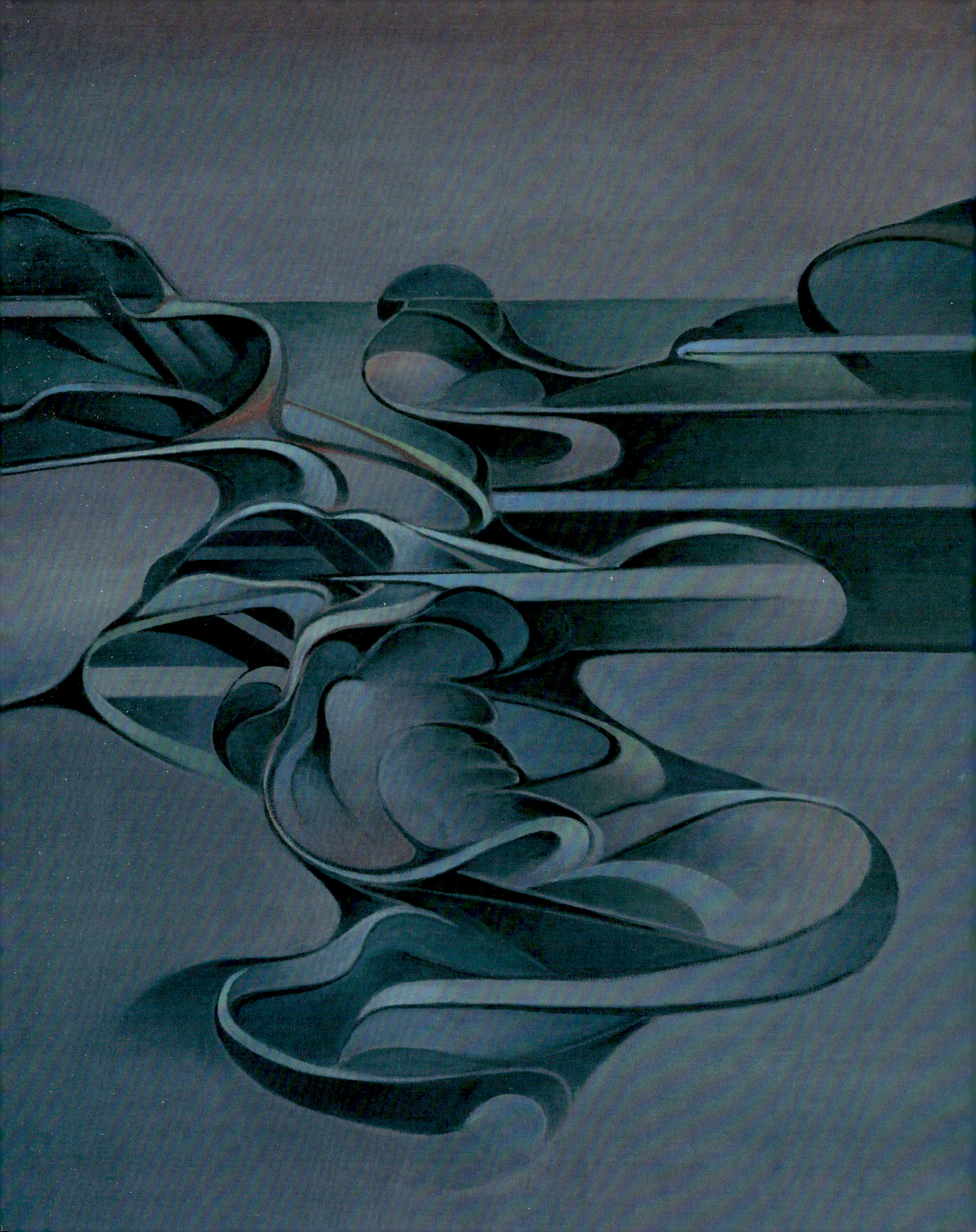

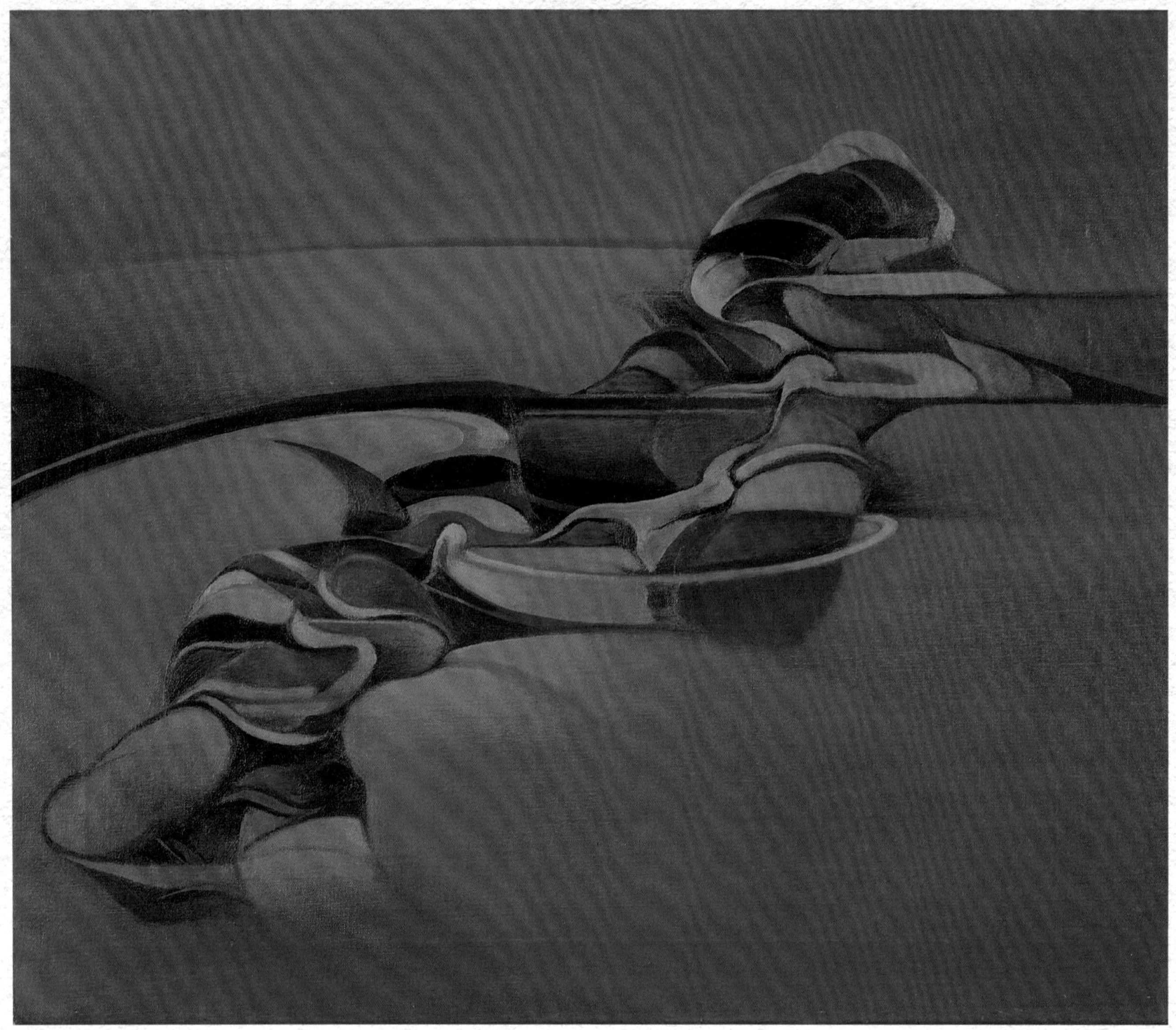

8:14 Counterpoint
1976
51 x 61 cm
Oil on canvas
(Towner Eastbourne)

LIVING IN LONDON 1967

It is fifteen years since I began living in London and it's as alien to me now as it was the first day I came here. This does not mean I do not like it or enjoy it even — one can like strange and unfamiliar things — but mainly that I do not ever feel at home.

Yet London has given me a great deal. My painting has made steady progress here, hurried along by this and that influence. I have met here the only person I have ever deeply loved and have experienced here most of the rich, sometimes strange, events that have shaped my adult life.

It would seem then that London is a place of rich association for me but this is not so. My sense of 'place' does not lie here. As I sit writing I look out at the straight lines of houses on the other side of the Square. I cannot see the sky unless I go to the window. Tiers of windows gaze blankly at me. I feel nowhere.

Once in London I lived with some sense of 'place'. By the river in Chelsea and later for a while on a hill in Swiss Cottage but here I dig up the tarmac daily with my mind searching for the lie of the land beneath. My mind is obsessed with wires and drains and tubes running under the streets. This pile of stones called London I cannot 'see'. I walk about amongst it trying sometimes to recall a sense of 'atmosphere' felt when I first came here but nothing happens. I am immune to it all.

Yet one must relate to one's surroundings. I keep my touchstone, found long ago on the pink clifftops and green hillsides of my childhood, strangely alive in me. Two days in the country and familiarity comes flooding back. I smell the countryside even in London. Sometimes I can sense it in the pink evening mist lying westward under the dark grey smudge of fumes and dirt at the far end of the farthest street.

But daffodils in the park mean nothing to me. My 'place' is not the blade of grass under my foot or the tree spreading its arms across the lawn. My place is the hills and the valley turning into the sea, the sea running into the land, the rocks running under the sea and running on to the curve of the horizon. My space and my place is where one glimpses for a moment the turning of the world and here among the houses it can never ever happen.

Wilfred Avery, Kensington Gardens Square, 1967

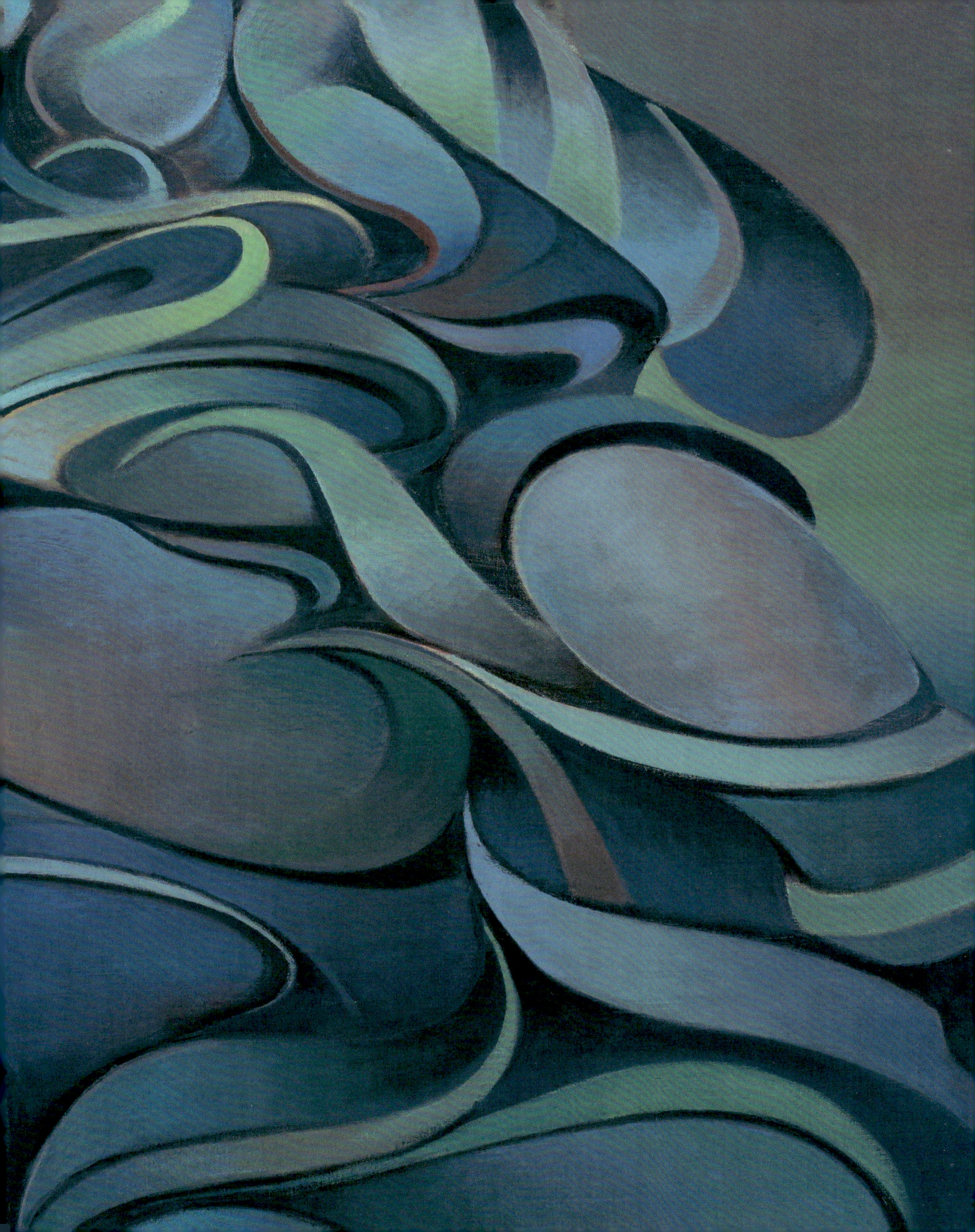

9 LEAVING LONDON: DOUBT

Twenty years from now I may well be dead. What is the point of hankering after recognition?[44]

DESPITE LIVING IN London for twenty-seven years, Wilfred never fully felt at home in the city. And so, in 1979 the couple relocated back to the West Country.

Although he termed the decision to leave London 'radical', the move was not so much a ripping off the plaster as a gradual unsticking. Wilfred and Ray had long considered leaving London, but felt they ought to stay until Wilfred had achieved some success, so as to be convenient for dealers wanting to view his work. Despite this, Wilfred had spent the last twenty years consistently turning away from the artistic circles who had made attempts to welcome him, in effect distancing himself both from galleries and from individual dealers. It is apparent, however, that he did not consider his own hand in this move, writing in 1975, 'I had never expected to be so isolated yet I try to accept now that I truly am.'[45] We know that Wilfred longed for commercial success, and would not have removed himself from any possibility of it had he not felt utterly rejected. He expanded on this feeling of being outside the popular sphere in both art and life three years later, by stating, 'I realise how falsely optimistic I am at times about the possibility of my work becoming more widely known.'[46]

Leaving London was not a particularly unusual decision. In fact, a number of twentieth-century artists made the move from city to countryside and Wilfred's relocation had a number of predecessors, with many urban galleries actually actively looking to support regional artists at the time. But unlike so many of his predecessors and contemporaries, Wilfred left the city with few connections on which he could fall back. His crucial error was moving away without a strong artist and dealer network to which he could return.

• • •

Like so many of the couple's decisions, their immediate move out of the city appeared 'meant'. Shortly after midnight one Saturday, Wilfred and Ray boarded a train at Paddington destined for Newton Abbot in South Devon. Arriving just before 7.00 the same morning, and with nothing open, they wandered around the empty town, exploring the small winding streets and peering into shop windows. In the front window of an estate agent, they saw a house in dire need of refurbishment up for sale in Ashburton, the only town in the Dartmoor National Park. And at the bus station, they discovered that the first bus due to leave that morning was to the town. The bus stopped immediately opposite the house itself, 77 East Street. On their return to the now open estate agent, Wilfred and Ray organised a viewing for the same afternoon, and by the time they had returned to London that evening, the offer they had made on viewing had been accepted.

Wilfred and Ray lived in Ashburton until 1985. Over the following seven years they moved four times, transforming each house with great care into peaceful and beautiful homes. Due to their many house moves, though there are a large number of works on paper, relatively few oils from this period exist, and most are comparatively small.

It was a difficult period of readjustment. Wilfred found the complexity of his new home landscape overwhelming; its rich colours and textures difficult to handle and put down in paint. For the first eighteen months after leaving London, he concentrated solely on doing up the house and produced no work. Later, he focused only on smaller inks and watercolour.

Thirty-five works dating from 1957 to 1982 were shown in a solo show held during the 1982 Ashburton Festival (*Images from Landscape: Selected Paintings and Drawings*, 5–13 June 1982). The accompanying exhibition text, written by Wilfred, reads, 'Landscape has been a continuous theme in my work though the images come more from the "inner eye" than from any objective view of Nature. In one way they are a digest of the Devonshire scenes that impressed in childhood, in another way they are of a mythical landscape where inner and outer reality meet.'[47] Looking, as ever, inwards rather than out, landscape forms and memories of early work returned, and Wilfred's style became increasingly linear and organic.

Despite both exhibiting and selling in this period, Wilfred's mood remained low. Reflecting in 1983 and again just a year later, he vocalised a great anxiety about his work and recent decisions, a crisis of confidence not seen since the breakdown he suffered in his mid-twenties. 'I don't much like who I am or what is happening to me,' he wrote in 1984, 'but I know that I can blame no one nor any circumstances for my dilemma. My situation is the result of my own choices.'[48]

Even without this self-narration, the work Wilfred was making at this time makes it clear that he had lost his footing. In work made in the years 1983 and 1984, Wilfred moved away from this theme of embodied landscapes and focused primarily on landscape instead. His work became brighter, and increasingly sinuous and meandering; in many ways far more visually appealing than it had been at any previous point. It veered dangerously, in fact, towards the decorative.

For Wilfred, the term 'decorative' was the most derogatory in his artistic vocabulary. It was at the forefront of a plague he believed had begun with the self-conscious design of Whistler, and had since crept over everything, from the work of Ben Nicholson, Barbara Hepworth and even to Henry Moore. Beauty, for Wilfred, was a by-product rather than an intention. 'Of course, we must make beautiful forms, powerful compositions, lovely surfaces,' he wrote in 1969, 'but not on some decorative object which has no meaning.'[49]

Sun Circle (1983–4 and reworked 1987–90) has been painted with none of the depth that Wilfred had spent so much of his career so painstakingly evolving. The work as a whole lacks plasticity; the tension between forms swapped for meandering curls and placidly pooling lakes. There is a gentleness here that does not sit well with what we know of the artist. Each landscape painted in this time frame bears a similar attractive sinuosity — paint application as liquid. Where is the psychological complexity? Wilfred's technique remained masterful, and surfaces glow.

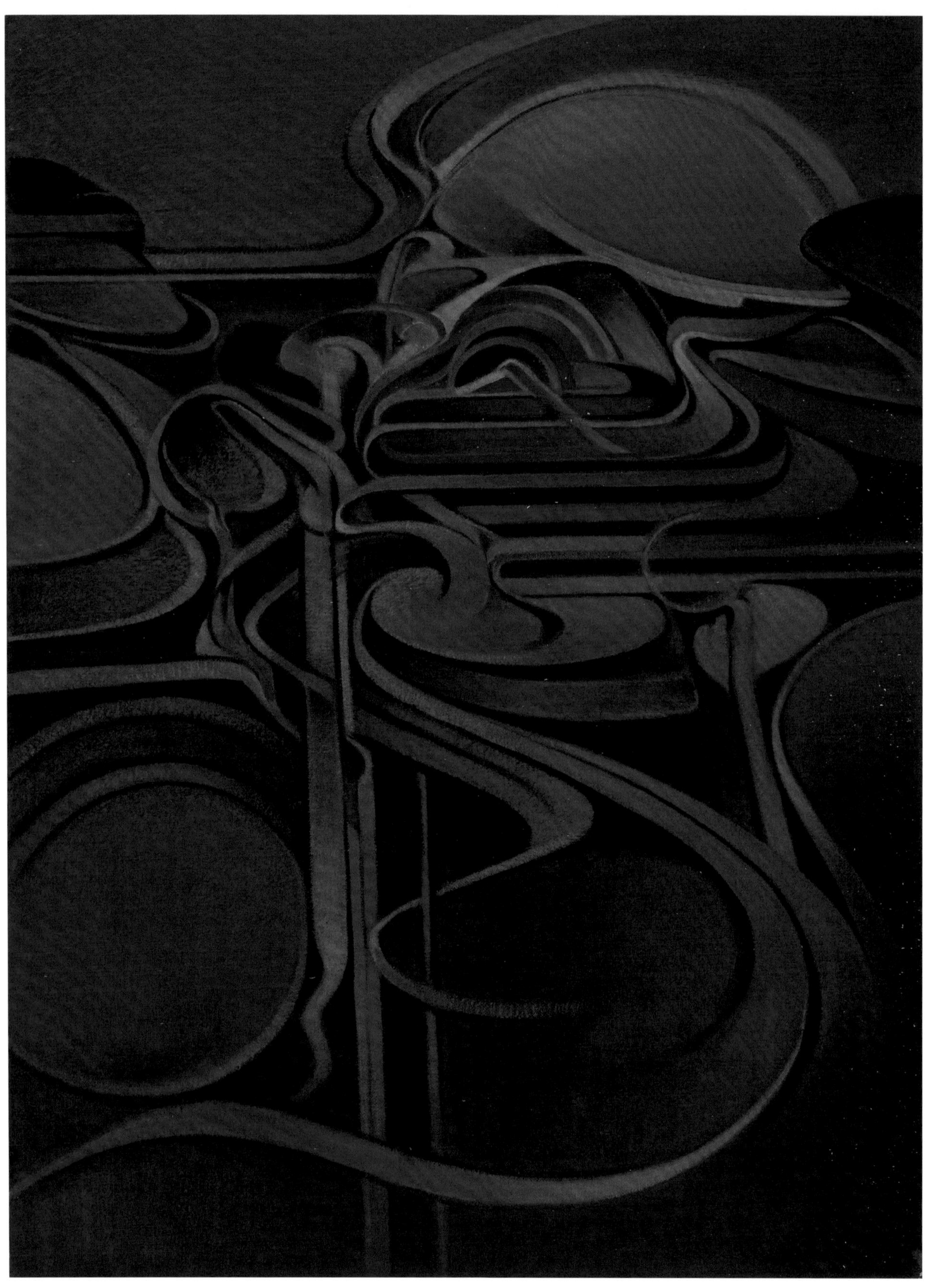

In none of the works made in this period have we lost any of the linear complexity — let your eye follow any painted line and you will see this for yourself. But what we are lacking is a sense of struggle — not because Wilfred had discovered what he had been searching for — instead, that he'd turned away from it.

But all was not lost. Coinciding with these landscapes, we see the continuation of this increased languidness, but now in Wilfred's once taut and twisted figures. Since the early 1970s we have seen his figures fall, settle as landscape, as if the tension thrumming in the tight-bound bodies of the 'Sixties Figures' finally became too great and snapped. Unknotted they recline, stretching out bodies momentous as mountain ranges.

Turning Figure (1983–7) is made up of gently coloured ribbons borrowed from the loose-limbed landscapes that Wilfred was struggling with at the same time. One thick leg, remarkably solid, and an arm bent almost at a right angle (to cushion the fall, perhaps?) tells us that this form is, or once was, human. Space has been alluded to much more successfully than in the concurrent landscapes. The figure has fallen backwards and at a diagonal, giving a depth to the image. Wilfred's composition draws our eye up to a head that is nothing more than flowing rivulets of blues, green and purple.

This break in the tension in both figure and landscape was vital in paving the way for the final period of Wilfred's work. His creative insecurity ended with a move away from Ashburton, and by the early 1990s he had taken up his theme of embodied landscape once again, beginning in earnest to once more weave together his figures and landscapes, ligaments phallic and abstracted, bringing them together into one cohesive whole.

• • •

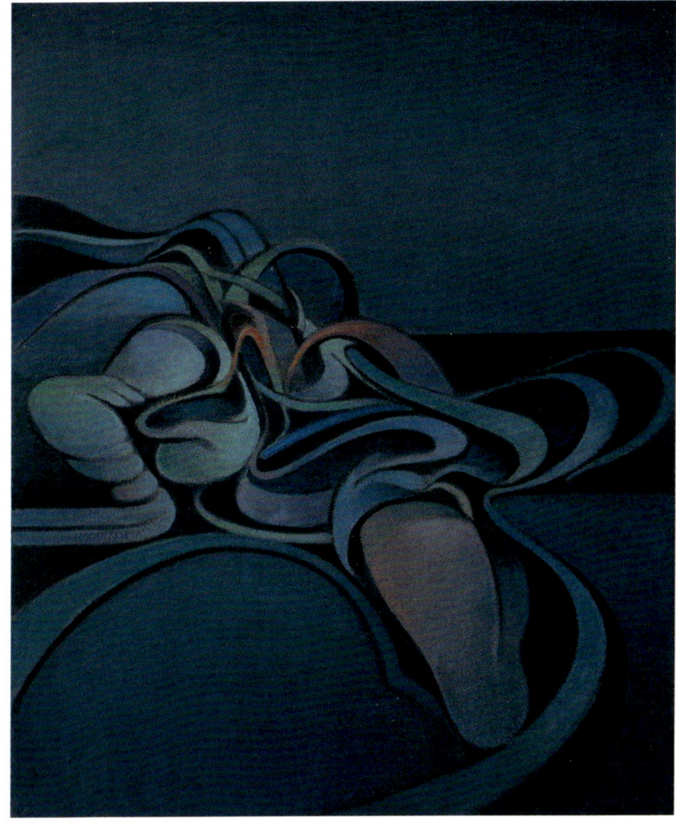

9:3/9:4/9:5/9:6
'Figure Elements'
LEFT TO RIGHT
Earth, Air, Fire, Water
1990
137 x 91.5 cm
Oil on canvas
(Studio)

In 1985 Wilfred and Ray decided it was time to move again. They both agreed that they wanted to live somewhere more accessible to London, and so moved to East Devon, to the small town of Budleigh Salterton. They had found their new house on another of their day trips, an unusual property at the very top of a steep road. It was the annexe to a hotel that had since been repurposed into a care home, with an accompanying chalet that Wilfred could use as a studio. The accompanying hotel grounds — a clifftop orchard and garden overlooking Lyme Bay — satisfied the artist's ongoing love for distant coastal views and, being a keen gardener, he turned his hand to nurturing the grounds. Having the sea in such close vicinity relaxed him and he produced a number of watercolours and drawings, many of which he showed in a mixed exhibition at the Fairlynch Museum, in 1986.

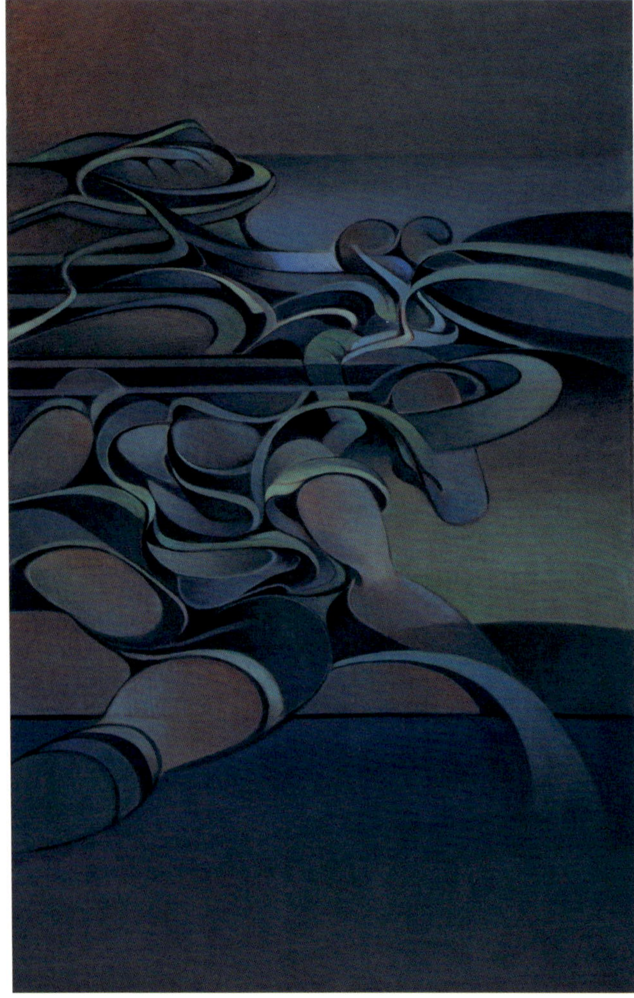

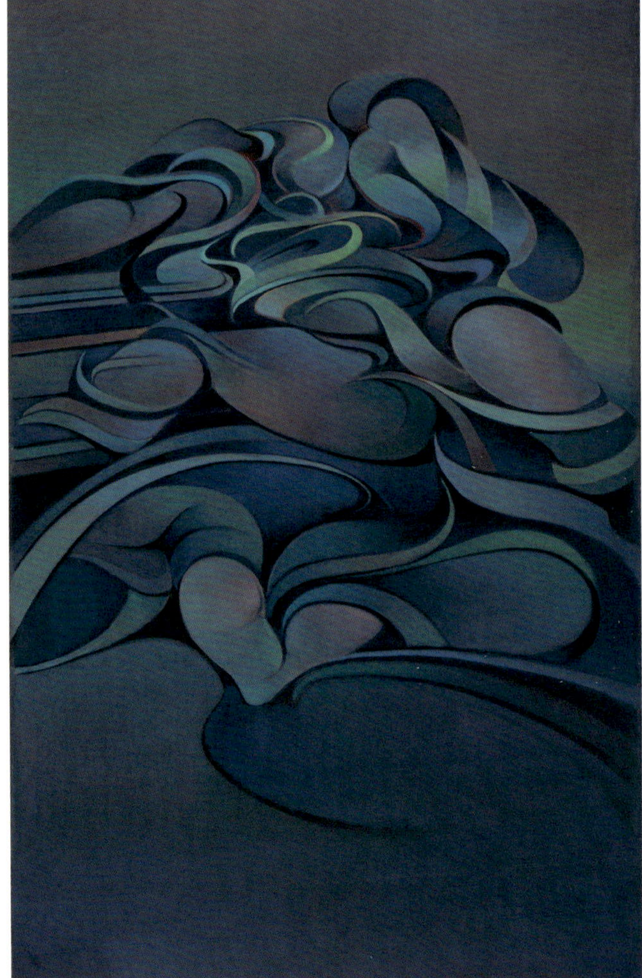

The couple lived at the property for three years before Wilfred began to feel his chalet studio was too limiting for his needs. After a short stint in a basement flat on St Leonards Road, Exeter, which only had space for a picture store rather than a studio, the couple moved in 1989 to St Andrew's Road in the suburb of Exwick. Here, they bought a beautifully ramshackle Arts and Crafts property. Wilfred's studio was in an octagonal tower at the very top of the building, with windows on every side. It was from this light-filled space that he began a very productive period of figure drawing and oils, the most important of which was a series of four luminescent paintings he titled 'Figure Elements' (1990), exploring the four elements of earth, air, fire and water.

The limpid bodies and Parma Violet tones of Wilfred's figure and

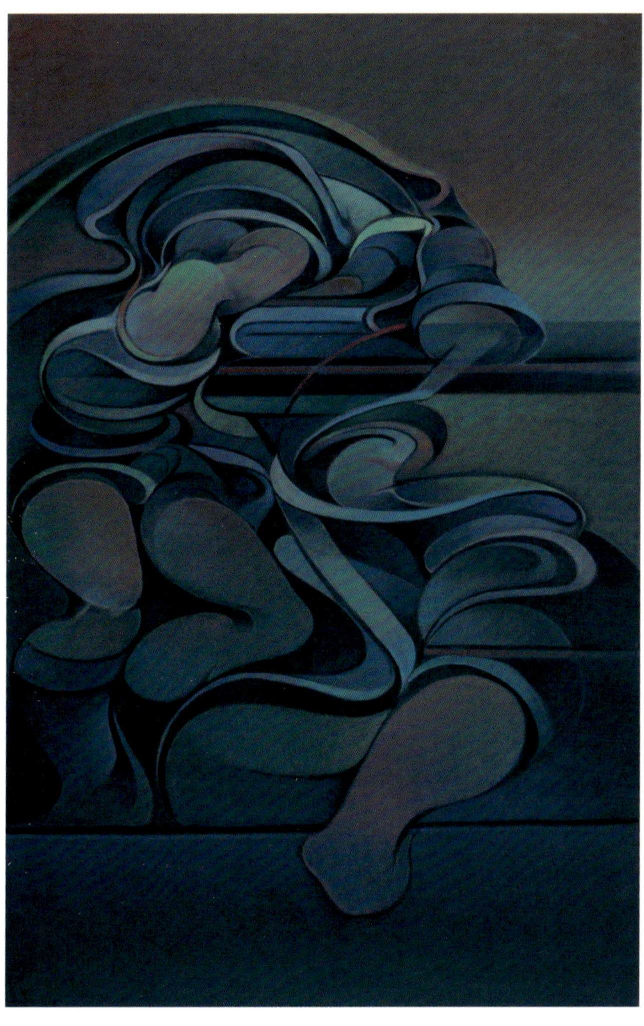
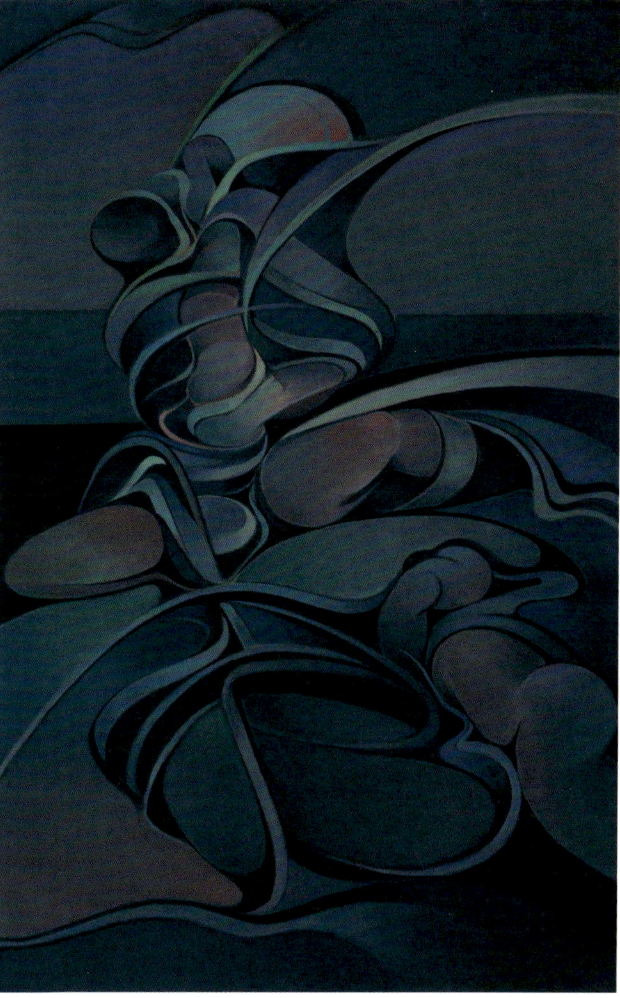

9:7 Octopus Triptych
1991–3
30 x 20 cm; 30 x 25.5 cm;
30 x 20 cm
Oil on canvas
(Studio)

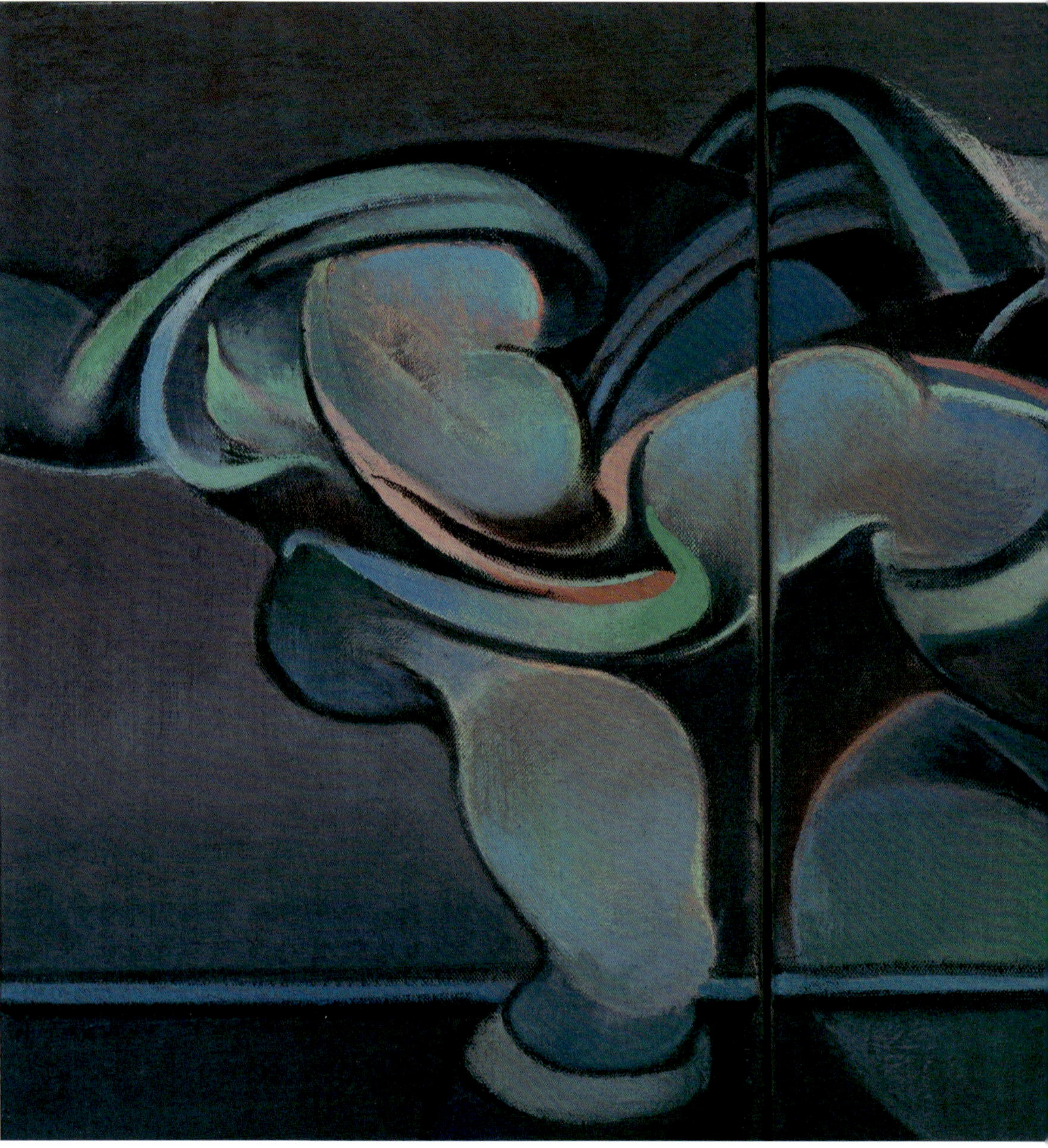

landscape works of the 1990s came into full force in this series. The painting quality in each is silky and limpid; semi-human forms merge with landscapes cherry-picked from earlier work.

In *Earth* and *Water*, Wilfred refers again right back to work made in the 1950s (compositions that had already been revisited in the mid-1970s). A wedge of ocean makes itself apparent in the background of both works; the surface of the water rendered in an unusually realistic blue. The human form is hinted at through disembodied thighs and knees, a shoulder and

10 SYNTHESIS

When all is said and done, our own existence is an experiment of nature, an attempt at a new synthesis.[52]
Carl Jung

How wonderful it will be if one can go on to the end, shedding one's mortality and lifting the spirit to a dimension that is always with us and yet always eludes us.[53]
Wilfred Avery

AFTER THIS LONG break away from the city, Wilfred decided it was time to move closer to London. In the last few years, he had been selling fairly regularly from the studio, and felt ready to attempt a reintegration into the London art scene. This move out of Devon was also prompted by the death of Adrien de Menasce. The loss of his sole creative partner was a devastating blow. An extract of the speech he gave at Adrien's funeral is included below:

> *I think of Adrien above all as a fellow artist; as a comrade in arms, as it were. His brave and dogged fight, to open painting again to the inner world of the spirit, is something that I share. He has been an inspiration and an ally at all times.*[54]

Wilfred wanted to be closer to his brother so that they could support each other through their shared grief, and as Ray had taken early retirement from his teaching position at Exeter College two years earlier, it was a good time for them both to relocate.

The word *synthesis* seems to sum up this final period of Wilfred's work. The term was used by Jung in the context of his theory of individuation: the technique of bringing about a psychological wholeness in one's being, of reconciling conflicting aspects into one single unit. And in this final period of his work, we can see Wilfred doing exactly this. Despite consistent doubt, this body of work ties together all the thoughts and experiments carried out over the last two decades, wrapping up Wilfred's career in the neat and deeply considered way that so characterises him.

In fact, it was only now that Wilfred managed to fully merge those two pivotal subjects of his — landscape and the male body.

● ● ●

A move out of Devon did not bring with it any less unusual living situations, and in 1995 Wilfred found them a flat and studio space right in a working mews above garages and a car wash in Kemptown, east Brighton. St Mark's Mews turned out to be one of the best studios he had ever had, and the freeholder allowed him to build a patio on the roof of the car wash. Being so much closer to London, Wilfred had easy access to art again, which inspired and motivated him to make new work. He was glad, too, to have escaped from what he would always refer to as the 'demanding' quality of the Devon landscape.

Living right on the coast, and surrounded by a constant stream of Brighton characters (after the generally staid inhabitants to be found in Devon), Wilfred began to make work on a theme he called 'figures by the sea'. The couple's proximity to the nudist beach no doubt inspired this, and brought with it memories of Wilfred's spectacular failure, *Figures on a Beach* — which now for the first time seemed quite prophetic (not least because of the mid-1990s fashion for shaved heads).

The theme also saw Wilfred, for the first time in his career, take the unclothed body outside into a realistic and exterior setting. This relocation brought with it a real sense of pride to his work, and, one might add, of the Pride movement too. Wilfred's palette became noticeably lighter, and extensive areas of bright colour — something not seen in these proportions since the very end of the 1950s — washed back on to the canvas.

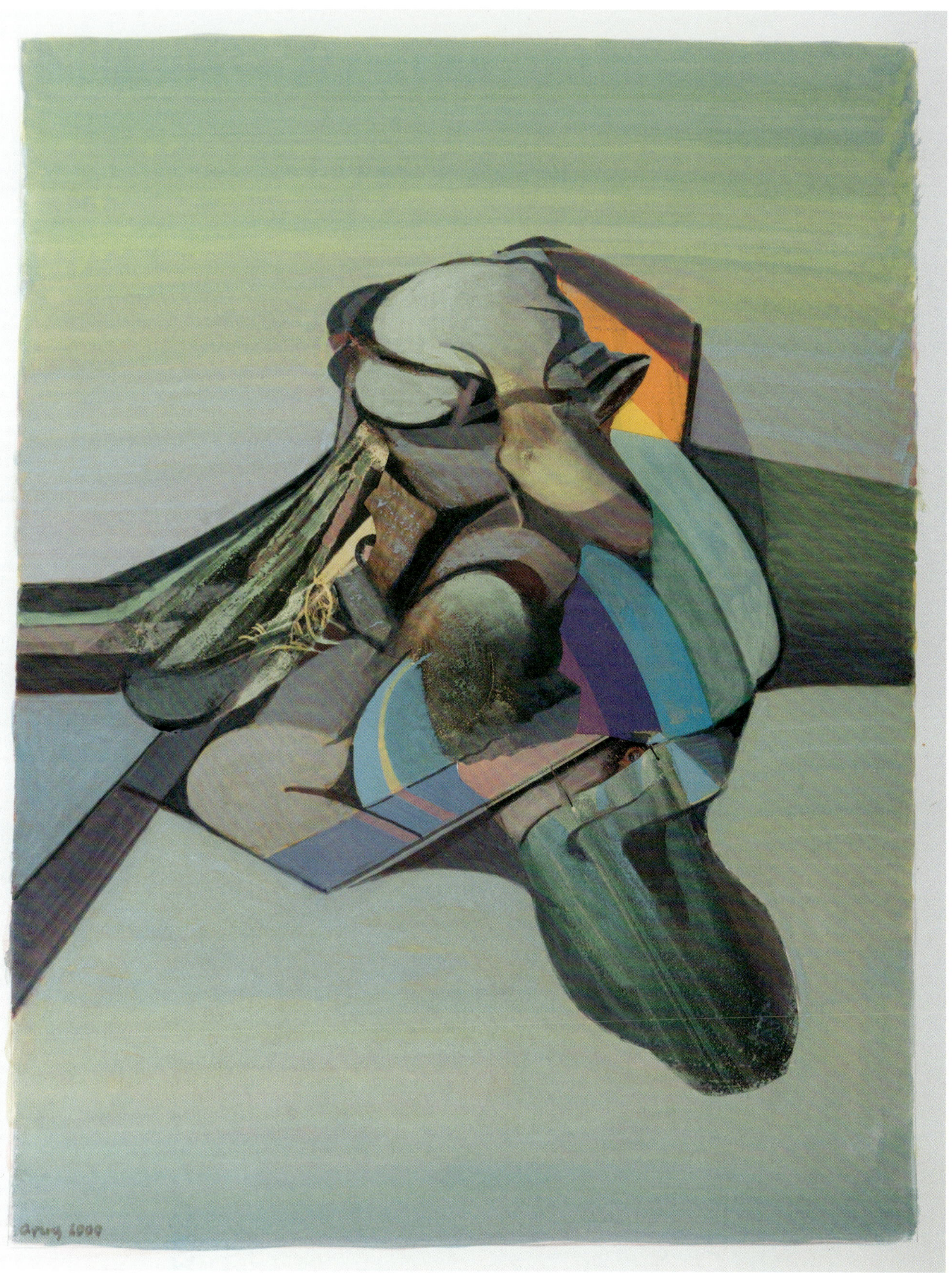

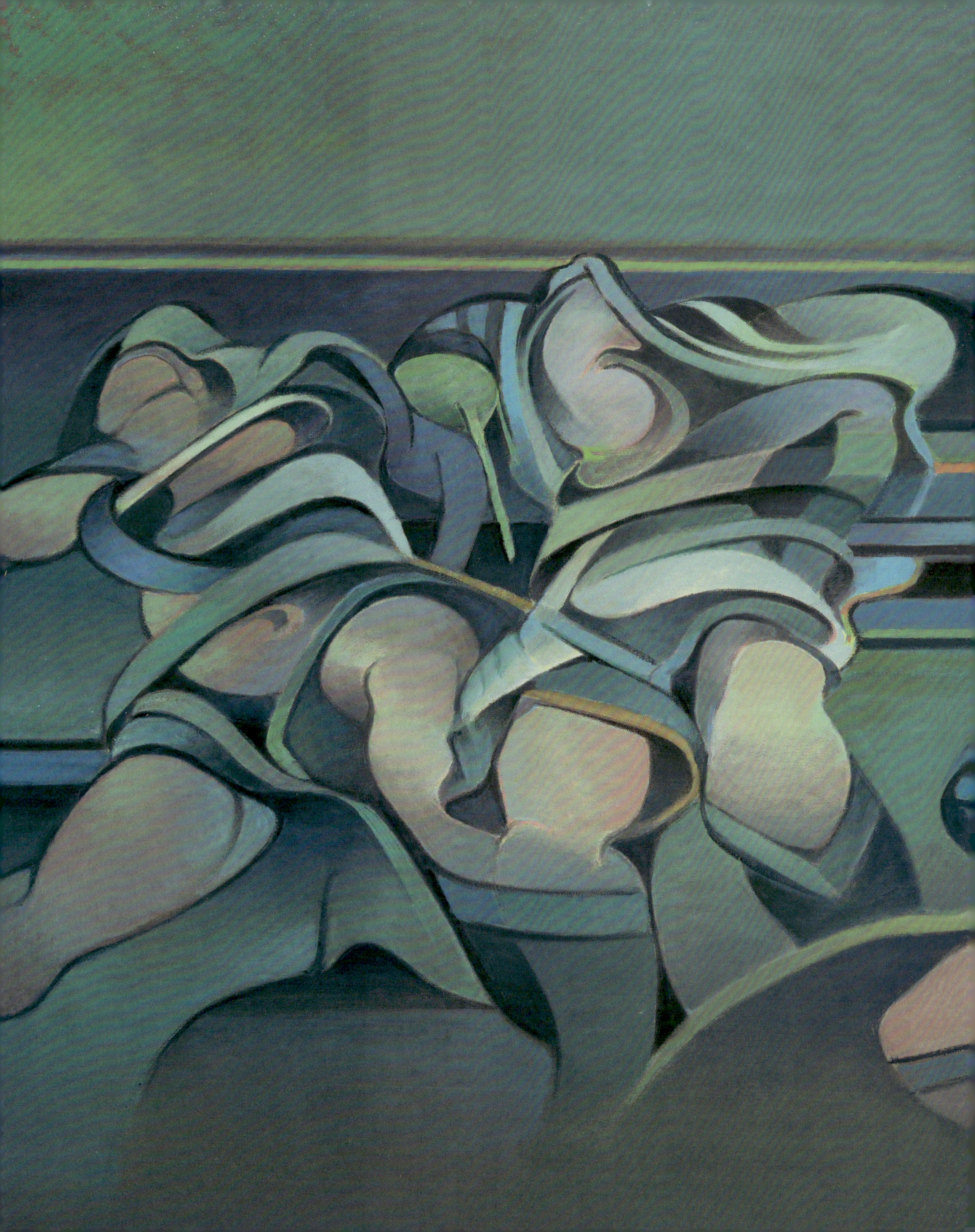

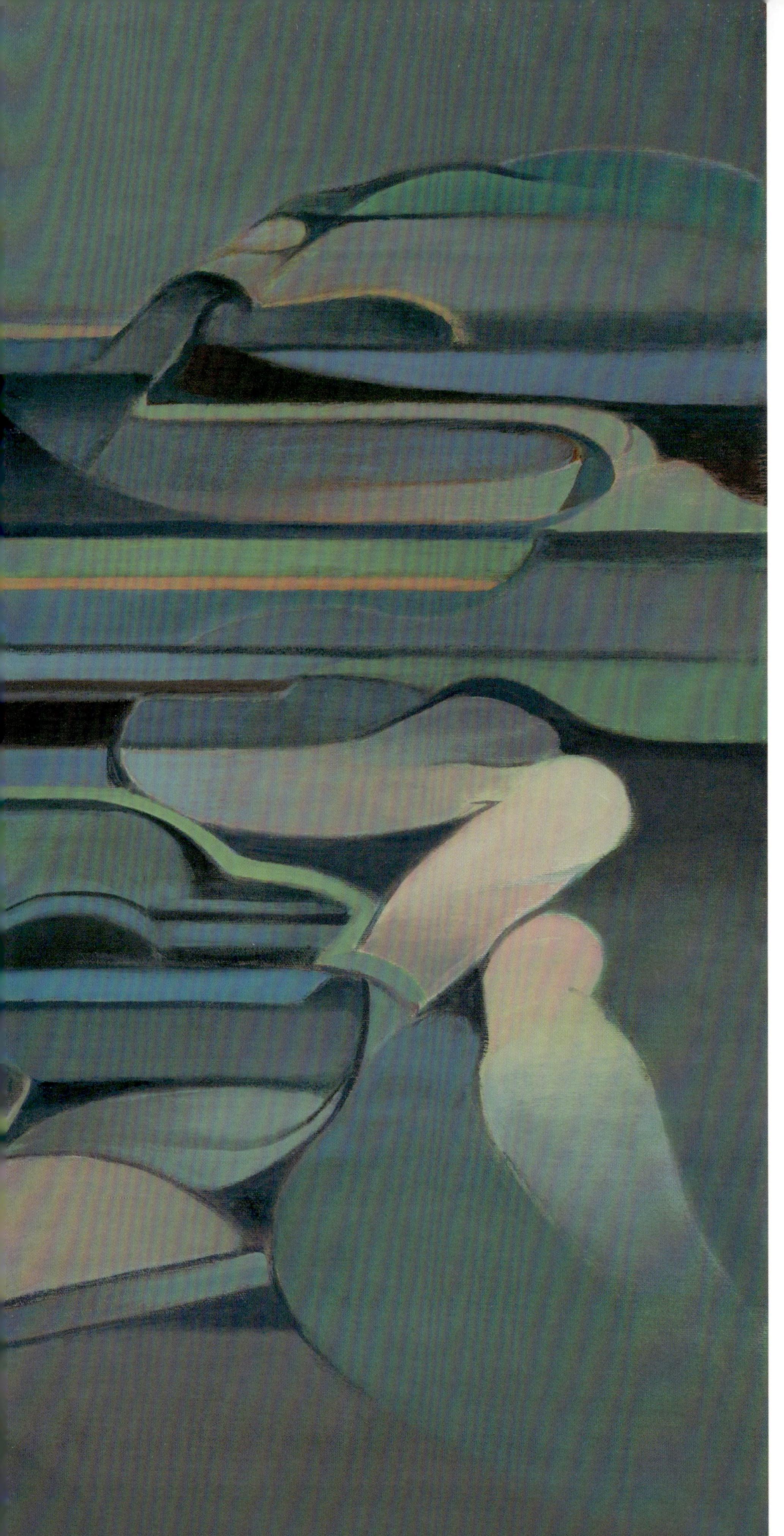

10:7 'Seasons':
Winter Green
2000
76 x 101.5 cm
Oil on canvas
(Studio)

Wilfred's bodies are broad and open, a pure confidence can be seen in their actions. Their buoyancy is mirrored in the colour scheme, a background of sunshine yellow appears for the first time.

• • •

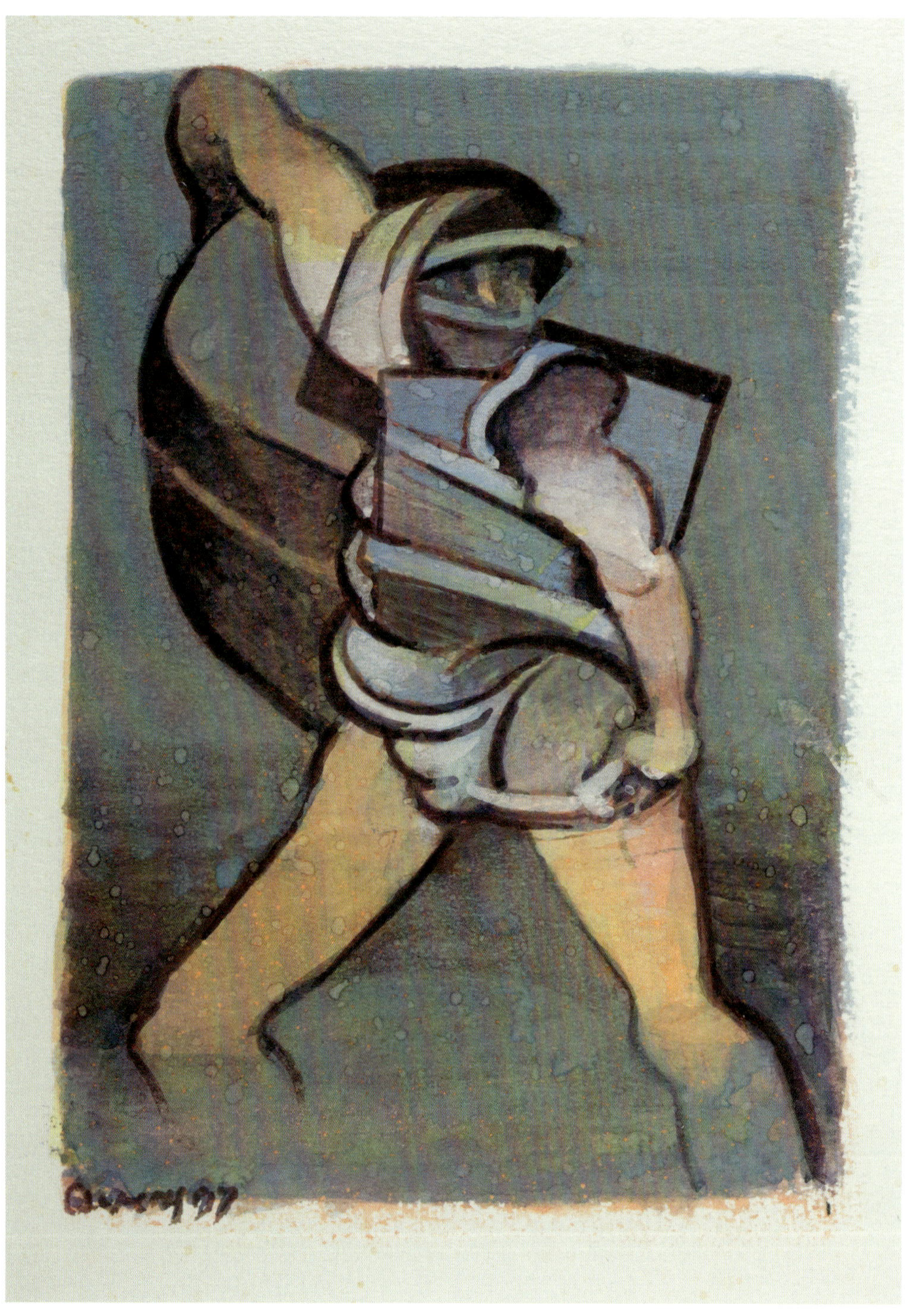

10:8 Small Figure Study 1
1997
18 x 12.5 cm
Gouache
(Studio)

After twenty-two years outside the capital, Wilfred moved back to London. His final two-and-a-half years in Brighton had been spent alone, trialling a separation from Ray. This was difficult for them both and they soon realised it was a mistake. In 2002, Wilfred moved into Ray's flat in

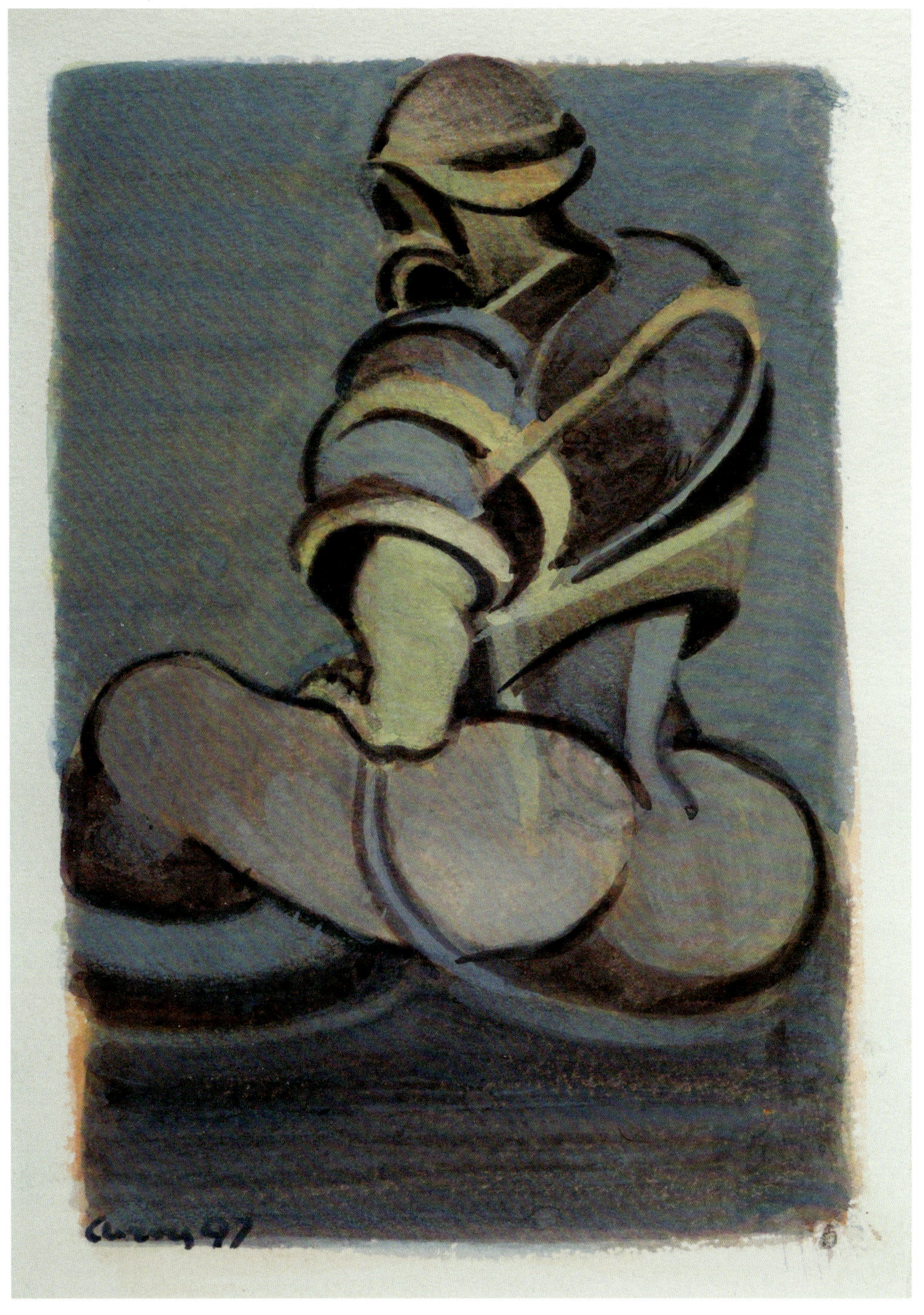

10:9 Small Figure Study 5
1997
18 x 12.5 cm
Gouache
(Studio)

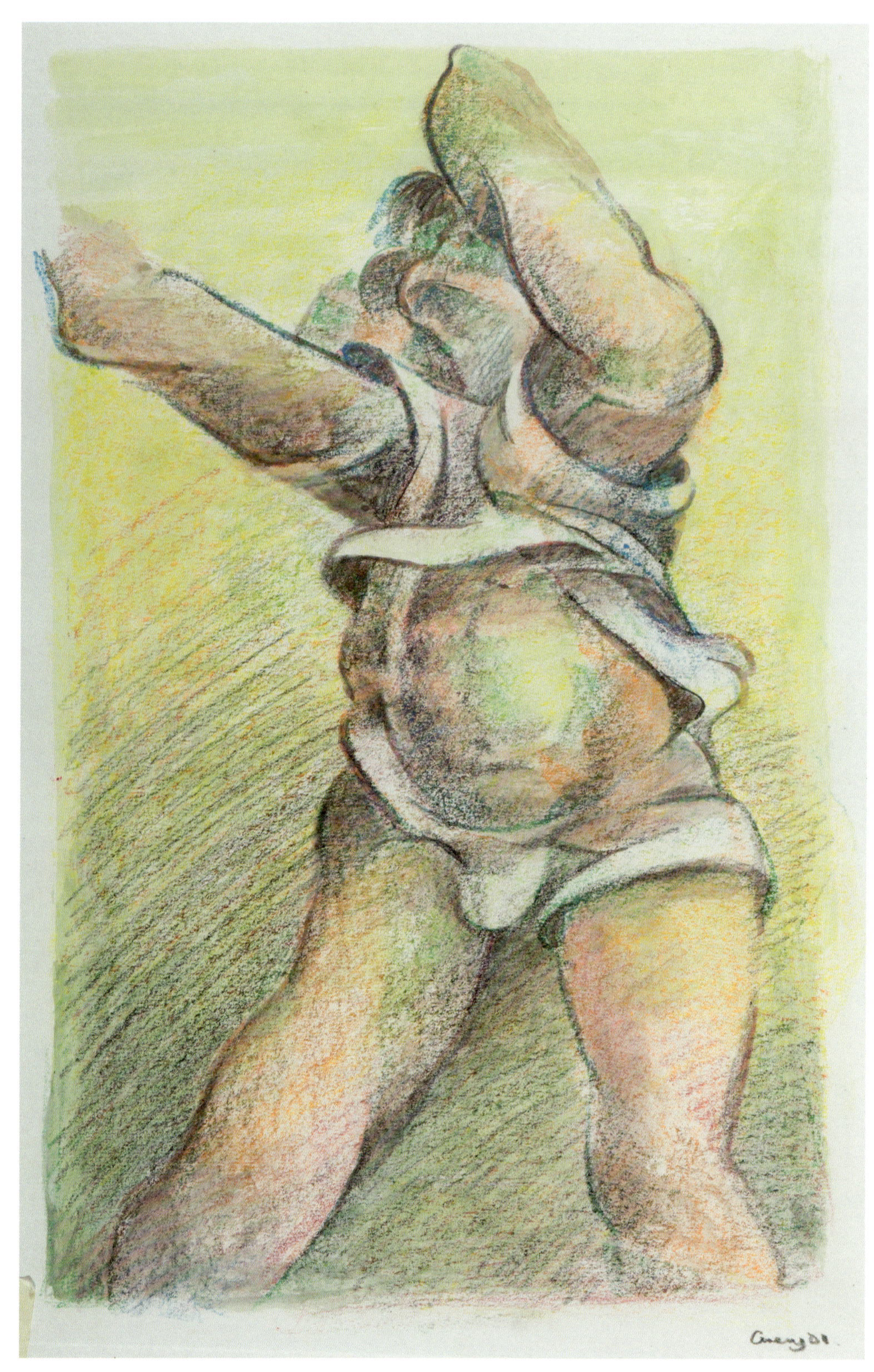

10:10 Study for Figure No 1
2001
38 x 25.5 cm
Coloured pencil on paper
(Studio)

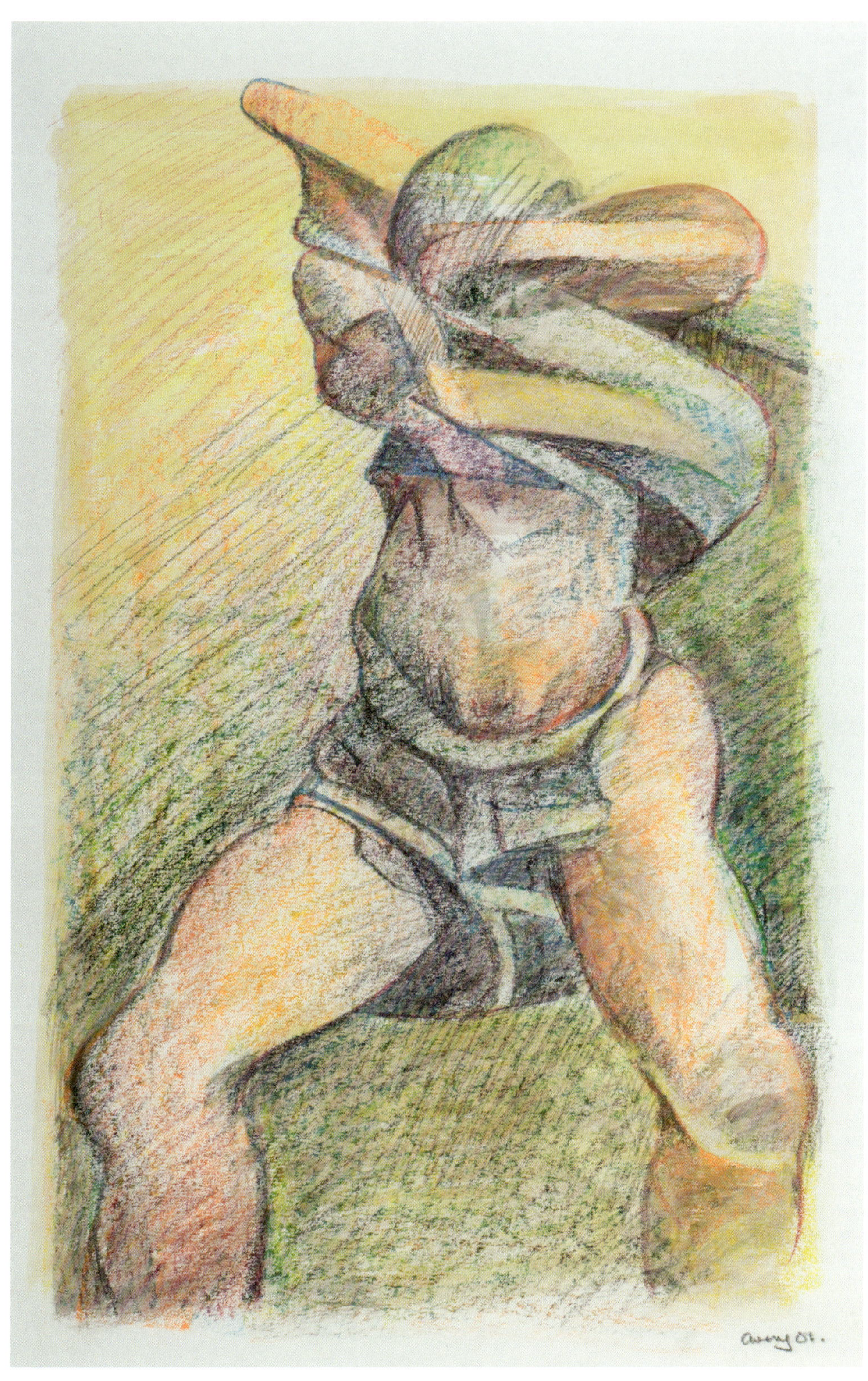

10:11 Study for Figure No 2
2001
38 x 25.5 cm
Coloured pencil on paper
(Studio)

Rowland Court, Croydon. They spent a year there together, during which time he was largely only able to make small works on paper (few of which survive).

In 2003, Wilfred sold St Mark's Mews, and the couple moved to Cintra Park, a small flat in Crystal Palace. Just six months after the move, Wilfred suffered a minor stroke. His health declined from that point onwards, and he found it increasingly difficult to make new work. *Parabola* (2001–07) is the final work he completed.

Wilfred had begun the diptych in Brighton, and continued working on it over a move back to London and then to Eastbourne from 2005. Its composition is an abstraction of *Figures by the Sea*. The two figures depicted here, are, however, composed of far more realistic and flesh-like body parts than many of Wilfred's contemporaneous works. Here are knees, shoulders and crossed arms; bulging stomachs repeated from earlier figure studies. Again, Wilfred tricks us. Assumed body parts are fragmented or made up of others; a bent arm comprises the stomach of the left figure. The colourful ribbons surrounding the same body appear again as clothing. Similar bright colours pick out sports socks, shoulder pads and a helmet; bright light, picked out in greys and a very pale lilac, gleams off its visor. Fragmented geometry, again not seen since the late 1950s and very early 1960s, is sharp and plasticky amongst the ever-moving flow of the two bodies. Each grows into, or perhaps out of, an abstracted landscape.

As the result of his stroke and ensuing health problems, living in London soon became too difficult for Wilfred, and in 2005 Ray and he found a flat in Eastbourne, just a few minutes' walk from the generous swathe of coastline that edges one side of the town. With the help of Simon Sherning from the Towner Gallery, whom Wilfred had met in 2011, he was able to review his archive, making small adjustments to works and, as ever, destroying whichever pieces with which he remained unhappy.

On 5 April 2008, Wilfred and Ray formed a civil partnership at Croydon Registry Office, with Sam as one of their witnesses.

• • •

It feels important here, right at the very end of this monograph, to touch upon an experience that Wilfred had a few years previously, an event that can perhaps be seen to sum up the entirety of his career.

In 1994, Wilfred experienced what he would later describe as the presence of Christ in his bedroom during the night. Their ensuing conversation, he elaborated afterwards, was about sexuality. Human relationships, Christ reassured Wilfred, exist in a circular formation. But rather than the circle being composed of man/woman/man/woman, its natural organisation was man/man/woman/woman. In this formation, any kind of relationship was possible and had equal standing.

It is perhaps more relevant to translate this visionary event in a psychological rather than religious context. Christ as a manifestation of his subconscious appears to have allowed Wilfred to justify his sexuality within a Christian context. Had the artist, after all these years, finally managed to link his spiritual nature to his sexuality?

This theory works equally well when we consider it within the context of this final period of work. The monumental and fancy-dressed figures that launch themselves across canvas, paper and card seem connected to more than just the landscape. They are more than just costumed bodies; Wilfred has instead brought in the whole and sweeping universe. That same body we saw hidden in his dark bedroom in the 1950s is now its own ringed planet. Standing proud and weighted and physical.

Person as planet as universe, monumental and central. Whole worlds, Wilfred tells us, are hidden inside each one of us; all and everything interconnected. He finally achieved what he spent his entire career attempting. Wilfred has done it. Full synthesis complete.

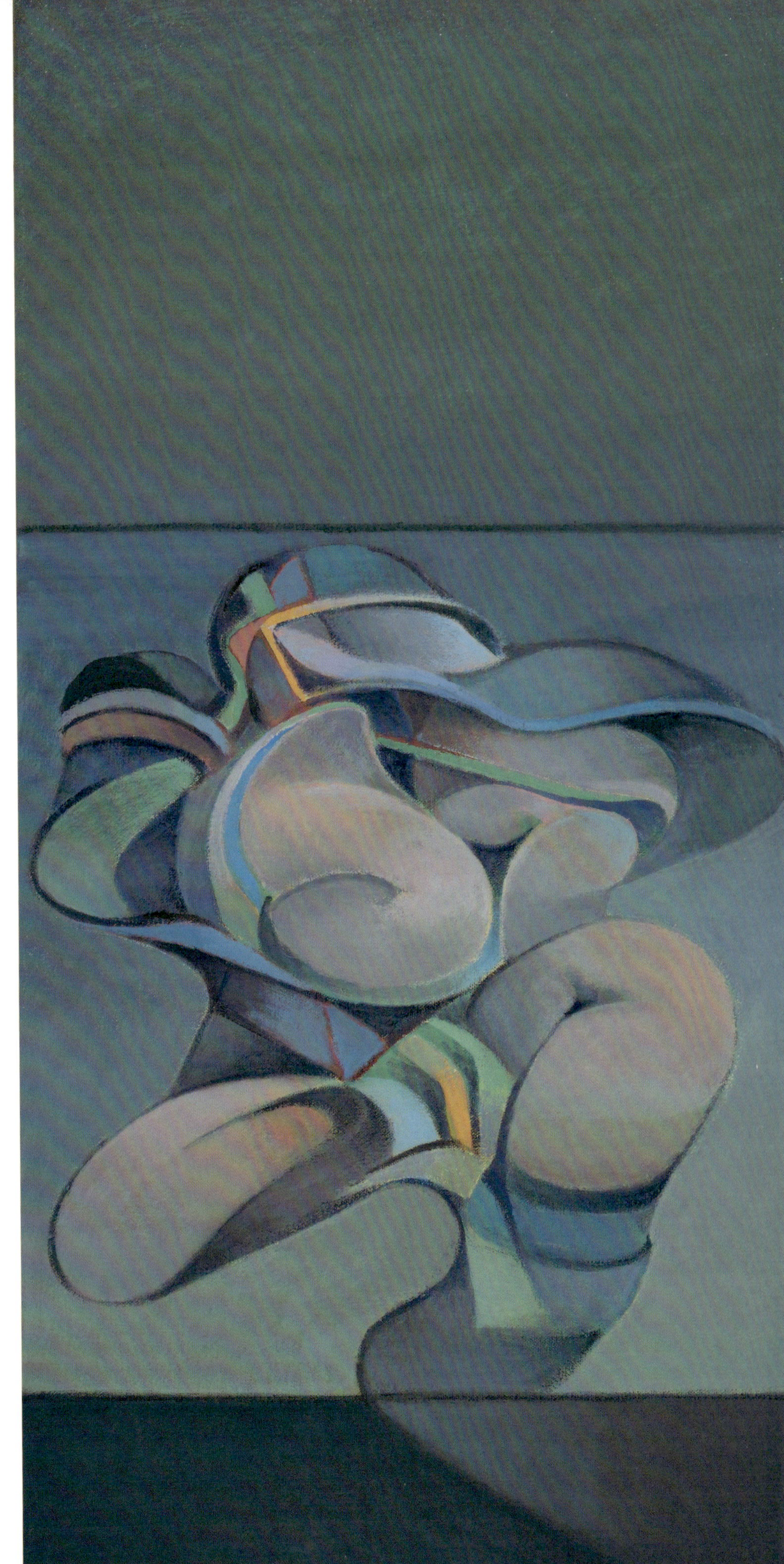

10:12 Parabola
2001–07
Each canvas 76 x 51 cm
Oil on canvas
(Studio)

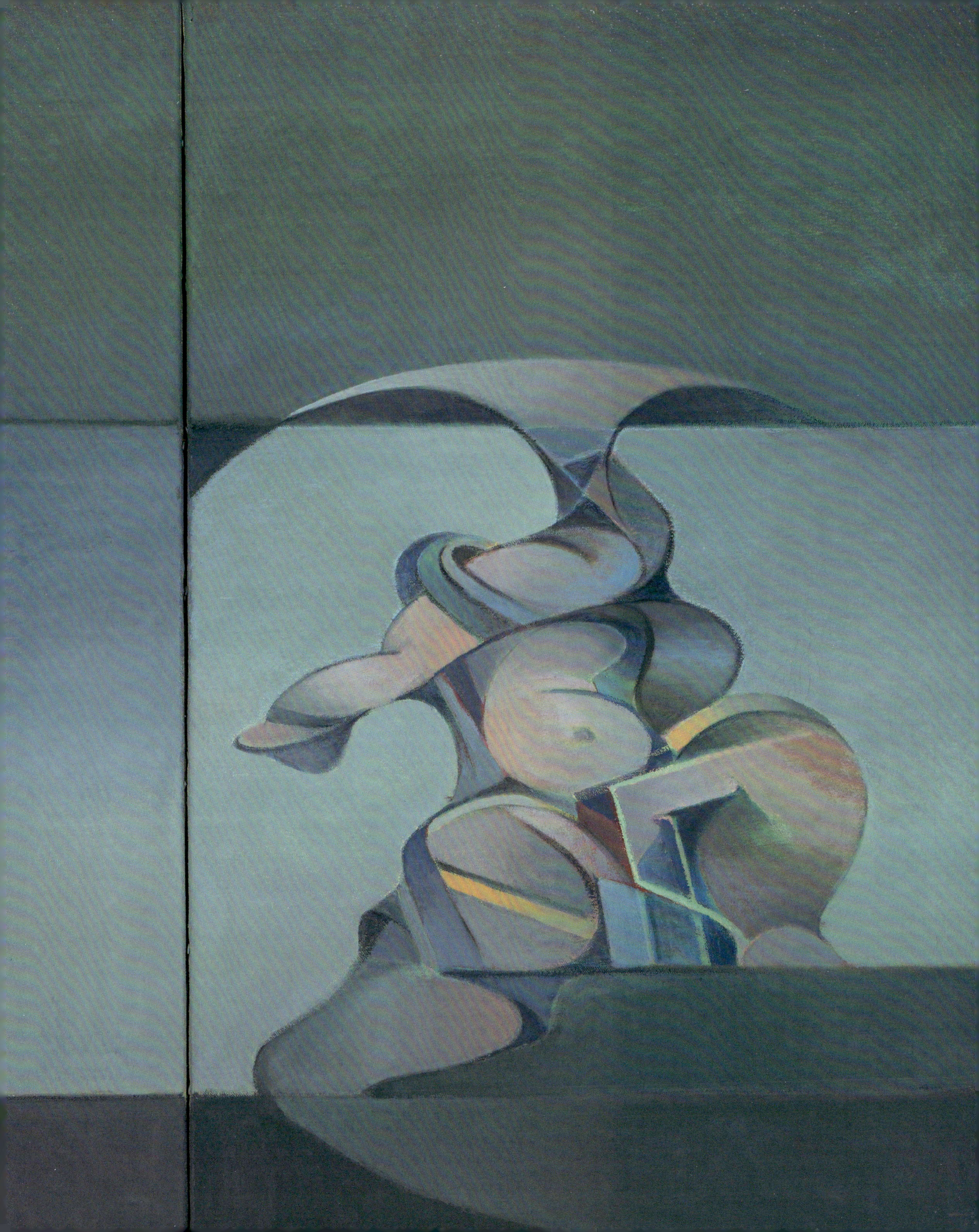

V STUDIO

Wilfred worked every day between 9.00 and 3.00. It was a practice almost religious in its structure and ritual; his work desk, paint pots, easels and mantelpiece decorations all organised with so much care that they seemed closer to altars than anything of strictly practical use. Ray would describe the atmosphere that pervaded each of Wilfred's studios as 'almost religious'; he had been introduced to the space the morning after they had first met, given a tour of Wilfred's work that he would admit afterwards he felt unequipped at that point to fully understand. Still, this atmosphere of dedication was evident, even to the least educated. As one can well imagine, Wilfred enjoyed this religious comparison, and would describe the preparation of his materials as a priest preparing for Mass. He even folded his rags, he would tell people, in the same way a priest would his own sacred cloth. Painting as a sacred practice – it seems Wilfred never strayed far from those early forays into the church. This palpable atmosphere of peace was enhanced by the soft slippers he would wear while painting. The door would be closed. All quiet.

And it was not until everything was ready, that he had mentally prepared in this way by slowly adjusting his equipment, by waiting until he felt the balance was just right, that Wilfred would turn to his canvas (the Mass has started; the painting begins). It was an immaculate studio practice, in more than one sense of the word.

Wilfred painted all of his studios pale grey throughout. Not just the walls but the work table, brush pots, easels, chairs, fireplace – all painted in the same unintrusive tone to ensure absolutely no visual distraction. Each mantelpiece in grey gloss. And pale grey slatted blinds that could be adjusted to allow the correct amount of light to fall on to his work while painting. Most of his studio floors were pale grey vinyl. Small stones gathered from the beach, painted meandering stripes in dulcet tones, were placed along the windowsill. His paintings announced themselves against the mellow walls.

A north-facing room was preferred for the quality of light. But in homes where this was not possible, Wilfred would place mirrors at tactical angles. He changed his medium according to the seasons; in spring and autumn focusing on oil painting, in the summer the balance tipping towards watercolour and collage, and making most of his drawings from Christmas and through deep winter.

Wilfred's methods of display were recorded by his friend Vicky Stewart. She and her husband Ken, living above Wilfred and Ray in the Red House on Topsham Road in Exeter, were invited into the studio many times. The routine was always the same. Before being admitted to the studio they were offered a drink or dinner. It was only after this socialising, when they had had the opportunity to get any catching-up out of the way, that Wilfred would invite them into the studio. Each showing was perfectly prepared for. Two chairs set out in the middle of the room, the artwork extracted from its place in the ordered stacks against the wall and laid out in the order it would be shown in. 'Every picture,' Vicky remembers, 'handled like something very precious.'[55] In order to refresh their vision, both members of this small audience were required to close their eyes in between each work. The works would always be shown without their titles – all distraction eliminated.

This intimate showcasing was a pivotal part of Wilfred's practice – all the more so during the periods he was selling and exhibiting little to nothing. Not only did the preparation for these sessions allow him to re-evaluate each of the works he chose to show, but in those great clouds of doubt it gave him a captivated audience to the artworks that otherwise might not have been seen at all. These viewings, doubtless, were a much-needed lifeline. ●

ENDNOTES

1. Wilfred Avery, *Myth and Symbol*, 1970 (unpublished).

2. Wilfred Avery, *Living in London 1967*, 1967 (unpublished).

3. Ibid.

4. Wilfred Avery, *One Eye Open – One Eye Shut*, 1978 (unpublished).

5. Wilfred Avery, *General Resume of Works Periods* (undated; unpublished).

6. Matt Houlbrook, *Queer London: perils and pleasures in the sexual metropolis, 1918–1957*, 2005, p. 237.

7. Gregory Salter, *Art and Masculinity in Post-War Britain: Reconstructing Home*, 2020, p. 86.

8. Houlbrook, *Queer London*, p. 110.

9. Lord, Catherine and Meyer, Richard, *Art & Queer Culture*, 2019, p. 99.

10. Stephenson, Andrew, 'Arcadia and Soho', in *Queer British Art, 1861–1967* (ed. Clare Barlow), 2017, p. 135.

11. Salter, *Art and Masculinity in Post-War Britain*, p. 143.

12. Ibid., pp. 82-86.

13. David Sylvester, 'The Kitchen Sink', in *Encounter*, 1954, p. 62.

14. Oswell Blakeston, 'Twin Successes' in *Art News*, November 1954.

15. Wilfred Avery, *Notes on Painting*, 1961 (unpublished).

16. Wilfred Avery, *Always Art – Art Always* (undated; unpublished).

17. Wilfred Avery, *Figures on a Beach*, 1960 (unpublished).

18. Wilfred Avery, *Figures on a Beach 1960*, 1999 (unpublished).

19. Ibid.

20. Wilfred Avery, *The Unpredictable Image*, 1960 (unpublished).

21. Wilfred Avery, *Time, Space and the Edge of Memory*, 1969 (unpublished).

22. Wilfred Avery, *That Certain Feeling*, 1969 (unpublished).

23. Wilfred Avery, *Fragments from a Journal of 1962*, 1962 (unpublished).

24. Wilfred Avery, *The Unpredictable Image*, 1969 (unpublished).

25. Carl Jung, 'Approaching the Unconscious', in Carl Jung and M.L. von Franz (eds), *Man and his Symbols*, 1964, p. 69.

26. Aniela Jaffé, 'Symbolism in the Visual Arts', in ibid, p. 310.

27. Wilfred Avery, *One Eye Open – One Eye Shut*, 1978 (unpublished).

28. Giorgio de Chirico, '"On Metaphysical Art," 1919', in Joshua C. Taylor (trans.), Herschel B. Chipp (ed.), *Theories of Modern Art: A Source Book by Artists and Critics*, 1968, p. 451.

29. Jaffé, 'Symbolism in the Visual Arts', p. 293.

30. Wilfred Avery, *Down to Earth*, 15 July 1969 (unpublished).

31. Wilfred Avery, *Notes from a Journal*, 1962 (unpublished).

32. Wilfred Avery, *General Resume of Works Periods* (undated; unpublished).

33. Catherine Malabou, *Plasticity at the Dusk of Writing*, Carolyn Shread (trans.), 2010, p. xviii.

34. Wilfred Avery, *Notes from a Journal*, 1962 (unpublished).

35. Wilfred Avery, *Drawing Circles*, 1973 (unpublished).

36. Wilfred Avery, *Down to Earth*, 1969 (unpublished).

37. Marsilio Ficino, II.7 in Sears, J. (trans.), *Commentary on Plato's Symposium on Love* (1985), p. 15.

38. Wilfred Avery, *The Erotic*, 1969 (unpublished).

39. Wilfred Avery, *Some Reflections on the Liberation Movement and My Work*, June 1975 (unpublished).

40. Wilfred Avery, *The Artist's Position: December 1975*, 1975 (unpublished).

41. Wilfred Avery, *Paul Cézanne: Thoughts after a visit to the Post-Impressionism exhibition. Feb. 1981*, 1981 (unpublished).

42. Wilfred Avery, *Myth and Symbol*, 1970 (unpublished).

43. 'Wilfred Avery: Painter' in Roger Day (ed.), *Proteus: A Magazine of the Arts from The Open University*, Nov. 1977, p. 41.

44. Wilfred Avery, *Epilogue – Saturday March 19th 1983*, 1983 (unpublished).

45. Wilfred Avery, *A Bigger Splash*, 1975 (unpublished).

46. Wilfred Avery, *Art and Society*, 1978 (unpublished).

47. Wilfred Avery, 'Images from Landscape: Selected Paintings and Drawings' (1982 exhibition leaflet).

48. Wilfred Avery, *Reflections – Ashburton 1984*, 1984 (unpublished).

49. Wilfred Avery, *Down to Earth*, 1969 (unpublished).

50. George Melly, letter to Garry Thorne, October 1990 (unpublished).

51. Vicky Stewart, diary entry, 31 January 1993 (unpublished).

52. Carl Jung, *Structure & Dynamics of the Psyche*, 2014, p. 377.

53. Wilfred Avery, *That Certain Feeling*, 1969 (unpublished).

54. Wilfred Avery, Adrien de Menasce funeral speech, 1995 (unpublished).

55. Vicky Stewart, diary entry, 11 June 1992 (unpublished).

BIBLIOGRAPHY

Avery, Wilfred, *A Bigger Splash*, 1975 (unpublished).

Avery, Wilfred, Adrien de Menasce funeral speech, 1995 (unpublished).

Avery, Wilfred, *Always Art – Art Always* (undated; unpublished).

Avery, Wilfred, *Art and Society*, 1978 (unpublished).

Avery, Wilfred, *Down to Earth*, 15 July 1969 (unpublished).

Avery, Wilfred, *Drawing Circles*, 1973 (unpublished).

Avery, Wilfred, *Epilogue – Saturday March 19th 1983*, 1983 (unpublished).

Avery, Wilfred, *Figures on a Beach*, 1960 (unpublished).

Avery, Wilfred, *Figures on a Beach (1960)*, 1999 (unpublished).

Avery, Wilfred, *Fragments from a Journal of 1962*, 1962 (unpublished).

Avery, Wilfred, 'Images from Landscape: Selected Paintings and Drawings' (1982 exhibition leaflet).

Avery, Wilfred, *General Resume of Works Periods* (undated; unpublished).

Avery, Wilfred, *Living in London 1967*, 1967 (unpublished).

Avery, Wilfred, *Myth and Symbol*, 1970 (unpublished).

Avery, Wilfred, *Notes from a Journal*, 1962 (unpublished).

Avery, Wilfred, *Notes on Painting*, 1961 (unpublished).

Avery, Wilfred, *One Eye Open – One Eye Shut*, 1978 (unpublished).

Avery, Wilfred, *Paul Cézanne: Thoughts after a visit to the Post-Impressionism exhibition. Feb. 1981*, 1981 (unpublished).

Avery, Wilfred, *Reflections – Ashburton 1984*, 1984 (unpublished).

Avery, Wilfred, *Some Reflections on the Liberation Movement and My Work*, June 1975 (unpublished).

Avery, Wilfred, *That Certain Feeling*, 1969 (unpublished).

Avery, Wilfred, *The Artist's Position: December 1975*, 1975 (unpublished).

Avery, Wilfred, *The Erotic*, 1969 (unpublished).

Avery, Wilfred, *The Unpredictable Image*, 1969 (unpublished).

Avery, Wilfred, *Time, Space and the Edge of Memory*, 1969 (unpublished).

Avery, Wilfred, 'Wilfred Avery: Painter' in Roger Day (ed.), *Proteus: A Magazine of the Arts from The Open University* (Nov. 1977, pp. 410-47).

Blakeston, Oswell, 'Twin Successes', in *Art News* (November 1954).

De Chirico, Giorgio, '"On Metaphysical Art," 1919', trans. Joshua C. Taylor, in Herschel B. Chipp (ed.) *Theories of Modern Art: A Source Book by Artists and Critics* (Berkeley, CA: University of California Press, 1968).

Ficino, Marsilio in Sears, J. (trans.), *Commentary on Plato's Symposium on Love* (Dallas, TX: Spring Publications, 1985).

Fisher, Nigel, *Harold Macmillan* (London: Weidenfeld & Nicolson: 1982).

Houlbrook, Matt, *Queer London: perils and pleasures in the sexual metropolis, 1918–1957* (Chicago: University of Chicago Press, 2005).

Jung, Carl, *Structure & Dynamics of the Psyche* (Abingdon-on-Thames: Taylor & Francis, 2014).

Jung, Carl, 'Approaching the Unconscious', in Jung, Carl and von Franz, M.L. (eds), *Man and His Symbols* (London: Dell Publishing, 1964).

Jaffé, Aniela, 'Symbolism in the Visual Arts', in Jung, Carl and von Franz, M.L. (eds), *Man and His Symbols* (London: Dell Publishing, 1964).

Lord, Catherine and Meyer, Richard, *Art & Queer Culture* (London: Phaidon Press Limited, 2013).

Malabou, Catherine, *Plasticity at the Dusk of Writing: Dialect, Destruction, Deconstruction*, Carolyn Shread (trans.) (New York: Columbia University Press, 2010).

Melly, George, letter to Garry Thorne, October 1990 (unpublished).

Salter, Gregory, *Art and Masculinity in Post-War Britain: Reconstructing Home* (London: Routledge, 2020).

Stephenson, Andrew, 'Arcadia and Soho' in Barlow, Clare (ed.), *Queer British Art, 1861–1967* (London: Tate Publishing, 2017).

Stewart, Vicky, diary entry, 31 January 1993 (unpublished).

Stewart, Vicky, diary entry, 11 June 1992 (unpublished).

Sylvester, David, 'The Kitchen Sink', in *Encounter* (December 1954), pp. 61-64.

ACKNOWLEDGEMENTS

First and foremost, I would like to thank Ray Crossley, for his open-minded and unendingly generous approach throughout. My gratitude extends to each one of Wilfred's family, friends and collectors I met along the way, many of whom welcomed me into their homes and shared countless stories and memories of the artist: Joan and Steven Fogel, Jack Humphries, Simon Janes, Tony Moore, Simon Sherning, Vicky Stewart and Nick Wood-Glover – thank you. Thanks also to those at Brighton and Hove Museums, The Hepworth Wakefield, The Ingram Collection, The Jerwood, The Museum of Barnstaple and North Devon, South Molton Museum, Sheffield Museums and the Towner Eastbourne. And finally, thanks to Alex Ramsay for the beautiful photography, and to all at Unicorn for turning this idea into the book you have in front of you.

This project benefited from the generous support of the Association for Art History.